A HISTORY OF THEATRICAL ART

A History of Theatrical Art

In Ancient and Modern Times by

Karl Mantzius

Authorised Translation by

Louise von Cossel

Volume II

The Middle Ages and The Renaissance

GLOUCESTER, MASS.

PETER SMITH

1970

First Published, 1903
Reprinted, 1937
Reprinted, 1970

CONTENTS

CONTENTS

CONTENTS

LIST OF ILLUSTRATIONS

x ILLUSTRATIONS

INTRODUCTION

THE present volume does not claim to present a complete picture of the theatrical art of the Renaissance, but limits itself to describing a few of its phenomena.

For several reasons I have preferred to reserve what remains for the next volume, which will treat of the great actors and playwrights of the sixteenth as well as of the seventeenth century, attempting to present a picture of dramatic art during the period of its fullest bloom.

K. M.

COPENHAGEN.

THEATRICAL ART
IN THE MIDDLE AGES

ECCLESIASTICAL PLAYS

I

THE drama and the dramatic art of the Middle Ages are no continuation of the antique. They are separated from it by a gap, a blank interval, and the Middle Ages, instead of continuing the edifice commenced by the Greek, leave it unheeded and forgotten, and create a new and characteristic drama of their own, springing from the tastes and capacities of the new times. It is true, we meet with a few traces which seem to contradict our statement about the perfect independence of the mediæval drama, among others the Latin plays imitated from Terence and found among the posthumous works of Hroswitha, the well-known Gandersheim nun. But these works merely prove that here and there behind the convent walls, which screened most of the learning of those times, quiet poetic minds eagerly studied and imitated their favourite classics to please themselves and perhaps a few of their colleagues, and we may be sure that such echoes of the classics did not pass beyond a very limited circle.

The mediæval drama is *popular poetry* written by authors and performed by actors sprung from the people ; a *popular amusement* growing out of the deepest interest

A

and concern of men's minds in those times—religion ; it had nothing to do with learned studies of ancient forms of art, which could only be appreciated by the few.

Not even the old ideas of tragedy and comedy are retained; the very words acquire a new meaning.   In the Middle Ages a tragedy means a *poetic tale* with a sad issue, a comedy one with a happy issue.[1]

Of course there are plays of a serious or of a cheerful character, but the two styles are mixed up with each other; in the former we find farcical scenes, the latter do not exclude serious reflections.   The merry plays offer many varieties, such as *farces, sotties, moralities* (these, however, may also frequently be of a serious character), *and shrovetide plays*.   The serious plays, which we will discuss first, are generally known by the name of *mysteries*.   At the time when they were written, however, this term was not used, and we do not meet with it till the fifteenth century.   Before that time the serious ecclesiastical plays go by various other names. Till the twelfth century, when the liturgical dramas were still written in Latin and performed in the church, the general terms were: *ludi, representationes, historiæ representandæ*.   After these Latin patterns the following titles were formed in the different countries ; in France : *jeu, représentation, miracle, histoire ;* in Italy : *rappresentazione, festa, funzione, storia, esempio ;* in Germany : *Spiel*; in England : *play, history ;* in Spain : *auto*.

Even the word mystery, which is not applied to any dramatic work before the fifteenth century, has in several

---

[1] Dante's famous work is called *Divina Commedia*, because it ends with bliss in Paradise.

ways been subject to considerable misconceptions. Originally it has nothing to do with the Greek μυστήριον or the Latin *mysterium*. In the Middle Ages it is mostly spelt with an *i*; Italian : *misterio*; French : *mistère*, and it is derived from the Latin *ministerium*, in the sense of "action," especially *ministerium sacrum*, "holy action." In old French *mistère* is often quite synonymous with *métier*,[1] which is the ordinary derivative from *ministerium*. Thus *mysterium* means exactly the same as "drama,"[2] simply "action"; as in Spanish *auto*, and in French *acte*, which no longer signifies the whole action, but only a division of it.

So much for the name. It is of more interest, however, to investigate the thing itself, to find out how the serious, that is, the ecclesiastical play of the Middle Ages originated and developed itself.

In the Middle Ages the Church was more than a refuge for sufferers and a house of worship for believers ; it embraced all the intellectual interests of the time and nourished all the higher aspirations of the people. It was the focus at which all artistic, literary and scientific efforts met, and in the service of which they worked. Architects exerted themselves to the utmost to raise the finest buildings, painters and sculptors to adorn these buildings more magnificently than the most beautiful palaces, musicians exercised their highest skill to render divine service as impressive as possible, and the people formed an enthusiastic public enjoying all these impressions as a mighty emanation of the wonderful power of the Church.

[1] See P. de Julleville : *Les Mystères*, i. p. 188 ff.
[2] From δράω : I act.

Where could dramatic art find another or a better origin than in the Church, which had drawn all other art into its service?

And there indeed its source is found. As the Greek drama was an expansion of the Dionysiac cult, so the serious mediæval drama originated in the Roman Catholic worship.

From the earliest times the mass of the Roman Church has borne a distinctly dramatic character. The beautifully decorated sanctuary, with the altar in its centre, separated from the choir by a rail, resembles a stage, on which the priest robed in his chasuble, the deacon and choristers with censers, seem to act before the silent audience of the congregation. The perfect symbolism carried out in every detail, which in former times was more generally understood than it is now, not only appertained to the building and adornments of the church, but to every item of the service; it was like a sublime spectacle, in which every part represented something different from what it was.

And the clergy, soon understanding what power precisely this dramatic element exercised over the minds of the people, did not hesitate to turn it to account, and by degrees to introduce dramatic action into the service, thus offering, in compensation for the incomprehensible Latin words, intelligible mimic and musical performances. The great religious festivals, Christmas in particular, gave special opportunity for liturgical dramas. Thus at a certain Christmas celebration, St Augustine (according to an apocryphal text) is represented addressing himself to the Jews in order to convince them of the divinity of

Christ. For this purpose he invokes all the old prophets, and makes them appear before him in succession in order to repeat their prophecies. After Isaiah, Jeremiah, Moses, Daniel and David, Augustine introduces some prophets of the New Covenant, Simeon, Zachariah, and Elizabeth, after which he has recourse to the testimony of the heathens, Virgil, Nebuchadnezzar and the Sibyl. All these solemn testimonies enable him to overwhelm the Jews with these words : "Is not this sufficient, O ye unbelievers ! Cannot ye be convinced by so many famous witnesses and such numerous testimonies ? "

This liturgical drama, which under different forms was acted all over Europe, was performed in Latin by priests, who distributed the parts amongst themselves.

In the same way other Christian subjects were represented at appropriate festivals, such as the Slaughter of the Innocents in Bethlehem, on the 28th of December. On this occasion the child-choristers, dressed in white and headed by a lamb, walked round the church in procession, after which they were murdered by order of Herod, then an angel called them to heaven, whither they pretended to ascend by rising up and walking into the choir. Here they sang a Te Deum, and the performance was ended.

The Wise Men of the East, The Resurrection of Lazarus, The Conversion of St Paul, are all favourite subjects for these religious dramas. In some of them the gestures to be made by the performers are very minutely described in the "rubrics," [1] which are written in Latin, as are the speeches of the play. Here is an example of a Latin Church play bearing the title *Planctus*

---

[1] The parenthetic indications serving as instructions for the actors.

Mariæ et aliorum.   The first verses are recited by
Magdalena and run as follows :—

> O fratres
> Et sorores
> Ubi est spes mea?
> Ubi consolatio mea ?
> Ubi tota salus, o magister mi ? [1]

The appended notes prescribe the following gestures,
which bear witness of their Italian origin :—

> Line 1. Magdalena shall turn towards the men with
> outstretched arms.
>   „   2. She turns towards the women.
>   „   3. She beats her breast.
>   „   4. She lifts her hands.
>   „   5. She bends her head and throws herself
> before the feet of Christ.

The Virgin Mary continues :—

> O dolor!
> Proh dolor
> Ergo quare
> Fili care
> Pendes ita
> Cum sis vita
> Manens ante secula ? [2]

---

[1] O brothers
O sisters
Where is my hope?
Where is my consolation?
Where is all my salvation, O my Master

[2] Oh pain ! Oh pain ! Why,
Oh beloved Son, doest thou hang thus,
Thou who art life and hast been from the beginning.

For these lines the following gestures are indicated :—

Line 1. } Mary wrings her hands.
   „ 2. }

   „ 3. } Opens her hands and points towards
   „ 4. }   Christ.
   „ 5.

   „ 6. } Beats her breast.
   „ 7. }

Sometimes also the rubric gives information about the style of the scenery, as in the play of *The Three Kings*, where we read that one of them "shall lift his hand and point to the star that hangs on a string." Or in another of *The Conversion of St Paul* which has the following introduction : "To represent the conversion of the blessed St Paul, a chair representing Jerusalem shall be placed on a suitable spot; on this chair the high priest shall stand. On another chair shall stand St Paul. He shall be accompanied by armed men. On the other side, at some distance, there shall be two chairs representing Damascus; on one of them a man named Judas shall be seated, on the other the chief of the synagogue in Damascus; and between these two chairs there shall be a bed, on which a man representing Ananias shall rest."

Most of all, these rubrics testify to the extreme care and love, and the comparatively full knowledge with which these naïve dramas were composed and studied.

In the long run, however, plays of this kind could not satisfy an audience whose sense for dramatic art was awake, not so much because of the deceptive *mise-en-*

scène—which was frequently more complicated than the above—as on account of the language. So by degrees the popular language was smuggled in; but from the moment when the plays were written entirely in the living tongue they slipped out of the grasp of the Church—quite gently and gradually, first moving out from inside the church to the space in front of it, though, no doubt, they were still performed by the clergy; then further away to the public street or market-place, written and performed in part by lay people, the clergy looking on or joining in the performance on an equal footing with the other actors.

In its essential points the development has been common to all the leading civilised European countries; not till later do the special national forms of dramatic literature develop themselves. France, however, takes the lead in the progress, and its dramatic poetry in the Middle Ages, besides being the best preserved and most employed, is the richest and most characteristic of all. Therefore we shall chiefly use French plays as examples of the art of dramatising during the first centuries—the twelfth to the fifteenth—and these plays and the manner in which they were performed are in the main representative of all civilised nations.

The earliest of all the surviving plays in the popular language has only been known for scarcely fifty years; it offers very interesting information about the kind of drama which has not yet quite detached itself from the Church, though it has ceased to be a Church service, and has raised itself to the level of real art.

The oldest French drama dates from the twelfth

century, and the MS. of it bears the title, *Representatio Adæ*, *The Representation of Adam*. It is, indeed, a trilogy, or at least a combination of three different pieces, the first of which treats of the *Fall of Adam and Eve*; the second of the *Murder of Abel*; the third contains *The Prophecies of Christ*. All three dramas are of Norman origin. The piece, which is entirely written in contemporary French—the Norman dialect— is accompanied by Latin rubrics indicating scenery, gestures and costumes. The introductory rubric, which shows a fairly good standard of scenic arrangement, runs, literally translated, as follows :—

" Paradise shall be situated in a rather prominent place, and is to be hung all round with draperies and silk curtains to such a height that the persons who find themselves in Paradise are seen from their shoulders upward. There shall be seen sweet smelling flowers and foliage ; there shall be different trees covered with fruit, so that the place may appear very agreeable. Then the Saviour [*Salvator*] shall appear, robed in a *dalmatica* ;[1] Adam and Eve place themselves in front of him, Adam dressed in a red tunic, Eve in a white garment and white silk veil ; both rise before *Figura* [term used for God in the MS., like *Salvator*], Adam nearest, bending his head, Eve lower down. Adam shall be trained well to speak at the right moment, so that he may come neither too soon nor too late. Not only he, but all shall be well practised in speaking calmly, and making gestures appropriate to the things they say ; they shall neither add nor omit any syllable

[1] The chasuble of the deacons.

of the metre; all shall express themselves in a distinct manner, and say in consecutive order all that is to be said."

The course of the play runs as follows : the reader begins by reading the text of the Bible which corresponds with the first situation : *In principio creavit Deus cœlum et terram*.[1]   The chorus grouped in the nave responds : "*Formavit igitur Dominus*. . . ."   God turns to the man and calls : "Adam!"   The man answers : "Lord!"   And the play begins.   The Lord explains to Adam his origin and his duties, shows him the garden of Paradise, and opens it to him while the chorus sings : "*Tulit ergo Dominus hominem*. . . ." Then follows the commandment of God forbidding man to touch the tree of knowledge.   Adam answers submissively like a vassal receiving an order from his liege lord.   God returns to the church (*vadit ad ecclesiam*), Adam and Eve play together in Paradise.

Then the devils appear; they run forward among the spectators, twisting their bodies and making horrid grimaces.   They sneak about in the garden, showing the forbidden fruit to Eve and tempting her to taste it.   Their prince, Satan, approaches Adam and tries to excite his curiosity; but Adam, with the prudence of a Norman peasant, replies evasively in monosyllables, and avoids the devil's snare.   Satan, discouraged, returns to hell, comes out again, cheers himself by a few capers, and then speaks to Eve.   In the subsequent scene, the best of the play, the unknown author shows a genuine psychological and dramatic sense, and even nowadays

[1] In the beginning God created the heaven and the earth.

we read this part with pleasure and respect. Satan successively plays upon all the weak points of woman— her appetite for dainties, her vanity, her curiosity, her jealousy, and her secret dislike of man. After having forbidden her to repeat his words to Adam, he commends the fruit. "The fruit possesses so great power that it will give them marvellous strength and might." [1]

> EVE (*interrupting him*).
>
> How is its taste?

> THE DEVIL.
>
> Heavenly!

> EVE.
>
> Is the fruit thus?

> THE DEVIL.
>
> Indeed it is.

> EVE.
>
> The mere look of it is pleasant to me.

While Eve is looking eagerly at the apple, "an artificial serpent shoots up along the stem of the tree of knowledge. Eve comes nearer and lends her ear, as if to listen to its advice. Then she takes the fruit and gives it to Adam."

When Adam has eaten, he is aware of his sin at once, and bends his head in repentance. "He cannot be seen by anybody, so he takes off his festal garments

---

[1] . . . si grande vertu qui les comblera de poesté et de seignorie.

and puts on poor clothes sewn of leaves, expressing the profoundest grief and beginning his lamentation." [1]

And while lamenting he prophesies the advent of Christ. The chorus chants: "*Dum ambularet. . . .*" God appears in His anger, Adam and Eve are expelled from Paradise, and the chorus sings : "*In sudore vultus tui. . . .*"

While the angel with his fiery sword watches the gate of Paradise, Adam and Eve till the soil with spade and rake ; the devil meanwhile plants thorns and sows thistles behind their backs. Then a host of devils rush in and catch hold of the poor wretches, put them in fetters and iron collars, and drag them off to hell. Shouting and hooting is heard from the infernal tower, a dense smoke comes out of it, kettles and pots are knocked against each other, and with this infernal noise the first part ends.

In the second part we see Cain's murder of his brother, contrary to the Bible, *after* the death of Adam and Eve. The first rubric says: " Then Cain and Abel appear. Cain wears a red garment, Abel a white one. They are to cultivate a field which shall be previously prepared, and after they have rested a moment from their work, Abel shall speak to his brother in an insinuating affectionate way."

The two brothers offer their sacrifices to God, but the gifts of Cain are not accepted. Cain gets into a rage, and threatens his brother with death.

[1] Tunc commedet Adam partem pomi ; quo comesto cognoscet statim peccatum suum et inclinabit se. Non posset a populo videri, et exuit sollempnes vestes et induit vestes pauperes consutas foliis, maximum simulans dolorem, incipiens lamentationem suam.

CAIN.

Abel, you are a dead man.

ABEL.

Why am I a dead man ?

CAIN.

I will take revenge on you.

ABEL.

I put all my trust in God!

CAIN.

He cannot free you from death.

ABEL.

I give myself entirely up to Him.

CAIN.

Do you wish to hear why I want to kill you?

ABEL.

Tell me, then.

CAIN.

I will tell you. You ingratiate yourself too much with God. For your sake He refuses me everything; for your sake He has rejected my sacrifice. Do you think I will not pay you out? Now I will give you your reward. You shall lie dead on the ground.

ABEL.

If you kill me, you do wrong; God will visit my death on you.

Cain in a fury throws himself on Abel and slays him. But in spite of his enthusiasm the prudent author does not forget the danger to which the performer of Abel's part is thus exposed ; he adds in the rubric:

"Abel shall have a saucepan [*olla*] beneath his garment, against which he (Cain) shall knock, when he pretends to kill Abel. Abel shall lie outstretched as if he were dead."

The chorus chants: "*Ubi est frater tuus?*" God appears and curses Cain. "Then He re-enters the church. The devils come and drag Cain away with them, covering him with blows ; they also carry away Abel, but more gently."

The third division of the play is a procession of the prophets who have predicted the advent of the Messiah, and who merely repeat the above described Christmas service in the popular language. This part is very inferior in dramatic interest to the two preceding divisions, and we will only mention a few of its rubrics. It is a peculiarity worth noticing that all the characters of the Old Testament are sent to hell, with the only difference that the *good* ones like Abel are better treated by the devils, who are not ignorant that salvation is in store for these, while the wicked ones can never expect to come out from the place of torment. As in the two first divisions, a Latin text corresponding with the subject of the play [1] is read and sung in the church, and

[1] This time it is the penitential sermon of St Augustine to the Jews.

it is the reader who summons the prophets to appear each in his turn. They have to keep ready in a hidden place each according to his "part." They shall step forward "with dignity and deliver their prophecy in a loud and distinct voice. The first who shall appear is Abraham, old, with a long beard and wide garments." After his speech there is a pause, then the devils shall come and carry him away to hell, and thus it is done with all the prophets. Among the number we notice Balaam, who comes in riding on his ass, from the back of which he delivers his prophecy. After all the prophecies follows a long sermon, a custom which is adhered to in the mysteries of several centuries and bears witness of their ecclesiastical character.

The *Adam Play* and the cycle of dramas which we must suppose to have been grouped round it, though they no longer exist, still remain under the auspices of the Church. These plays were entirely or partly performed in the church, and the actors as well as the authors were probably clerics ; in subject they kept quite close to the Scriptures, merely illustrating them and rendering them intelligible to the people. In the thirteenth century, however, these plays began to emancipate themselves from the guardianship of the clergy. For some time already the middle classes had attempted to increase their social and political power by enrolling themselves in guilds according to their different trades and means of livelihood, and they soon discovered that it was possible for dramatic art to flourish apart from the protection of the Church. Therefore brotherhoods were founded with the purpose of representing dramas at their own expense and for their own pleasure. This, however, was not effected entirely without the assistance of the clergy, nor was the religious character altogether lost. The subjects, though not drawn directly from the Bible, continued to treat of religious events, especially of the miracles which the Virgin Mary and other saints were supposed to have worked. These plays were called *miracles*, as well as the stories about the miraculous deeds of holy men and women. However, we soon see that the spirit of the Church had departed from these dramas, by the irreverent way in which the clergymen are frequently represented, and by the licentious, sometimes very vulgar scenes which occur in these otherwise so serious plays. From the fourteenth century onwards we find in France a complete cycle of such miracles about the most diverse subjects, yet all with one distinctive mark, that it is the Virgin Mary, who as a *dea ex machina* in the hour of need comes to the rescue of the hero or heroine in distress. This cycle of plays was called " The Miracles of our Lady" (*les miracles de Notre-Dame*). In Germany they were called *Marienspiele*.

The part which the holy Virgin plays in these dramas is often very peculiar, according to our ideas. It seems to be a point of honour with her to save every ruffian, whatever outrageous crimes he may have committed, if he only invokes her assistance at the critical moment. In one drama she takes a lively interest in a woman who has suffocated her son-in-law, in another a queen of Portugal is rescued and pardoned, though she has murdered two persons, while her confessor, who with her permission has disclosed the fact, is burned alive. In a third one the all-bounteous Virgin helps a hermit who has drowned the king's daughter after having violated her.

This exaggerated belief in the omnipotent influence of the Virgin Mary, characteristic of the thirteenth and fourteenth centuries, finds its strongest expression in a speech in which the devil, who is always at war with the Mother of Christ, indicates the fear of our Lord to act against her will. He says: "If he did anything to displease her, he would be beaten when he came home."

The clergy—as we have already observed—are not spoken of in flattering terms; not only monks and nuns are accused of being as subject to worldly tendencies as other sinful mortals, but the Pope himself is frequently taken to task for his cupidity. Kings and princes are generally represented as stupid, brutal and ludicrous; warriors and judges as a scourge; the lower classes alone find favour with the authors, which distinctly proves the democratic origin of these plays.

In order to give an idea of the dramatic literature of this period, which, with all its absurdities, its ludicrous anachronisms and its childish technique, is very interesting, and gives a vivid image of the opinions and everyday life of those times, we will describe the contents of some miracles which form part of the above-mentioned French series.

One of the most generally known is *Robert le Diable*, with which some years ago the interesting—though of course unsuccessful—experiment was made of having it

performed in modern language on a Parisian stage.[1]
The play contains forty-seven characters, and bears the
following title: "Here begins the *Miracle of our Lady
with Robert the Devil*, son of the Duke of Normandy,
who was ordered, on account of his misdeeds, to simulate
madness and dumbness; afterwards God had mercy on
him, and he married the Emperor's daughter."

The story is briefly as follows :—

The Duke of Normandy takes his son Robert to
task on account of the abominable life he leads.   " I
have knighted you," he says, "that you might cease
from evil and think of doing good, as behoves every
good knight."   But Robert answers that he does not
want to do good at all; on the contrary, he means to
go on robbing and murdering as hitherto.   Then he
summons his companions ; they march out together and
lay waste the property of a rich peasant; yet they expect
the man to thank them for having spared his life.   The
poor man answers naïvely : "Gentlemen, I pray God
heartily to give you all good health!"[2]

Whereupon the amiable company pillage an abbey,
and return home laden with booty.

The squires complain to the duke that his son
Robert ravages all property and violates all women.
The duke answers that he will put his son in prison, and
he sends two messengers to him ; the playful Robert
sends them home each the poorer by one eye.   Then
the duke makes his son an outlaw; anyone who meets

---

[1] It was performed on the 2nd of March 1879 in the "Gaité" Theatre in
an adaptation by E. Fournier.

[2] Seigneurs, je pri Dieu bonement
   Qu'il vous tiegne tous en santé.

him within the boundaries of the duchy is allowed to imprison him.

This merely increases Robert's fury. In the wood where he lives he finds some hermits engaged in prayer, and kills them all. A wayfarer tells him that his mother is staying in the castle of Arques. Sword in hand he rushes up to the castle, mad with rage, but his mother hides herself in terror from her son.

But this fact, that even his mother is afraid of him, seems to make him think ; he wonders why he has become so wicked that he is a horror to all.

" To be sure, I see it clearly now ; all men bear me a deadly hatred. And if God does likewise, it is not unjust. All shun me, all keep away from me. Shame and disgrace are my due for all the crimes and misdeeds with which I have defiled myself. Even my mother flees from me, and that grieves me much. Madam, speak to me, and beware of hiding from me again. I beseech you to tell me why I am so full of wickedness that I cannot abstain from it. I believe it comes from some hideous sin with which you or my father must have been infected at the hour when you conceived me."

Then the duchess confesses the terrible secret to him. As God would not give her a child, she had asked the devil to do so.

" I said in my anger : As God will not lay a baby in my lap, I wish the devil would do it. At that same hour and moment your father came home from the wood and found me bathed in tears. And the good man, who wished to comfort me in my distress, began caressing me, and then and there you were conceived."

This revelation immediately changes Robert into another man ; a fear seizes him that he will be damned, and he determines to go to Rome to obtain pardon of the Pope.   But before starting he tries to persuade his companions in crime to join him in his pious design, but these hardened ruffians have not the slightest desire to convert themselves.

Then Robert, who is already longing to do a good work, kills them all.   Upon which he entrusts the abbot he has just robbed with all his accumulated treasures, desiring him to return each thing to its lawful owner, and as a beggar he starts on his way to Rome.

The scene is removed to that city, where Robert confesses his crimes to the Pope, tells him his sad history, and owns his devilish origin.   But the Pope, who dares not give him absolution himself, sends the sinner to his own confessor, a hermit, whom Heaven has chosen to announce to Robert what penance he has to do.

Now we are taken into the presence of the hermit, who, in a prayer, is just beseeching God to let him know how he shall treat the great sinner who is coming to seek his help.   Then God, the Virgin Mary and the Angels come from Paradise, and God dictates the following conditions for his salvation : " Thou shalt tell him that he shall feign to be mad, and that in whatever place he finds himself he shall not speak any more than a mute person ; moreover thou shalt impress upon him that however hungry he may be, he shall never eat anything except what he can take from the dogs." These conditions the hermit imparts to Robert when he comes, and he gladly submits to them.

Then we see him in his new guise at the imperial court. The emperor is at table when the madman appears, followed by the mob hooting and hissing at his ludicrous gestures and idiotic grin. One boxes his ears, another blacks his face, but he only laughs and holds his tongue. The emperor pities him, and sends his equerry to make him sit down to table, but he refuses all the food offered to him. Only when the emperor throws a bone to his dog, the maniac jumps up and tears it away from the animal. Afterwards he establishes himself beneath the stairs close by the dog, with which he makes friends. The emperor sends him a bed, but he refuses to rest on it, and lies down on straw.

But now the empire is attacked by heathens ; the emperor, being in great danger, calls his whole people, clergy and laity, to arms. The angel Gabriel reveals himself to Robert, tells him that he is destined to save the empire from destruction, and shows him where to find weapons and armour. Robert puts them on, and without being recognised by anybody in his bright, white armour, he marches out with the emperor to war against the heathens, who meanwhile have inflamed their courage for battle by the following remarkable war-song :—

> Sabaudo bahe fuzaille,
> Draquitone baraquita,
> Arabium malaquita,
> Hermes zalo.

Nevertheless they are defeated by the mighty valour of the unknown knight. The emperor, after having gained the victory, asks everybody who the gallant fighter was, but he is nowhere to be found, and Robert lies again in his old rags on the straw.

The emperor's daughter appears; she cannot speak, but indicates by gestures that the knight they are seeking is the madman. All burst out laughing, nobody believes her.

Meanwhile the Saracens (or heathens; these two terms are always synonymous in mediæval folk-lore) try a fresh attack; the emperor goes to war again, and for the second time the mysterious white champion appears in his ranks, and his wonderful feats again secure victory to the Christians. One of the emperor's men tries to discover who the stranger is, and wounds him with his lance; the point of the weapon remains in the wound, but the shaft breaks and the stranger disappears. Now the emperor promises his daughter and half of his kingdom to him who can bring back the missing point, and the seneschal, who is in love with the princess, tries to pass himself off as the unknown hero by putting on white armour and wounding his leg. High honours are bestowed upon him, and his wedding with the princess is about to take place, when his trick is discovered, for the princess, suddenly recovering her power of speech, reveals that she has twice seen the maniac put on his armour and pull the point of the lance out of his wound.

Now all the court gather round Robert who, lying on straw with the dog, goes on playing the madman and making wanton grimaces even at the pope and the emperor[1] (fig. 1 p. 30).

[1] Il fait la figue au pape et jeux de l'estrennie d'un festu à l'empereur.

But at this moment the hermit appears and relieves the penitent from his vow by announcing that God has forgiven his sin. The emperor is glad to give his daughter and half of his kingdom to the son of the Duke of Normandy. Robert would prefer to go away with the hermit, but is persuaded by him to consent to the marriage and to inherit the imperial throne.

While this miracle for the most part preserves the character of the romance of chivalry from which it is drawn, the miracle of *Jean le Paulu* offers an example of a genuine saint's drama. It has this title: " Here begins a *Miracle of the Virgin* about *St John the Shaggy* [*Paulu = poilu, velu* ; = shaggy], the hermit, who, tempted by the fiend, killed a king's daughter and threw her into a well; but afterwards, because of his penitence, our Lady called her back to life."

As an introduction to the play St John comes to listen to the sermon which, as we have observed, is nearly always attached to these miracles. He seems very pleased with it and returns to his hermitage.

Here now appears the *enemy*; he has frequently, but in vain, tried to lead John into temptation. This time he has changed his face and name and comes in the guise of a handsome young man named Huet, who is engaged as servant by the hermit.

The king has lost his wife a short while ago; he leads a quiet lonely life. In order to divert his thoughts, his men persuade him to go out hunting with them, and his daughter accompanies him. They hunt a stag, but the princess loses her way; her father and his attendants seek her in great anxiety.

The young girl is terrified at finding herself alone in
the dense wood, and prays to the holy Virgin to come to
her assistance.

She discovers a light in the hermit's cottage, and goes
and knocks at the door.   The devil opens it to her, and
she accepts John's offer of hospitality.   Here is the
opportunity for which the fiend has been looking out so ·
long, to lead the holy man into temptation ; and this time
he is successful.   The pious John is caught in the snare
and seduces the princess.

The next morning the false servant reproaches [1] him
for his deed, and he is very much frightened indeed.   No
doubt the king will learn the truth, says the disguised
devil, and the culprit will be punished with death.   In
his distress John asks the devil what he shall do.
" Throw the girl into the deep well, and nobody will
speak of her again."   The hermit immediately takes hold
of the young princess, who is still asleep, and with the
assistance of the servant throws her into the well.   This
is no sooner done than the devil reveals his true nature,
and runs away with a sneer.

Now John is seized with remorse.   He falls on his
knees, and implores the mercy of the holy Virgin ; he
imposes upon himself the terrible penance of living
naked in the woods without shelter, and walking on all
fours like a beast.

[1] Vous avez bien fait vos degois *
　　　Père ennuit de celle pucelle
　　　Osté li avez la plus belle
　　　Chose qu'elle en son corps eust
　　　Et done miex priser se deust
　　　　　C'est pucelage.

　　　　* Amused yourself.

Then we are suddenly transported to a very different scene; a woman in travail, who sends her husband to fetch the midwife, and afterwards gives birth to a fine boy.

Seven years have elapsed since John began his penance, and God sends him forgiveness by the holy Virgin and the angels.

The king is out hunting again; he visits the same country where his daughter once disappeared, and sad memories fill his mind. "I cannot help weeping, for it occurs to me that I have not been in this place since I lost my child who was my great joy and delight. . . ."

Meanwhile the hunters have discovered a strange animal, the like of which they have never seen; it is the four-legged hermit; they are going to chase him, but John allows them to seize him without resistance, and he is taken to the king. At the same moment a merry procession passes them; it is the new-born child being taken to church to be baptised. To the general amazement the boy in the arms of the midwife raises its voice and speaks to John the Shaggy, asking to be baptised by him in the name of God.

The king, who is deeply impressed by this miracle, questions John about his past life, and the penitent sinner confesses all without reserve, viz., that he has violated the king's daughter and thrown her into a well. The king receives this heart-rending news with a sublime calmness worthy of imitation, and says: "Since God has forgiven you, gallant knight, I will also forgive you." He only wishes to find his child's body, and is taken to the well in which she was drowned. Here they all

kneel down in prayer.   John in particular prays with
the burning faith and eagerness of a repentant sinner.

In response to his prayer God and the holy Virgin
descend from heaven, and God orders him to raise his
voice and call the woman he has killed, and the princess
answers from the bottom of the well.   The knights
rush forward and drag her up, and her father, though
never abandoned by his admirable self-control, cannot
help feeling a very natural curiosity, and asks what she
has been doing all these seven years.   She answers that
she has been living with a lady who was so beautiful
that she could not be any other than the Virgin Mary.
All are delighted, and the king is so pleased that he
orders John to be consecrated as a bishop, after which
the princess is conducted to the church with great pomp
and splendour, and the play ends with joyful songs.

About the *mise-en-scène* and mode of performance
of these Mary-plays we know nothing for certain,
even less than about the drama of the twelfth century,
with regard to which the Latin rubric of the Adam-play
gives pretty good information.   A detailed *mise-en-
scène* would have required a most complicated machinery
and equipment; for without a moment's notice we are
transported from Normandy to Rome, from Italy to
Hungary, from the wild forest to the seashore, or to a
poor cottage.   There are battles, processions, church-
going.   But it is to be supposed that all this scenery was
mostly left to be imagined by the fancy of the audience,
and that with child-like naïveté the spectators were contented to take a fight between half a score of men for
the great campaign between the Saracens and the

emperor, that a dozen steps between two points on the stage represented the way from Rome to Normandy; also that they were in the habit of assuming that a certain period had elapsed when the actor declared that it was so.

In a future chapter we will try to put before our readers the probable course of development of the stage from the Adam plays through the miracles down to the great passion plays, and to explain what conclusions may be drawn from these plays with regard to scenic peculiarities. Here we have only aimed at giving a loose outline of these characteristic dramas in order to prepare the reader for understanding the purely technical scenic phenomena, the treatment of which is even more the object of this work than the history of the drama proper.[1]

II

The Great Mysteries—The Passion of Christ on the Stage—Form of the Mysteries and their Representation of Characters—Comic Scenes— The Blind Man and the Fool—The Devil and the Various Forms under which he appears—The Prologue.

THE ecclesiastical plays of the fifteenth century do not differ essentially from their nearest predecessors ; on the contrary they are a direct development of them in form as well as in subject. They do not show any tendency to a more concise artistic form, or to what we understand by a more concentrated dramatic action. We feel much

[1] Yet the Mary-plays are well worth studying. Readers who wish to make acquaintance with them are referred among other books to P. de Julleville's important work *Les Mystères*, or to Creizenach's *Geschichte des neuern Dramas*.

more inclined to look upon the fifteenth and part of the sixteenth century as the period of decline of the ecclesiastical play, though outwardly the latter flourished more than ever during that time.

What in the previous centuries had been simple and pious on account of the naïve faith with which the subjects were treated, and effective and impressive through the solemn semi-liturgical manner of its representation, assumed in the fifteenth century the more ostentatious, less religious character of a popular amusement without becoming richer or more refined even in its mere outward artistic form.

It would be absurd to measure the mediæval drama by the standard of modern or classical principles; and it is quite ludicrous to hear literary authorities reproach the authors of mysteries for neglecting the theory of the three dramatic unities which they did not know, and which, if valuable at all, at any rate would not have been appropriate to this kind of subjects. But it cannot be denied that the mysteries of the fifteenth century are spun out to such a length and filled with such an abundance of irrelevant and superfluous details, that it seems impossible to attribute the success which, as a matter of fact, attended these plays, to their intrinsic poetical value.

While, as we have seen, the plays of the earlier Middle Ages and the miracles of the fourteenth century —though by no means short—yet keep within measurable dimensions, the mysteries, properly so-called, swell to an inconceivable size. Several of them amount to thirty or forty thousand lines, and one—the longest of all—*The Acts of the Apostles*, a monster mystery performed in Bourges and lasting forty days, contains no less than 61,908 lines. By way of comparison we may remind the reader of the fact that the longest Greek tragedies do not contain much more than two thousand lines, and the modern ones generally about double the number.

Of course this enormous length could only be obtained by a merely external accumulation of subjects, originally perhaps by linking together separate plays. Instead of each being represented by itself, the stories of Adam and Eve, Cain and Abel, Noah and his sons, etc., were all fused into one great symphony about *The Old Testament*; however, it was no fusion in the proper sense of the word, but merely a loosely connected succession of the events related in the Holy Scripture. In this way originated what in English literature are called *Collective Mysteries* and in French *Cycles de Mystères*, those unshapely monuments of the peculiar theatrical indulgence and greedy desire of shows characteristic of the later Middle Ages.

A new and grand subject offered itself to the writers of mysteries in the history of the Passion of Christ; and the *Passion plays*, as they are called because of their divine origin, probably gave this dramatic period its peculiar stamp. We do not mean to say that the power of the authors increased in proportion to the sublime nature of the subject; on the contrary, it seemed to oppress them, and we cannot say that their art culminated in the figure of Christ. But in spite of all artistic imperfections, the story, grand and profoundly touching as it is in itself, represented with the devotion and zeal peculiar to mediæval amateur actors, could not help impressing the naïve, believing public with overwhelming power. Even in the present day the same play draws thousands of less naïve and less believing tourists to the small Bavarian town of Oberammergau, where the peasants are allowed to represent the human tragedy of the Son of God every tenth year, and the testimonies of experts are unanimous in describing the deep effect of these performances [1] (fig. 2).

Of course these modern mysteries leave out everything that might scandalise the spectators by its too profane or simply ludicrous character, all those quaint and amusing little details which in our eyes add to the attraction of mediæval plays.

Ancient authors, as may be imagined, never attempted to obtain what we call true local colour, which is altogether of much later date than we generally suppose. On the contrary, they assimilated, perhaps on purpose, everything to their own time. Costumes, habits and expressions were brought as close to everyday life as possible. In this respect the Middle Ages form an

[1] It must be observed, however, that the Oberammergau Passion plays do not date from the Middle Ages, but are of comparatively recent origin. In the year 1633 the country was afflicted by a pestiferous disease, and the peasants of Oberammergau made a vow to God that, to appease His anger, they would every tenth year represent in public the sufferings of His Son. The plague ceased, and the very next year the peasants, assisted by the monks from the neighbouring Benedictine monastery of Ettal, kept their vow, and these performances were continued pretty regularly during the subsequent decennaries, till they were forbidden during the Bavarian period of enlightenment under Montgelas. In 1811 they were resumed by permission of King Maximilian, and since then have been continued every tenth year amid an ever increasing concourse of curious visitors of various nationalities. Comp., e.g., Eduard Devrient : *Das Passionsschauspiel in Oberammergau u. seine Bedeutung für die neue Zeit*, Leipzig, 1851; and Karl Hase: *Das geistliche Schauspiel*, Leipzig, 1858.

1

2

1—Robert the Devil at the Emperor's Court (from a miniature).
2—The Passion Play at Oberammergau.

absolute contrast to Greek classical antiquity. While the dramatists of ancient Greece took pains to make everything as unreal, sublime, or conventional as possible, the mediæval dramatic author aims directly at everyday life, picks up and takes note of every detail, and retails it in the most ordinary language of real life. And as he was least of all capable of restraining himself, of modelling and condensing his subject, his efforts resulted in the chaotic dramas of the great mysteries. Though they contain beautiful and amusing details, perhaps a good deal more than they are credited with, they are not likely ever to become important, either to the theatre or to any but learned readers.

These plays, however, which differ so widely from those of our own time, cannot be measured by a modern standard; and it must be confessed that though the authors of those times did not treat their material according to our taste, in other respects they took great pains to work out its details. These plays are all composed in rhymed verse—as a rule in lines of eight or ten feet, with regularly alternating rhymes—and these verses are generally quite fluent and well constructed, especially in the French mysteries. As an example we quote part of a dialogue between Jesus and Mary in a Passion play of the fifteenth century (by Jean Michel). Mary prays to be deprived of the sense of hearing while her Son must suffer. But Jesus answers that it would do her but little honour if she did not show grief or pity on seeing her Son nailed to the cross. Besides "good Symeon" had prophesied that she would suffer. So she has to submit.

JESUS.

. . . Pour ce contentés vous, ma mère,
Et confortés en Dieu vostre ame.
Soyés forte, car oncques femme
Ne souffrit tant que vous ferés ;
Mais en souffrant meriterés
La laureole du martire. . . .

NOSTRE-DAME.

Au moins veuillés, de vostre grace,
Mourir de mort brefve et legiere.

JESUS.

Je mourray de mort très amere.

NOSTRE-DAME.

Non pas fort villayne et honteuse.

JESUS.

Mais très fort ignominieuse.

NOSTRE-DAME.

Doncques bien loing, s'il est permis.

JESUS.

Au milleu de tous mes amys.

NOSTRE-DAME.

Soit doncques de nuyt, je vous pry.

JESUS.

Mès en plaine heure de midy.

NOSTRE-DAME.

Móurés donc comme les barons.

JESUS.

Je mourrai entre deux larrons.

NOSTRE-DAME.

Que ce soit soubz terre et sans voix.

JESUS.

Ce sera hault pendu en croix.

NOSTRE-DAME.

Vous serez au moins revestu.

JESUS.

Je seray ataché tout nu.

NOSTRE-DAME.

Attendés l'aage de viellesse.

JESUS.

En la force de ma jeunesse.

NOSTRE-DAME.

C'est très ardente charité ;
Mès pour l'onneur d'umanité
Ne soit vostre sanc respendu.

JESUS.

Je seray tiré et tendu.
Tant qu'on nombrera tous mes os ;
Et dessus tout mon humain dos
Forgeront pecheurs de mal plains.
Puis fouyront et piez et mains
De fosses et playes très grandes.

NOSTRE-DAME.

A mes maternelles demandes
Ne donnés que responces dures.

JESUS.

Accomplir fault les escriptures.[1]

[1] Be contented, dear Mother, and let your heart find comfort in
  God.
  Be strong, for never did a woman endure what you will come to
    suffer, but in suffering you will gain the halo of martyrdom.
N. D. At least you will have mercy and die a short and easy death.
J. I shall die a very bitter death.
N. D. But not a low disgraceful death.
J. Indeed, a very shameful death.
N. D. But far away then, you will promise.
J. In the midst of all my friends.
N. D. Let it be in the night, I pray.
J. No, in the very hour of noon.
N. D. But then, do die like the barons.
J. I shall die between two thieves.
N. D. Let it be under the earth and in silence.
J. I shall hang high up on a cross.
N. D. At least you will have clothes on.
J. I shall be nailed to the cross quite naked.
N. D. Wait till you are an old man.
J. In the bloom of my youth.
N. D. It is ardent charity ; but for the honour of mankind, do not allow
    your blood to be shed.
J. I shall be pulled and stretched so that they can count my bones ;
    and above my human back sinful criminals will plant nails, and

It cannot be denied, however, that besides these beauties, the mysteries abound in passages of almost incredibly bad taste, in the coarsest platitudes and the most ludicrous anachronisms. Every opportunity of creating comic situations is eagerly embraced. We remember the short episode related in the Bible about St Peter cutting off the ear of Malchus, the servant of the high priest, and Jesus restoring it. This event is at once made use of for a humorous scene.

In a German Easter play[1] the scene is represented as follows :—

> O weh, schanden und schaden!
> mit denen bin ich wohl beladen,
> ich han hier verloren mein Ohr,
> darumb heiszt man mich einen Thor.

JHESUS.

(ad Petrum dicit.)
Peter, thu din Schwerdt wieder in,
denn du sollst desz sicher sin.
Wer rache will erwerben
mit Schwerdten, der soll verderben.

JHESUS.

(ad Judæos.)
Führet mir her den wunden Mann,
sin Ohr setze ich ihme wieder an.

they will pierce my feet and hands with great holes and wounds.

N. D. To my maternal prayers you have nothing but harsh replies.

J. The Scriptures must be fulfilled.

[1] Quot. fr. Ed. Devrient, *Geschichte der deutschen Schauspielkunst,* i. p. 27 f.

MALCHUS.

Meister, ich bitte dich,
dasz du wollest heilen mich.

JHESUS.

Din Ohre setzen ich dir wieder an,
als ich wohl meisterliche kann.

MALCHUS.

(*dicit socio suo.*)
Geselle lieber Freund, nimm wahr
wie es um min Ohr war.
Zuch hin, merke, ob es feste steh,
denn es thut mir allzu weh.

SOCIUS.

(*trahit aurem, dicens.*)
Dein Ohr steht dir fest sicherlich
Geselle, also dunket mich.

MALCHUS.

Jhesus ist ein viel guder Mann,
er kann wohl setzen Ohren an.[1]

---

[1] Woe is me, shame and damage, with them I am well laden. I hav lost my ear, therefore they call me a fool.—J. (*says to Peter*) : Peter, put you sword back again, for you may be sure that he who will take revenge with his sword shall perish.—J. (*to the Jews*) : Bring me the wounded man, I will put on his ear again.—M. : Master, I pray that you will heal me.—J. : Your ear I shall put back again as I can do perfectly well.—M. (*says to his companion*) : Comrade, dear friend! look what was the matter with my ear. Pull it and try if it is all right, it hurts me too much.   Companion (*pulls the ear, saying*) : Your ear is all right indeed, comrade, so it seems to me.—M.: Jesus is a very good man ; he knows how to put on an ear.

Not even a situation of the sublimest nature, such as the crucifixion of our Lord, escapes the general desire for vulgar realism. The act of nailing our Saviour to the cross is spun out with long dialogues between the executioners, who pull his limbs with all their might to make them reach the place where the nails are to enter, and the hard work is accompanied by merry jokes. Thus in one of the English collective mysteries (the Towneley collection), where the conversation runs as follows between the torturers (*tortores*) :—

Pr. Hald downe his knees. *Sec.* That shalle I do. His noryshe yede never better to. Lay on alle your hende. *Terc.* Draw out hys lymmes, let se, have at. *Quart.* That was welle drawen that. Fare falle hym that so puld! For to have getten it to the marke. I trow lewde man ne clerk nothing better shuld.[1]

Very similar scenes are found in German and French mysteries, though perhaps the English, especially those of the Towneley collection,[2] surpass the others in mixing up the serious subject with irrelevant humorous matter. For instance, it is in this mystery that a comic intermezzo is introduced after the crucifixion, the *Processus Talentorum*, where Pilate plays at dice with the executioners for the coat of Christ, of which he possesses himself, though he does not make the highest throw, whereupon the cheated torturers end

[1] [The Towneley Mysteries (Publications of the Surtees Society), London, 1836.]

[2] Of the English collective plays four sets are preserved—the so-called *York plays*, *Chester plays*, *Towneley plays* and *Coventry plays*. The two last-mentioned are supposed to have been written by citizens, and are strongly flavoured with comic elements. The Towneley collection, it is clear, was particularly adapted for rustic spectators.

the play with comic reflections on the immorality of gambling.

Though the Passion plays properly so-called are probably the most distinguishing characteristic of this period of the Middle Ages, other subjects are not neglected. Subjects from the Old Testament are as frequently used as before, with the addition of several new episodes, some of which are quite apocryphal, as, *e.g.*, that about Octavian and the Sibylline prophecies, which were supposed to have foretold the coming of the Messiah, and therefore were counted among sacred subjects. Further, *The Acts of the Apostles* provided an immense and diffuse subject, in which the authors accompanied their heroes all through their mission journeys in India, Spain, Rome, Egypt, etc., and did not leave them till they had made them suffer terrible martyrdom, preceded by elaborate tortures. On the whole, the chief attraction of these plays, their *clou*, as it is called in modern theatrical language, consisted of scenes of torture, and—quite contrary to the Greek tragedy, which does not lack horrors either, but hides the actual execution behind the scenes—the mediæval mystery represented the horrors before the eyes of the audience, who did not wish to be spared a single detail (fig. 3). There was indeed such an ac- cumulation of cruelties and torments that we may sup- pose them to have lasted longer on the stage than they would have done in real life. In the above-mentioned great mystery by Arnoul and Simon Greban, *The Acts of the Apostles*, we meet with a curious instance of economy ; one and the same executioner is charged with

3—A scene of torture in a Passion Play (from a picture by Albrecht Dürer).

the killing of all the twelve apostles ; in whatever country the holy men are to suffer martyrdom, it is invariably the same man who appears and kills them.[1]

There were also a few secular subjects which obtained the privilege of being represented under the form of mysteries, but the few profane dramas are quite lost in the uniform multitude of religious motives. Thus among old classical subjects France possesses a *Destruction of Troy*, by Jacques Milet (fifteenth century), the most popular—before the Renaissance—of all ancient Greek subjects. The author, however, does not take his story from the *Iliad*, but, after the fashion of his time, he uses the favourite spurious history which pretends to be the genuine work of Dares the Phrygian (*Daretis Phrygii de excidio Trojæ Historia*), and, as a loyal Frenchman,[2] he sides entirely with the Trojans, and looks upon the Greeks as a crafty villainous race. Achilles, in particular, is the object of his hatred, and he describes him as a traitor and a coward.

Another classical subject is found in the Swiss play *Of the noble Roman Lady Lucretia*,[3] by Heinrich Bullinger, a noted author of the Reformation, a successor of Zwingli, who, being a learned man, knew more of classical history than his French colleague. He even introduces his play by reading the story out of Livy, his principal authority, just as the biblical text was read

---

[1] Julleville : *Les Mystères*, i. p. 228.

[2] According to legend the Trojans were the ancestors of the French.

[3] "Ein schön Spiel von der geschicht der Edlen Römerin Lucretiæ und wie der Tyrannisch küng Tarquinius Superbus von Rhom vertriben und sunderlich von der standhafftigkeit Junij Bruti," etc. Basel, 1533. Reprinted in Bächtold's *Schweizerische Schauspiele*, i.

previously to the performance of the liturgical dramas. However, the drama turns less upon Lucretia and the disgrace inflicted upon her, than upon the political action which follows the outrage committed by Tarquinius; in fact, the principal character is Brutus, the "Burger-meyster," as the author calls him. The play has a very political and moralising tendency, and in this respect does not differ from the other dramas of the time of the Swiss Reformation.

An interesting point of this drama is that it has an appendix containing directions for the right understanding and performance of its characters. They are very brief, we must say, and conceived in quite general terms, and their object is more to explain the author's view of his characters than to offer technical instruction for their representation.

" The essence and life," it begins by saying, "of this and other plays not only reveals itself in speech, but rather in manners [*sic*], bearing and gestures. Namely, that great application be devoted to the habits, manners [*sic*] and emotions of the persons represented, the result of which will be that they will be lifelike in bearing and movements, while otherwise they will be dead."

" First of all Brutus is the principal character of this play; he shall be mentally and physically a splendid, brave man—grave, calm, just, full of scorn of what is wrong, so that nothing can shake him, yet kind to those who are good. The same qualities shall be shown in Valerius." . . .

. . . " S. Tarquinius (the king's son) shall be an

impudent, shameless scoundrel, physically exuberant, tyrannical and debauched." . . .

. . . " Lucretia and her servants, men and women, shall be perfectly chaste, modest and bashful, decently attired in black, without any luxury." . . .

We meet with a single (probably unique) instance where the mysteries even take up a subject of modern history : the French *Mistère du siège d'Orléans*, by an unknown author, who is supposed to have written the play about 1440, a few years after the death of Joan of Arc. Of course the famous maiden plays a prominent part in this remarkable drama, but the principal character is the town of Orleans itself, in honour of which the author, who is a native of this town, has evidently composed his play.[1] As may be imagined, a great number of Englishmen appear in this mystery, but all of them under curious qualified names, such as Sallebry for Salisbury, Suffort for Suffolk, Estuart for Stuart, and Fouquamberge for Faulconbridge. The religious element, which was naturally wanting in the classical mysteries, is strangely enough also less important in this play than we should have supposed from the nature of the subject. Nevertheless, God the Father, the Virgin Mary, Michael the Archangel, and the patron saints of Orleans, appear in it.

These enormous serious dramas, ecclesiastical and other, naturally required an immense number of performers ; two hundred was no unusual figure, and the longest mysteries even required as many as five hundred. It would, then, seem as if this branch of literature

[1] Julleville : *Les Mystères*, ii. p. 578.

offered an abundance of varied parts for the actors of those times, and to a certain extent this was indeed the case. Each tolerably large mystery contained a multitude of different characters, from God the Father down to the fiend, and all classes of men, peasants, artisans, soldiers, etc., etc.

However, on a closer examination the variety is not so great after all. To begin with, the subjects being nearly always the same, the characters could not vary much either. Naturally in a Passion play the central characters were always Jesus, Mary, Pilate, etc., round whom, among others, a certain number of traditional secondary characters were grouped ; and likewise in religious plays with other subjects.

What signifies more, however, is the fact that individual characterisation is the weakest point of the mysteries. It is this astonishing deficiency in particular which makes the dramas of that period such tedious reading. All the speeches flow on in one monotonous strain without arresting the attention of the spectator by any salient features of character, expression or thought.

The most indispensable features are just sketched with the coarsest pencil, so that Christ does not speak like a merry peasant, or the Virgin Mary like the hangman. But apart from these general outlines, which even in a child's drawing allow us to distinguish a man from a woman, nearly all characterisation is neglected. Thus, for instance, it is quite impossible to distinguish the apostles from each other by anything but their acts. They all speak in the same way without individual stamp.

The same applies to all the other characters : God, Christ, the holy men and women, in fact all the serious persons represented. It is precisely this deficiency more than anything else which shows the imperfection of the dramatic poetry of those times, indeed much more than the awkward and, in our eyes, very strange construction of the action. Whether a tragedy has five acts or four or seven is, from the artistic point of view, a very indifferent question ; whether it observes the three unities, or two, or none at all, is, to say the most of it, a technical question which depends on varying taste ; but whether the poet has the gift of describing the inner life and character of his persons through the proper choice of words and ingenuity of thought is a question of principle, of which neither difference of time nor of custom can allow the evasion. And this was just the point where the mediæval dramatic authors failed, though they might have learned inventiveness and the art of individualisation of their brethren in art, the painters and wood carvers.

In the less elevated characters, as a rule, there was a little more variety. It has been said that every opportunity was seized of producing a comic situation ; this however, must not be understood as if the characters who were meant to be serious ever fell out of their solemn monotony, but the secondary traditional parts, such as servants, peasants, beggars and executioners always brought in some animation, and were now and then painted with a rough comic touch. The safest and therefore most frequently used means of exciting gaiety was to represent a person with some physical or mental defect. A blind, a deaf or a lame man, or, better still, a fool or a maniac, was a standing comic character in mediæval mysteries.

It is interesting to notice that while deafness and lameness are still favourite means of effect with the modern dramatic author and actor, blindness and madness have long since fallen to the share of tragic poetry. But it was precisely these two lamentable complaints which created most mirth among the public of those times. The madman or fool—*le fou, der Thor*—excited so much laughter that finally he became indispensable, and was used as independent intermezzo to cheer up the spectators after the serious scenes. His part was not always written ; sometimes the MS. only indicated that it was the turn of the fool to speak (*stultus loquitur*), and it was left to the ingenuity of the actor to improvise his follies. By degrees, however, as the fool becomes a fixed comic type who performs his jokes independently of the action of the play, he loses his original character of "fool," and becomes the merry-maker. A more detailed development of this character will be given in a future chapter.

The part of the blind, as a rule, stands in a somewhat closer connection with the play. It is not quite unusual, for instance, that the miraculous cure of a blind person offers opportunities for comic scenes. In a mystery about St Bernard (*Saint Bernard de Menthon*) a man born blind is cured by touching some relics of saints. The servant who has hitherto guided his steps, but who is now superfluous, asks the blind man for his reward. His master looks at him attentively and then replies

with gravity : "My friend, I do not know who you are.
I have never seen you before." In another mystery a
blind and a lame man have recovered their health by
similar means. Here, however, the cure is effected
against their own desire, and after their recovery they
complain bitterly of having lost the comfortable and
lucrative living which they had enjoyed hitherto by
means of their infirmities.

Another characteristic figure of the mediæval plays
was the devil. The importance of the devil in the
ecclesiastical plays we may say lay near at hand, and
was a necessary consequence of their subjects. The
firm belief of the Middle Ages not only in *one* personal
devil but in numberless multitudes [1] of messengers of
hell, who—more or less successfully—were constantly
hunting for human souls, imparted to the devil of the
stage an interest mixed with horror, with which scarcely
any of the other favourite parts could compete. And
we must say the authors devoted rather more ingenuity
to the description of these horrible, but exciting creatures
than to that of most of the other parts, and they showed
greater variety in picturing the different evil spirits.
We find clever, stupid, pathetic and comic devils, we
might almost say good and bad devils. We see the
grand Prince of Hell and the poor subdued devil-servant,
who always gets into scrapes and is the constant laugh-
ing-stock of the audience.

In the beginning, however, the devil was scarcely

[1] A professor of theology in Basle, Martin Borrhaus, we know, took the
undoubtedly considerable trouble of counting them, and found that their
number must be exactly 2,665,866,746,664. Comp. S. Birket Smith : *Studier
paa det gamle danske Skuespils Omraade,* p. 46.

meant to be a comic figure, and it is a quite erroneous conception with which we meet not unfrequently—that he was nothing but a kind of jester, whose business afterwards devolved upon the fool.

In fact, the two characters are by no means identical, and frequently appear side by side in the later mysteries without in any way being mixed up with each other. There is, for one thing, this very essential distinction between their positions in the plays : that the devil constantly interferes in the action, and not unfrequently plays a principal part in it, whereas the part of the fool is but loosely connected with it and, as we have said already, in many cases is not even written, and in some cases is composed by another person than the writer of the mystery.

Finally, the devil is by no means always portrayed as a jester.   As we have said, he appears in very different guises.   In the earliest mysteries about Adam, Satan—as he is called there—was by no means intended to produce gaiety.   He is represented as cunning and seductive in a dignified moderate style, and in his speeches does not bear the burlesque character which became so common in later times.

The *Towneley Mysteries*, like Goethe's Faust, begin with a kind of prologue in Heaven, where God is seated on an elevated throne, and in a long monologue describes Himself to the spectators :—

> " Ego sum Alpha et O,
> I am the first and last also,
> Oone God in mageste ;

Marvelose, of myght most,
Fader, and Sone, and Holy Goost,
    One God in Trinyte," etc., etc.

When God has left His throne, Lucifer appears and
sits down in blasphemous scorn on the seat of the Lord,
whence he speaks to the fallen angels in mocking, but
by no means ludicrous terms. He finishes with the
following lines :—

" Say, felows, how semys now me
To sit in seyte of trynyty?
I am so bright of ich a lym
I trow me seme as welle as hym."

Sometimes the devil even assumes a tragic and
pathetic tone, as, for instance, in the French Passion
play by Arnoul Greban, or in a Low-German play about
the fall of man. In the introduction of the former the
fall of Lucifer is represented, and the " Prince of devils "
expresses his despair in stirring words. Satan, his
servant, asks why he howls like a starving wolf instead
of singing and laughing as he meant to do, and this
is part of his answer : " My laughter and my song are
fatal and wicked. My nobility and my great beauty
have turned into deformity, my song into a wail, my
laughter into despair, my light into dark shadow, my
honour into pain and fury, my joy into irremediable
grief. My pride only is left and will never change."
At the close of the same scene all the devils join in
howling a song, in which there breathes a really gloomy
and diabolical poetic power. It runs thus :—

" La dure mort eternelle
    C'est la chançon des dampnés.
    Bien nous tient à sa cordelle
    La dure mort éternelle.
    Nous l'avons desservy telle
    Et a luy sommes donnés ;
    La dure mort eternelle
    C'est la chançon des dampnés." [1]

In these verses there is a high conception of the evil
spirit, which rises far beyond the ludicrous grimacing
popular devil, whose hocus-pocus excited the laughter
of the public.   But, as a rule, there was a marked
difference between the Prince of devils and his subjects.
In certain mysteries there are a large number of devils
which are not all drawn with the same lines; in *The
Acts of the Apostles* by the brothers Greban there
are no less than nineteen different devils.   Like a pet
child this figure had many names.   In early times the
chief devil himself no doubt generally went by the
name of Satan, *e.g.*, in the Adam-play; later Lucifer
became the general term, while Satan was lowered to
the rank of one of his principal servants, who also was
frequently a comic character, was sent on fool's errands
and got beaten.   Other favourite names of devils were
Astaroth, Belzebuth, Belphegor, Asmodeus, Belial, and
many others.   We may mention as a curiosity that *The
Acts of the Apostles* has a devil named Pantagruel, the

---

[1] The hard eternal death—is the song of the damned.   It holds us tight
in its rope—the hard eternal death.   We have deserved it as it is, and we
are given up to it.   The hard eternal death—is the song of the damned.

same name which was chosen by Rabelais for the principal character of his famous novel.

The division into acts and scenes was unknown in the mysteries, at least in the earlier times. This change was not introduced till Latin plays became known. However, there had to be pauses here and there in the long pieces, and so they were interrupted in a quite arbitrary way, whenever the author thought that audience and actors might want a rest. Thus in the German play by Jac. Ruef, in which a division ends in the following way :—

> " Nun redet all der Ordnung nach,
> Doch lieben Fründ, lass euch nit irren
> Wir wolln en wenig jetzt pausiren." [1]

Then follows a "musica," and the play goes on from where it stopped. Otherwise the mysteries were naturally divided into "days," viz., into parts, each of which might be performed in one day. This division, however, was very irregular, and sometimes these "days" contained as many as twelve thousand lines, sometimes much less.

Almost the only characteristic feature which the ecclesiastical play of the Middle Ages has in common with the Roman play is the *prologue*. This, however, is no imitation; the man who speaks is not called *Prologue*, but—where he bears a title at all—it is that of a *Precursor* or *Prelocutor*. Sometimes it was the author himself who recited the prologue, sometimes the manager

---

[1] " Now, let each one speak in his turn. But, dear friends, don't misunderstand it. We are going to make a short pause."

of the play.   Very often—especially in   Germany—the
introduction was the business of a messenger or herald,
if not of one of the actors in the play.

The prologue for one thing had to explain the
subject of the piece to the audience or, where this was
superfluous, to tune their minds to devotion ; in this
case it became a little versified sermon ; and last, not
least, it had to secure silence.

The latter task, no doubt, was the most troublesome,
to judge from the innumerable means which were used
to arrest the attention of the noisy, chattering, ever
restless audience.   Sometimes we hear the frequently
repeated persuasive appeal : " Doulces gens, un pou de
silence ! " or : " Nun schweiget still." [1]   Sometimes the
better feelings of the public are appealed to, and those
who are not amused are desired to leave the theatre
and not to disturb the others ; [2] sometimes a little joke
is attempted ; it is explained that silence is not really so
difficult : " Chacun n'a que sa bouche à taire." [3]   But
stronger means are also resorted to.   Thus one of the
Towneley mysteries (*Processus crucis*) begins with the
appearance of Pilate, who, with drawn sword, swearing
and loading the audience with abuse, demands silence
in the name of the devil and the blood of Mahomet.
And *vice versâ* blessings are called down on the heads
of those who keep silence, and the prologue promises
to implore the forgiveness of God for the sins of those

---

[1] " Now be quiet."

[2]   Et se d'aventure en nos jeux
         Quelqu'un s'ennuye ou se travaille,
         Je luy conseille qu'il s'en aille
         Et laisse les aultres en paix.—Jean Michel's *Resurrection*.

[3] Each has but his own tongue to hold.

who secure silence. The most ingenious expedient, however, was invented by an Alsatian author, Jörg Wickram (sixteenth century). His play *God-fearing Tobias* begins with the appearance of a devil as messenger from Lucifer with a letter to the citizens of Colmar.[1] Lucifer writes that he has heard of this play which is to be performed in Colmar; but as ecclesiastical plays of this kind are not to his taste, he would like the audience to make a great noise and behave indecently during the performance, so as to prevent the texts of the Bible from being heard. Then the messenger adds, after having read his master's letter out loud, that he will take good care to put down and give Lucifer a list of all those who speak loud and make a noise.

III

Ancient and Later Theories about the Construction of the Mystery-stage— Development of the Stage from the time of the Adam-plays down to the Sixteenth Century—Auditorium, Scenery and Mechanical Contrivances—English and Spanish Street Performances.

OUR knowledge of the construction of the mystery-stage is not extensive, and the ideas which grew up in the course of time have—like those about the Greek theatre —by an ingenious combination of misunderstandings, produced a completely perverted image which has nothing whatever to do with the reality. Though these mistakes were proved many years ago, and correcter views of

[1] Jörg Wickram was a fertile author who lived in this town ; besides *Tobias*, his most important plays are the *Gospel play of the Prodigal Son*, the Shrovetide play, *Das Narrengiessen*, and *Der treue Eckart*. Though dating from the sixteenth century they are quite mediæval in form.

the mediæval theatre have been put forward, the erroneous conceptions recur over and over again, not only in
the brilliant descriptions of the more superficial authors,
but even in the works of otherwise very trustworthy and
highly esteemed scholars.   So it may not be quite superfluous once more to drive a stake through this persistent
spectre, which has disported itself in Danish stage-his-
tories among others, and which in Germany brought the
confusion to such a pitch that, a few years ago, an
imaginary mystery-stage, three storeys high, was built in
a modern theatre at great expense, and Goethe's *Faust*
performed on it.

Our sources for the study of external stage equipment are not very numerous.   The performances, we
know, were quite sporadic.   Mysteries were performed
now in one town, now in another ; much time and money
were spent in building fine theatres, but in the Middle
Ages proper stationary buildings and regular representations were entirely out of the question.   When the play
was over, the edifice—of course made of wood and other
light substances—was pulled down, the material, which
might be used elsewhere, was sold by auction, and so
every trace of the theatre disappeared.   A particularly
solid and well constructed theatre might exceptionally
be allowed to stand some years in order to save the
trouble of rebuilding it for a new performance.   Otherwise the stage was not considered—like the church—
to require a permanent house.   Theatrical performances
were seldom recurring festivals in the towns which could
afford to pay for them at all, and they required each
time a new and special equipment.

This circumstance deprives us of a very important source of knowledge with regard to the appearance and use of the mystery-stage. While in Greece the ruins of theatres offer the most essential support for researches, and at all events leave but little doubt as to the character of the building, though of course they can give no direct information about the manner in which it was used, the Middle Ages leave us entirely on bare ground. There is not a flight of stairs, not a beam, not the slightest remains of a theatre to give us a hint or any information. On the other hand we possess, besides the actual dramas, a number of contemporary—not very detailed or intelligible—descriptions, and a very few pictures representing mystery-stages and performances.

Now, despite these three sources of information, there may be points on which it is difficult enough to obtain full light ; but there is one thing on which we soon acquire perfect certainty, viz., that the former and still prevailing conceptions have no foundation at all.

To pursue the different phases under which these erroneous hypotheses have appeared in the course of time, and to show how they originated, would scarcely be of sufficient interest in proportion to the time and space it would occupy. Here we will content ourselves with stating that finally it was considered an established fact that the stage consisted of a high scaffolding leaning against a firm background, such as the façade of a house, and that this structure was divided into three spaces, one on the top of the other—this tripartition at the same time being a religious symbol—the uppermost space representing Heaven, the middle one Earth, and the lowest one Hell. These three storeys were supposed to be connected by stairs or ladders, so that the inhabitants of one of these realms might be able to enter into the others by these means of communication.

This conception of the mystery - stage needs no refutation, as it is not supported by any authority at all, but has its origin merely in the fancy of earlier authors, influenced by previous misconceptions of old texts. The false theory about the three storeys is essentially built on a passage in the chronicle of the town of Metz, which mentions a Passion play performed there in the year 1437. The passage in question runs briefly thus : " Lan dessusdit, au mois de Jullet fut jué en Mets le jeu de la passion de nostre Seigneur Jhesu crist, en la place en Change et fut faict le paircque d'une très noble façon ; car il estoit de neuf sièges de hault ainsi comme degrés tout à lentour ; et par derrière estoient grands sièges et longs pour les seigneurs et pour les dames."

The literal translation is as follows : " In the month of July of the above-mentioned year was performed in Metz the Passion play of our Lord Jesus Christ on the Place of the Exchange, and the auditorium was arranged in a very noble way ; for it was nine seats (benches) deep like steps all round ; and behind them were high and long seats for distinguished gentlemen and ladies."

The brothers Parfaict,[1] the well-known eighteenth century writers of stage history, probably supposed *paircque* to mean " stage," whereas in this place it is

---

[1] *Histoire du Théâtre François, depuis son origine jusqú à présent*, i. 51 ff.

meant for "auditorium"—*parquet*, as it is still called. They fancied that *sièges* meant storeys, and drew the conclusion that the stage consisted of a number of storeys one on the top of the other; this number was afterwards reduced to three, without any other reason than its greater convenience—hence the whole story.

It is much more difficult to establish with certainty how the stage was constructed at the different periods than to refute the mistaken ideas about its arrangement, and the attempts to solve the question which have been made hitherto have not been quite successful, as they are contradictory, and none of them very clear in itself. However, they are invaluable in so far as they have brought to light an abundance of hitherto unknown matter which helps to throw light on the general conditions of the stage. This is the case, in particular, with Petit de Julleville's large book on the Mysteries, the principal work on this subject, the second part of which is a treasury of interesting and admirably arranged details.

The attempt we are about to make here to reproduce the image of the mediæval theatre in tolerably sharp outline may possibly share the fate of earlier works upon the subject; new discoveries of authorities or of other instructive remains may obliterate or correct the attempted reconstruction. Yet, with the resources available at present, I do not think it would be possible to produce a perfectly trustworthy and universally received description. Our principal object shall be to add authentic features to the image, avoiding all non-contemporary essays at reconstruction, which, as a rule, especially in theatrical questions, have given too free scope to a somewhat confused imagination.

The first description of a mediæval stage is given in the Adam play mentioned above at some length. It will be remembered that the rubrics gave details about one locality, Paradise, and contained numerous very instructive remarks besides. It is true, there is no evidence at all to prove that these instructions were carried out, or that the play was performed at all in the above-stated manner, for the unknown author everywhere contents himself with saying how the localities in question ought to be arranged. However, the firm and practical grasp which reveals itself in the written instructions certainly does not point to inexperienced attempts; on the contrary, it seems to prove that the arrangement proposed by the author is one which he has seen and tried elsewhere and found to be good.

We learn that the stage was set up in front of a church, with which it was always closely connected. When the Lord has spoken He always retires into the church, and the texts and chorals which interrupted the action were invariably spoken or sung from the church. So the church forms the permanent background of the stage.

We get information, moreover, about two established localities, Paradise and Hell, but we are not told where they were situated. All we hear is that Paradise shall be in a rather prominent place,[1] and that it shall be hung with drapery, so that the persons in it are only seen from their shoulders upwards, and so as to allow dresses to be

---

[1] *Loco eminenciori.*   Comp. the whole rubric translated above, pp. 9, 10.

changed and mechanical tricks to be performed behind the drapery. It seems to have been at some distance from the porch of the church, for God, speaking from the church, points to it, saying: "Dost thou see this garden?" and Adam replies: "What is its name?" God: "Paradise." Adam: "It is very beautiful." God: "I have planted it myself," etc. And then He places them in Paradise."

About Hell we learn less, or rather nothing at all. We can only conclude that Hell was also placed so as to allow persons to enter or to be taken into it and be concealed from the spectators, for nearly all the persons represented in the play are taken to Hell successively to disappear for ever. In fact the rubrics give plain directions to this effect, for instance where Adam and Eve are to be conducted to Hell by the devils. The passage runs as follows: " . . . and they are to place them in Hell, where they shall then produce a great smoke. In Hell they shall scream joyfully all at once, and knock kettles and pots against each other so as to be heard outside." The piece gives no information either about the situation or outward appearance of Hell; all we have a right to suppose is that it was as far removed from Paradise as possible, so if the latter was situated as a sort of prominent box to the left, seen by the spectators, we must suppose Hell to have been placed at the opposite wing, to the right of the church door.

We gather, besides, from the texts and the rubrics that in front of the church between the two extremities, Paradise and Hell, there was a flat stage, where those parts of the action were performed which were not

limited to these two localities.   To this place Adam and
Eve are driven after having forfeited Paradise.   We see
that from Paradise, which we suppose to have been on a
level with this central place—this supposition at least is
nowhere contradicted—a door led out to the place, and
this door, after the fall of man, was guarded by an angel
with a fiery sword.   The place seems to have been of
earth, as it is tilled by Adam and Eve with spade and
rake, so perhaps it was the actual soil in front of the
real church.   At least there is nothing to prove that the
ground was elevated; on the contrary the fact that the
devils are frequently described as running out among
the public, by way of interlude, seems to indicate that
the stage, and at least the front part of the auditorium,
were on the same level, viz., on the flat ground in front
of the church.   On the central place some permanent
properties are indicated, two large stones used by Cain
and Abel as sacrificial altars.   They are placed there
from the beginning, that of Abel to the right-hand side
of God, left-hand of the spectators, on the same side
where we suppose Paradise to have been situated; that
of Cain to the left of God, the side where we imagine
Hell to have been.   Besides these stones, mention is
made of benches, on which Adam and Eve and—in the
last part of the play—all the prophets sit, except Balaam,
who comes in riding on his ass, on which he sits while
delivering his prophecy.

This is all the information about outward scenic
conditions found in this old play.   About the auditorium
we learn nothing at all.   One fact, however, must be
pointed out; it is perfectly clear that at the time of this

play all the actors were *not* the whole time visibly present on the stage. It is expressly mentioned both that they enter and leave successively, and that they dress in a "hidden place." We do not find the Lord seated on His throne as an immovable spectator during the whole action; during the intervals between His speaking or acting He retires into the church. And as it is said that the prophets dress in a hidden (secret) place, which must mean a place behind the fixed localities, Paradise and Hell, it cannot very well be supposed that the actors marched to the place of the festival in procession and full costume, as became the custom afterwards.

To sum up in a few words the description of this earliest known scenic arrangement. A background consisting of the front wall of the church, with the porch as its centre. The choral song emanating from the nave of the church, God appearing on the stage through the church door. To the left (of the spectators who sit opposite to the church door) a projecting sort of platform or box representing the garden of Paradise, the lower part of which is covered with drapery, the upper part exhibiting trees with fruits. The platform is arranged so as to hide from the public what is going on behind the curtain. To the right, Hell, likewise concealed from the eyes of the public. In front of the church, between these two extremities, a level plane with a few fixed properties and seats. The audience must be supposed to have surrounded the stage on *three* sides; the fourth (the back) of course being unavailable for spectators, as part of it was formed by the wall of the church, and the performers changed their costumes there behind the scenes, where also those mechanical tricks were performed which had to be concealed from the eyes of the spectators.

The next information we get about a mystery-stage is contained in a fragment of a Resurrection-play, which from linguistic reasons is supposed by philologists to date from the same (twelfth) century as the Adam-play, but which nevertheless marks a great advance in scenic development.   The play, which is in French like its predecessor, is distinguished by having its rubrics composed in verse and in the popular language, not in Latin prose like the Adam-play, and it commences with the description of a stage which is much more elaborately equipped, and has a much greater number of localities than the one described above.   The introductory description translated into English runs thus : " In the following way we present the holy Resurrection.   To begin with, we place all the localities and houses [*les mansions*]; first the crucifix, then the sepulchre.   There must be a prison to shut up the prisoner; Hell shall be placed on this side, the houses on the other, and then Heaven.   And, in the boxes [*les estals, i.e.* boxes, divisions, the same as *les lieux*], first Pilate with his vassals; he shall have six or seven knights; Caiaphas shall be in the second; with him the Jews.   Then Joseph, he from Arimathæa. In the fourth stall shall be Mr Nicodemus.   Each has with him those who belong to him.   In the fifth the disciples of Christ.   The three Marys shall be in the sixth.   Care shall be taken that Galilee be in the middle of the place.   Emmaus shall also be set up, where Jesus was recognised in the inn. And when all the people are seated and silence is secured, then Joseph, he from Arimathæa, shall come to Pilate and say to him : "— Then follows the dialogue, which is here and there interrupted by explanatory observations, all in verse.

The above description, I think, gives a clear idea both of this particular stage and of the development since the Adam-play, though it must be confessed that the previous interpretations have been anything but clear. Now, as before, we see Heaven and Hell each at one extremity of the background; as before, we imagine Hell to be to the right of the spectator. Its appearance and construction are not described. The theatre, by this time, seems to be quite detached from the church, and instead of the background formed by the church wall, we find a row of boxes or houses (*estals, mansions, lieux*) in which some of the principal characters are seated, surrounded by supers. Near Hell is a prison, a dungeon. This locality also recurs in later mysteries in the close vicinity of Hell; it is the limbo where unbaptised souls are tormented. Next after the dungeon follow six localities, which are undescribed like all the rest, but which, judging from the term *estals*, must be supposed to have been a kind of boxes placed side by side so as to form a background to the stage. In these stalls are seated, first Pilate nearest Hell, then Caiaphas, while the three Marys and the disciples sit nearest Heaven, which in this piece replaces Paradise, and forms the extremity of the stage to the left. We need not imagine this background as a regular straight wall; on the contrary, it harmonises better with the later style to fancy it as an irregular curve round the stage—*la place*, as it is called in the original description.

Also in this *place* we notice a considerable development.

The middle part of it is meant for Galilee, where Jesus appeared to the Apostles after His resurrection. Perhaps it formed a hill representing the mountain on which, according to St Mark,[1] Christ made His appearance, or perhaps rather a lake, near which, according to the more dramatic account of St John,[2] Christ watched the fishing of His disciples. For, in later times lakes are a favourite and effective item on the mediæval stage. There is further a place representing the lodging-house in Emmaus, limited, we imagine, to a table and a few benches or chairs. About these two places, however, no positive information is given; the scenes which are laid in Galilee and Emmaus are lost, and the fragmentary manuscript gives no further instruction. Finally we see on the stage the cross of Christ planted in the ground, and the body of the Saviour fixed on it; a stone monument represents the sepulchre.[3] Both seem to indicate that the stage was on firm ground, not on a wooden platform. The places of the cross and the sepulchre are not precisely indicated. A later plan of a German play of the fifteenth century, published by Mone,[4] shows both these objects in close vicinity of Heaven, the cross nearest.

What we gather from this piece is: (1) that the

---

[1] Chap. xxviii. 16.
[2] Chap. xxi. 4 ff.
[3] Joseph says: " I have here a fine monument made of stone."
[4] *Schauspiele des Mittelalters*, ii. p. 154.

stage became detached from the church; (2) that the façade of the church has been replaced by a row of buildings, a kind of scaffolding divided into boxes, in which the persons represented are seated before the performance begins; (3) that the stage proper is provided with different accessories and indicated localities. Finally, we are given to suppose that the wicked souls are placed on the side of Hell, which at the time of the Adam-play would have been on the left-hand side of God the Father, while Heaven and the good souls find their place to the right of God and to the left of the spectators.

The two following centuries scarcely offer any information with regard to *mise-en-scène*. The rich collection of French Miracles of the fourteenth century contains no descriptions of external scenic conditions; only a few passages in the text enable us to draw conclusions as to the existence of some scenery, and these agree, on the whole, pretty well with the image we have hitherto formed. Thus Heaven and Hell continue as the two extreme points opposite to each other. As we said above, the Virgin plays a prominent part in these pieces. When the plot is most complicated she "descends" from Heaven with her angels and solves it. We frequently read that she "comes down from" or "ascends up again" to Heaven. Here we must suppose that from the box representing Heaven a ladder or flight of stairs led down to the level stage. Such stairs are seen in later illustrations, leading sometimes to Heaven, sometimes to the other localities. From some of the miracles we see clearly that a lake with a boat or ship was actually represented on the stage by real water and a real vessel. Of course it could only be of small size. Of the extent of the stage we do not know anything, but in those times it cannot have been very large. The plays we know of the period between the twelfth and the fourteenth centuries do not contain a great number of characters : the Adam-play eighteen ; the Resurrection thirteen ; some of the miracles only ten or twelve ; others run up to between twenty and thirty ; and a single one, *Robert le Diable*, to forty-seven. To these must indeed be added a number of supers, but it does not require a very large space to contain some fifty persons, especially if we consider that part of the performers were grouped in the boxes while the others were acting on the level place. On our modern stages we frequently see two hundred persons, or many more, appear simultaneously without giving them the effect of being crammed, though wings, furniture and other accessories help to fill them up.

In passing on to the fifteenth century, the flourishing period of the *mysteries*, we find much more distinct points of support, which fully confirm our conclusions based on earlier records. Particularly instructive in this respect is an illustration of a mystery belonging to the middle of the fifteenth century. This highly interesting picture originally formed the title-page of a prayer-book, and was composed by Jehan Fouquet, a special expert in matters concerning the stage, the same who was entrusted with the arrangement of the theatrical performance on the occasion of the entry into Tours of Louis XI. Evidently this illustration was unknown to the

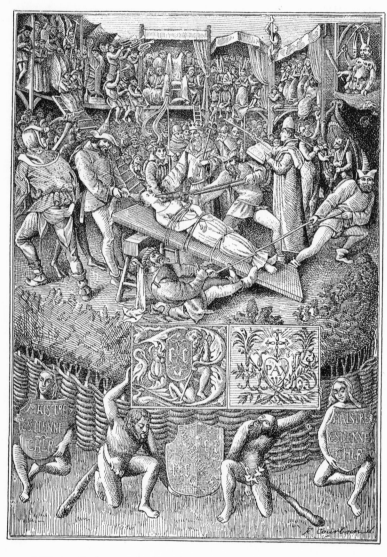

4 – A Mystery Performance in the 15th century.　The martyrdom of St Apollonia
(after a title-page by Jehan Fouquet).

various scholars whose works have hitherto served as bases for the generally received ideas about scenic conditions, but was brought to light for the first time by M. Germain Bapst,[1] whose explanation of it, however, does not hit the mark.

The picture (fig. 4) represents one of the popular scenes of torture, and is taken from the mystery of *St Apollonia*, a play which unfortunately is lost, but of the existence of which we are informed by a library catalogue of the fifteenth century. In the foreground the holy woman lies out-stretched on a sloping board, the upper end of which is supported by a trestle. Two torturers are tying her to the board and drawing together her feet with a rope with a violence that shows the passion exhibited in such scenes of torture. A third torturer, armed with enormous pincers, is pulling her teeth or tongue out of her mouth, while a fourth one, evidently inspired by the devil behind him, pulls her hair with all his might, and finally, a fifth is going away in a costume and with a gesture which suggests a scene, the coarseness of which is beyond description. Behind the stretcher on which St Apollonia is tortured, we see the emperor Decius and his suite; he seems to be dictating the torments, while an officer of justice, with a staff in his hand, reads out the sentence to the assembled people which crowds in the background.

The stage on which this action is represented consists of a platform raised at most four to five feet above the surrounding level and resting on a gabion-like struc-

---

[1] *Essai sur l'histoire du théâtre*, Paris 1893, p. 33.

ture. The stage projects in an irregular oval, and is bounded at the back by a row of stalls, which seem to be arranged exactly as described above in the Resurrection play.

Furthest to the right, somewhat advancing towards the centre of the stage, we see the gigantic head of a dragon with open mouth and large sparkling eyes. This is the entrance of hell as it used to be represented during this and the following period. We learn from several contemporary descriptions that this mouth opened and closed. Thus, for instance, in a report of 1437 about a Passion-play in Metz we read: "The mouth and entrance of hell in this place was extremely well made, for by some mechanism it opened and closed of itself, when the devils wanted to go in or out. In this head there were two eyes of steel which sparkled magnificently." In the mouth we see a devil with an animal head and a cudgel in his hand, while the other devils, who move on the stage and probably have speaking parts, wear no animal masks. Behind and above the dragon's head we see a great phantastic diabolical figure with many heads and supplied with horns; he holds a scourge in his right hand. This is perhaps a representation of the Prince of Hell.

Behind this figure, whose abode is not clearly defined, we see the wooden partition which surrounds the stage in a curve and forms its background. The height of the scaffolding does not seem to have exceeded twelve or fourteen feet; it is divided in the middle by a floor so as to form two storeys, the lower one of which is on a level with the floor of the stage, but does not seem to have been used, except perhaps for dressing. What took place there would have been excluded from view by the persons on the stage. But the upper storey is divided into stalls or boxes, separated by partitions and hung with various draperies. I cannot make out for certain what each box is meant for. The localities they are supposed to represent of course depend on the play, of which, as I said above, we know nothing. The box furthest to the left, however, clearly enough represents part of Heaven, where the Virgin Mary sits on a throne surrounded by angels, and seems to make a sign with her hand as if to stop the awful tortures of Apollonia. From this division a broad flight of stairs leads down to the stage.

To the left of the abode of the holy Virgin we are allowed to see a small part of another box, most likely the dwelling-place of God the Father. To the right of the Virgin Mary there is a box containing a band of music, which consists of an organ and six trumpets of different shapes, and close to them we discover to our amusement a bottle and a basket, evidently a hamper containing food. We scarcely venture to take this as a proof that even in those early times trumpeters felt the professional craving for liquids, of which they are accused at the present day. In front of the organ a man is seen blowing the bellows in the old-fashioned way.

The next box—the central one—shows an empty draped throne surrounded by ladies and gentlemen. A small ladder, which seems to be practicable, allowing it to be used successively for all the localities which have no fixed stairs leading up to them, is leaning against the floor of the box and indicates that the throne has been recently left. Evidently this throne is the seat of the emperor. The two boxes nearest to Hell are full of persons of both sexes, though most of them are women. What they are meant for is not quite clear.

Our illustration does not present the mystery-stage in its whole extent. Perhaps the draughtsman meant to simplify his reproductions by only drawing a small number of boxes against the background. Even the play of the "Resurrection" had more of them, and we see from contemporary accounts that sometimes, at any rate, it was the custom to have a much larger number of divisions; thus, for instance, in a Christmas play performed in Rouen in 1474 no less than twenty-four different localities are enumerated, invariably with Paradise and Hell as the extremities.

No doubt also the equipment was frequently much more luxurious than in this illustration. At the above-mentioned performance in Rouen "Paradise was open and represented as a throne surrounded by a halo of beams. In the middle God the Father was seated on a decorated chair; on His right hand Peace, and beneath her Charity. To the left Justice, and beneath her Truth; and all round them nine rows of angels, one above the other." The mysteries, properly so called, which treated the Bible from beginning to end, also required a somewhat richer scenery, and especially a number of mechanical con-trivances. Therefore the art of the machinist was pretty highly valued during this century. Still it is particularly the next — the sixteenth — century, which

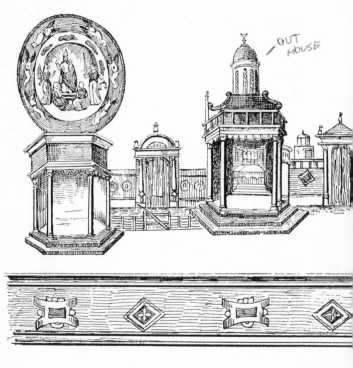

OUT
HOUSE

16th century.

presents at the same time the decline of the drama and the highest perfection in the domain of scenery.

Of this period, too, we are fortunate enough to possess an illustration (fig. 5) which shows the stage where a very celebrated mystery was performed, the Passion-play in Valenciennes, 1547, which lasted twenty-five days, and was famed widely abroad. Our illustration is a reproduction of a water-colour drawing, which is prefixed to the MS., and represents "le téâtre ou hourdement pourtraict comme il estoit quand fut joué le mystere de la Passion Nostre Seigneur Jesus-Christ."

In this drawing we notice an appreciable development since the fifteenth century. The principle is indeed the same, inasmuch as it shows a flat stage surrounded in a curve by the different localities in which the action successively takes place, and which form the divisions of the background, being the whole time visible to the spectators. But instead of the plain draped boxes, we now see buildings with towers and spires, with magnificent gates, pillars and stairs. Compared with the earlier illustration, which otherwise, from an artistic point of view, is much more interesting, it has the great advantage that each of its divisions is provided with an inscription indicating what it is meant to represent. Now, as hitherto, Heaven and Hell form the extremities of the whole series of localities. Hell, furthest to the right, is here represented as a large building of two storeys, the entrance of which, as in the picture of Jean Fouquet, is formed by an immense dragon's head. This head is grotesquely painted in red, green and brown.

Inside the large bow windows in the upper storey of Hell we see two red wheels, to which two naked sinners are attached. The top of the building is guarded by three variegated fire-spitting dragons, and above these monsters again his Majesty Lucifer himself rides astride on another fire-spitting dragon with a splendid curled tail. He seems to be borne by a pillar of fire. From hell a bridge leads to the "fore-court," inside the prison windows of which our unbaptised ancestors are sitting in sad expectation, with a background of flames rising behind their abode. A cannon with upward - turned mouth stands on the roof of the building. Then follow in succession a number of earthly localities : "the Golden Gate," "the House of the Bishops," "the Castle" —a sort of large canopy resting on pillars and projecting far towards the front of the stage—"Jerusalem," "the Temple"—constructed in a similar way to the castle —and "Nazareth," a wall with a gate, in front of which there is a level plane, raised and bordered by gabions. Finally, to the outermost left, "Heaven" or Paradise, surmounting a third canopy-like structure bearing the inscription, "a Hall." Heaven is circular; in the middle of it we see God the Father on His throne, surrounded by the four allegorical figures which we know from the Christmas play in Rouen. Behind the Lord—as we read in the MS. — "a golden wheel is turning incessantly," and the outermost circle is formed by flying angels. On the stage proper, evidently a terrace of earth, there is a lake, in which a comparatively good-sized ship is anchored. This lake is marked "The Sea." Otherwise the stage is empty, which, of course, does not prove that accessories like the cross of Christ, the Holy Communion table, or other objects, were not placed there. The draughtsman may have omitted such accessories on purpose, as they probably changed from day to day, according to the requirements of each play.

In combining the above-described testimonies we find a continuous progressive development following the same groove from the twelfth to the sixteenth century. We nowhere discover the slightest trace of a stage consisting of a vertical scaffolding in three storeys ; but neither do we find a construction resembling the now generally accepted idea of a stage consisting of an enormous square wooden platform, meant to be seen from all sides, and having various buildings scattered over it like toy-houses on a table, with Hell as a kind of foreground and Heaven as an elevated background.

All the various accounts and illustrations show a stage on the level ground, occasionally raised about four feet or more, forming a terrace supported by gabions. The purpose of this elevation may have been partly to give a better view of the stage to spectators who were placed on the surrounding level ground, not on amphitheatrical seats, where an elevated stage offered no advantage ; partly to allow of placing machinery underneath the stage for the execution of various scenic devices. Thus we find in an account of the expenses incurred by the performance of *Les Trois Doms* in Romans, in 1509, an item of 1 florin 6 sous, paid to six men for digging a passage beneath the stage from Hell to Heaven ; and in the Resurrection play by Jean Michel the actor representing Jesus was " seen to jump up suddenly and nimbly from beneath the ground by a small trap-door which was *covered with earth* and closed without being noticed."

This last remark proves most clearly that the floor of the stage was earth and not a wooden platform; why cover the trap-door with earth, if the surrounding parts of the floor were not part of the natural soil of earth?

The accessories used in each part of the mystery are placed on the terrace whenever they are wanted, but otherwise the stage is without decorations.

The background, which originally was formed by the church, afterwards—when it became the custom for the actors to walk to the place of the festival in procession and in full costume—consisted of a series of "houses" or rooms, in which the performers were placed during the intervals of their acting.   As late as the fifteenth century these compartments were only plain wooden boxes hung with drapery, and nothing in their outward appearance indicated what kind of dwellings they were meant to represent.   Sometimes, however, the prologue had to give the public this information, or each division was provided with a poster bearing its name.   Thus, for instance, in a mystery performed in Rouen in 1474, the prologue says : " In order to avoid tediousness we will say nothing about the localities this time. You may know them by the inscriptions found at the top of them." [1]   This way of indicating the localities continued in use for a considerable period.

---

[1] " Affin d'ennuy fuir nous nous tarions
    Present des lieux.   Vous les povez cognoistre
    Par l'escritel que dessus voyez estre."

The sixteenth century, which does not otherwise alter the construction of the stage, replaces—at any rate in the great expensive mysteries—the modest draped partitions by large magnificent buildings, which to a certain degree show by their appearance what they are supposed to represent, and we may also take for granted that the pieces of decoration and other accessories were richer and more true to nature.

Just as the sixteenth century marks a considerable progress in the development of scenic decoration, it also carried the mechanical devices, the machinery, or, as it was called by the French theatrical technicians of those times, *les secrets*, to a perfection hitherto unknown. Whereas people had formerly been satisfied with some fire-spouting dragons, hellish pits which opened and closed, and so forth, now the machinery took up a principal share of the general interest and degenerated into mere conjuror's tricks, which were enjoyed as such by the wondering public. Therefore the master of the machinery[1] was a most important person, and for great mystery-performances several of such artists were engaged, each of whom had his own secrets to manage; thus at a Passion play in Vienna, in 1510, there were no less than eight masters of machinery.

And, indeed, the feats were of a nature to rack the brains of more than one. At the above-mentioned performance in Valenciennes, in 1647, angels were seen flying in the air, singing, and irradiated with magnificent light. This was effected in the following way: in their

---

[1] *Le maître des secrets* or *des feintes*, as he was called in France.

hands they held golden staves, "which at the end had the shape of a lamp, out of which came the said flame, on blowing a little into the said staff."

"Item," we further read about the same performances, "at the slaughter of the Innocents in Bethlehem" the blood was seen to come out of their bodies. . . . "Item, about Sathan, who carried Jesus in climbing up a wall about forty to fifty feet high. . . . Item at the wedding [in Cana], where the water which was poured out in the presence of all was changed into wine, of which more than a hundred of the spectators drank ; likewise at the multiplication of the loaves, bread was given to more than one thousand persons, and twelve baskets were filled with the fragments." The dry, barren staff of Moses was seen suddenly to shoot out flowers and leaves, and the contrary happened with the fig-tree, which dried up visibly under the curse of the Lord.   Also the eclipse of the sun, the earthquake and the bursting of the tomb-stones, were represented in a way which appeared miraculous to the naïve spectators.

In another celebrated play, *The Acts of the Apostles*, performed in the old Roman amphitheatre in Bourges, which on this occasion was transformed according to mediæval scenic requirements, still more wonderful miracles were worked.   Artificial camels and dromedaries came forward.   A vessel full of all kinds of animals descended from Paradise and returned up to it again.   Devils and fire-spouting monsters flew about in the air ; two tigers came up from the earth to pursue the apostles, and by means of a trap-door in the ground were converted into sheep. Barnabas was burned alive on the stage, which was done in the following way : an artificial body full of bones and bowels was thrust on the pile, by which trick at least the spectators had their sense of smell tickled. For pulling out the eyes of St Matthew two artificial bores had been made, which were so constructed that the eyes came out of them after the operation, as if they had been pulled out of the orbs of the living saint. Simon Magus changed his face several times before the eyes of the spectators, and a fire-spitting serpent crept up an oak-tree. The play, which lasted forty days in all, is divided into nine books, and the movable accessories seem to have been shifted as many times. The last decoration required among other things the following *faincte*: "There shall be a high tower in shape like the Capitolium on which Simon Magus shall mount when he is going to fly, and there shall come a 'cloud-wing,'[1] semi-circular, to carry him away in the air; then the cloud shall be taken away and show the body of the said Simon Magus quite openly; then on the prayer of St Peter he shall fall to the ground and break his head and his bones. . . . St Paul shall be decapitated, and his head shall make three bounds, at each of which a well shall appear and flow with milk, blood and water."

And many more tricks show both that the task of the machinist was no sinecure, and that the technical resources were not inconsiderable, also that what the mediæval public demanded was not so much an artistic illusion, such as modern times try to produce — for,

[1] *Une nue collisse*, *i.e.* a cloud gliding on ropes.

however successfully these things were carried out, they could not in the open air and clear daylight produce what we understand by illusion—as the excitement of seeing a direct imitation of the coarsest details of real life—therefore they wished to see real eyes pulled out of the tortured martyrs—and to be surprised by the mechanical skill which produced these imitations. In this respect the mediæval stage is equally far removed from the ancient Greek and from the modern theatre. The Greek theatre indeed has horrors enough, but in its too scrupulous fear of exhibiting the ugly reality it always leaves them out of sight, and the stage continues to be a symbolic, sublime and unreal place. Our modern theatre, which represents the dramatic scenes as pictures in a frame, is able to hide much unreality and produce great illusion by effects of light and other scenic resources.

We learn that sometimes the spectators—like those of a modern conjuror's performances—control and interfere with the secrets of the stage. They do not care to accept the illusion that Jesus changed the water into wine at the wedding of Cana ; they expect to taste if it is real wine, and if the machinist has indeed been capable of imitating the miracle of Jesus.

The very fact that the public was enabled to watch the manœuvres of the actors could not help destroying all illusion ; it shows at the same time how close was the connection between actors and spectators. We know much less about the construction of the auditorium than about that of the stage. As there were no permanent theatres, we naturally suppose that the auditorium was always accommodated to the local conditions and to the larger or smaller dimensions required by the play. So much is certain, however, that the above-described scenic arrangement did not allow of the public surrounding the stage on all sides in the way described by several authors.

As background the stage required a solid and tolerably high building. If we imagine the stage to have been rectangular—nothing proves that it had this shape—we must suppose one of the sides to have been occupied by the scenery of the background, whereas the three other sides were left for the spectators. If the stage forms an oval with a curved background, a still greater part of it will be excluded from the eyes of the public. Moreover, there can be no doubt whatever that the machinery required a number of people working in concealment, unseen by the spectators, and this circumstance in itself excludes the theory of spectators surrounding the stage on all sides.

Nevertheless, it is not quite impossible that stages may have been constructed so as to allow the localities to be seen from all sides, especially where there was no need of very complicated machinery, but we must emphasise the fact that as yet the existence of such a construction has not been positively proved.

At the great important mystery-performances, which lasted several days, tribunes with several storeys were erected, either opposite to or on three sides of the stage, as a rule at some distance, so that the low seats closest to the stage were for the ordinary public, whereas the tribunes contained closed boxes for persons of distinction. At the above-mentioned performance in Vienna in 1560 there was a scaffolding of two storeys with ninety-six "chambers," each of which could be closed with a key, and was let for four "sundollars." Above the tribune awnings were put up to afford protection against the weather; otherwise stage as well as auditorium was open to the sky, and it happened occasionally that the performances had to be put off on account of violent showers of rain or otherwise bad weather, so that the public had to go away disappointed.

An auditorium more luxurious and spacious than any other seems to have been constructed by the inhabitants of Autun in the year 1516 for the performance of *The Life of St Lazarus*. Though we cannot entirely trust the assertion of our authority, the lawyer Chassanée, who describes this playhouse in a Latin work,[1] that it held no less than eighty thousand people, his account deserves attention, not least because here we meet with an attempt to imitate the Roman amphitheatrical style. This is how he describes the building: "We, Aedui [Gauls, Frenchmen], constructed in the year 1516 an excellent and magnificent amphitheatre on the field of St Lazarus, which is in the middle of our town. It was made of hewn beams, worked with great art, at the expense of the Church and the citizens. There has never been the like of it in France. The theatre contained in its upper part two hundred and forty cells,

---

[1] D. Bartholomæi Chassanæi Burgundi : *Catalogus gloriæ mundi*, Geneva, 1649. Quot. by Julleville, i. 405.

all divided by wooden partitions, and with their walls papered. These were the seats destined for churchmen, noblemen, senators, knights, gentlemen of distinction, and the patricians of the town. In the *cavea*, or lower parts, steps and benches were placed in circles, which increased in circumference in proportion to their height. Here the people assembled in crowds, sitting or standing, protected against rain by cloth awnings, which covered both spectators and actors; the latter played in the centre of the *cavea* or stage, and were always separated from the audience by a moat filled with water and by other obstacles. In this amphitheatre eighty thousand men could easily assemble, and when the play had been announced in the neighbouring districts the spectators rushed to the place in almost innumerable crowds. The performance was perfect; it was given in honour of St Lazarus, the patron saint of the Aedui, whose life, written in excellent verse, not from empty vanity, but for the honour of God and St Lazarus was represented full of life and gratis [sic]. God also granted that on this occasion there was heard neither whistling nor noise, mockery or scornful laughter. It rained in the night, but during the day it was the finest and clearest weather ever seen."

We see the good lawyer is not quite clear; in one place he understands by *cavea* the lower part of the auditorium, in another the "stage," in the middle of which the actors appear. Otherwise the construction of the stage is not mentioned; it need not have been circular like the Roman arena or the Greek orchestra, but may quite well have had the usual background, in which case, of course, the rows of amphitheatrical benches did not close all round.

For the above description of the scenic construction of this time, we see, the examples are chiefly derived from France, as also both the illustrations of the fifteenth and sixteenth centuries respectively date from this country. From other countries the contemporary information is much more sparing, and we must say on the whole that the mysteries nowhere reach such perfection as in France. However, a few rather defective designs from Germany seem to indicate that there the construction was essentially the same as in France. In the rough sketch published by Mone in his book *Schauspiele des Mittelalters*, we again find Heaven and Hell opposite to each other, and forming the extremities, with a curving row of buildings between them. What we are in the habit of calling the stage proper is pretty closely covered with different localities, such as the three crosses and *das hailig grab* close up to Heaven ; in the middle ground, pillars, one for the scourging of Christ, the other, curiously enough, for the cock that announces the denial of St Peter ; in the foreground a house for the Holy Supper ; finally, near Hell, and on the same level, the "house of Caiaphas" (*Kaivas Husz*) and the "house of Annas" (*Annas Husz*).[1]

We meet with a similar, but much more complicated, arrangement in the plan of a stage for a two days' Easter play performed in Lucerne in the year 1583. At the international exhibition of musical and theatrical objects held in Vienna in 1892, a model composed after the

[1] Comp. Mone, ii. 157.

afore-mentioned plans was exhibited, in which the stage was supposed to be surrounded by spectators on all sides. Without a close knowledge of the area of the ancient market-place in Lucerne, it is scarcely possible to prove that the stage, as supposed, occupied the whole place, while the spectators were seated partly at the surrounding windows, partly on scaffoldings constructed for the purpose. Still, judging from the plan, which in many points is not clear, it might seem as if this had been the case, though it is quite possible that our general theory holds good in this case also. A reduced and simplified reproduction is found in Rudolf Genée's *Lehr- und Wanderjahre des deutschen Schauspiels.*

In England, on the contrary, we find a decided deviation from the general construction. Whether the latter was known there is a question we cannot answer; but of the performances of the great collective plays we possess accounts which reveal quite peculiar scenic arrangements.

It was customary for the citizens of the town which was going to perform an ecclesiastical play to divide the different parts of it between them, so that each class or trade had its particular division to provide for. They defrayed the costs of equipment, stage, costume and all, and in the distribution of the sacred subjects the truly English practical sense was shown in the taking into account the pecuniary capacity of each trade. Thus the goldsmiths undertook the part about the three Magi, where crown and precious jewels were employed. The Deluge was acted in two divisions, the first of which, where Noah and his family had to build the Ark, was undertaken by the shipbuilders; the second part, where the scene was laid on the sea, was in the hands of sea-men and fishmongers. The Passover meal was the business of the bakers; the vintners, of course, were the very men for the Wedding in Cana.[1]

The scaffoldings on which these plays were per-formed were called "pageants,"[2] and the plays them-selves got the same name. An eye-witness—Archdeacon Rogers, who died in 1595—gives a tolerably graphic description of a pageant theatre. He writes: "The season of their performance was Monday, Tuesday and Wednesday in Whitsun - week. The maner of these playes weare, every company had his pagiant, or p'te, wch pagiants weare a high scafolde w'th 2 rowmes, a higher and a lower, upon 4 wheeles. In the lower they apparelled themselves, and in the higher rowme they played, beinge all open on the tope, that all behoulders might heare and see them. The places where they played them was in every streete. They begane first at the Abay gates, and when the first pagiante was played, it was wheeled to the highe crosse before the Mayor, and so to every streete, and soe every streete had a pagiant playinge before them at one time, till all the pagiantes for the daye appoynted weare played, and when one pagiant was neere ended, worde was broughte from streete to streete, that soe they mighte come in place thereof, excedinge orderlye, and all the streetes

[1] Comp. Miss Toulmin Smith: *York Plays*, containing an exact dis-tribution of all these (48) separate plays, after a list of 1415, composed by a town clerk.

[2] The word has been differently explained; nowadays, however, it is generally supposed to originate in the Latin *pagina* in its signification of scaffolding.

have their pagiantes afore them all at one time playinge togeather ; to se w'ch playes was great resorte, and also scafoldes and stages made in the streetes in those places where they determined to playe theire pagiantes." [1]

We see from these descriptions that the Pageant-stages somewhat resembled the strolling puppet-shows ; at the bottom a space (of course covered) where the actors dressed, and whither they retired during the intervals of acting ; at the top an open stage where the performance took place. About the size of such a scaffold we have no idea. It goes without saying that all the scenery must have been utterly primitive. Though no doubt much time and care were lavished on the study of these plays, and though the honest citizens and artisans certainly were not stingy where the glory of God and the honour of their class were concerned, these plays at once remind us of Shakespeare's beautiful satire in the " Midsummer-Night's Dream," and we see Bottom the Weaver and Snug the Joiner exert themselves on the scaffold to the astonishment of their equals.

The English mysteries in themselves—at least as far as I can see—are very inferior to the best contemporary French plays, and bear altogether the stamp of a simpler origin and simpler execution. Nor do the English accounts mention any great luxury in equipment or in the arrangement of the auditorium, such as is the constant burthen of the reports about the more important

---

[1] Archdeacon Rogers' (d. 1595) account of the Whitsun-plays at Chester, quoted by Sharp, *Dissertation on the Pageants or Dramatic Mysteries anciently performed at Coventry*, pp. 17, 18.

French performances. We are scarcely mistaken in assuming that the average English plays of those times were of a simpler, more exclusively popular character than those of other European countries. There can hardly be any doubt that besides the travelling stages used for pageants, England possessed larger, grander stages of the French style, on which the entire Collective Mystery could be performed in succession, but we do not—at least not yet—possess exact information about them. We know so much, however: that the three Magi appeared on horseback, which, as a matter of course, would have been impossible on the high pageants, and a few notes in the plays refer to an arrangement which is inconsistent with travelling stages. Thus in the play about the Last Supper, in the Coventry collection, we read: "Here Christ entereth into the house with His disciples and eateth the Paschal lamb; and in the meantime the '*counsel-house*' before said shall suddenly unclose, shewing the bishops, priests and Jews sitting in their state, like as it were a '*convocation*.'" And further on, when the bishops have left the house: " and then the place where Christ is in shall suddenly unclose round about, shewing Christ sitting at the table and His disciples each in their degree."[1] It has been proved by the English scholar, F. T. Ordish, that plays of this kind were performed in the old amphitheatres of the time of the Romans, or in later imitations of them.

We have still to observe that the travelling pageants, which, like large cars, moved from street to street, and

[1] A. W. Pollard : *English Miracle Plays*, xxvi.

as it were in a mighty procession furnished the public with a complete play, find their parallels in Spain, where the so - called *fiestas de los carros*, carriage - plays or festivals, were arranged in a similar manner. However, about the mediæval Spanish plays we possess scarcely any information, and what we know about these carriage-plays dates from a later time. It has been maintained in an earlier chapter of this book[1] that the Japanese have a kind of procession-play which in many ways reminds us of the European mediæval street mysteries. Nor are these procession-plays quite unknown in France, but as a rule the representations on these carriage stages only consisted of tableaux or mimic scenes of mysteries. In Chaumont, however, the people celebrated every fifth or sixth year a festival in honour of St John the Baptist, and on this occasion it became the custom to perform fragments of plays in connection with the procession all over the town.

IV

The Actors of the Mysteries—Whence they came—Participation of the Different Classes of Society—Children and Women as Dramatic Performers—Contracts and Penal Clauses—Toil and Dangers of the Performances—Costumes.

ORIGINATING in the Church, the mediæval plays drew their first actors from the priesthood itself. From the beginning of the mystery-plays and quite down to the period of their culmination, there existed no professional class of actors. It is true, jugglers and minstrels

[1] Vol. i. p. 50.

travelled through the countries delivering their songs and stories, but dramatic representations performed by specially trained actors, who considered dramatic art as their principal work and their means of livelihood, were not known till the fifteenth century.

And even if such a class had existed, they would scarcely have been entrusted with the performance of what we call ecclesiastical plays. For these were—and continued to be—a kind of religious festivals, and even after having been detached from the Church, they were considered neither as a mere popular amusement nor as a special art; their occasion and purpose were always the glorification of the Virgin Mary and the Saints, in which the whole people—all classes of society—wished to share, and which they did not wish to leave in the hands of a paid company.

Probably the conception of dramatic art as such did not even exist in the mediæval mind. In order to avert a general scourge, such as a plague, etc., or to honour the saint of the town, or to commemorate the great religious festivals, such as Whitsuntide or Ascension, scenes from the Holy Scriptures or episodes in the lives of the saints were represented " in figures," without any idea of practising one of the fine arts; the object was to please God, and finally—but this was never publicly acknowledged—to gratify the people with a festival, which they enjoyed more than anything else, and for which there was a general craving.

Let us hear how the good town of Seurre in the fifteenth century understood the task which we should call the composition and staging of a drama. It is

André de la Vigne, the composer of the mystery himself, who describes how his play about St Martin originated: "In honour of God, the Virgin Mary and the glorious patron of this town of Seurre, Monseigneur [*sic*] St Martin, assembled in the year 1496, on the ninth day of the month of May, the day before the Ascension of Christ, in the house of Master André de la Vigne . . . [here follow the names of the members of the committee] . . . who held a council about making and composing a register [*sic*], in which was to be recounted and explained in figures [*par personnaiges*] the life of Monseigneur St Martin, so that in seeing it acted the common people might easily hear and see how the noble patron saint of the said town of Seurre led a pious and holy life; which register was made and composed, such as it now appears, five weeks after the said day. . . ."

But though the actors did not conceive their work as an art, they took it nevertheless very seriously. It must not be imagined that Shakespeare's witty satire on the amateur acting of citizens applied even to the average of mediæval performances. On the contrary, immense application and care and the most self-sacrificing devotion were bestowed on these representations. Even now we see the veneration with which the Oberammergau peasants devote themselves to their dramatic work; their zeal, however, is nothing compared with the interest—we may say, the passion—exhibited by the ancient amateur performers of the mystery-plays.

All classes contributed their share to the staff, nobility, clergy and citizens of every rank. In French accounts we find a number of noble names among the performers of different kinds of parts. The clergy naturally took a very active part in these plays; not the highest clergy, however, but mostly deacons, ordinary priests and monks. They preferred in particular the most sublime parts, such as God, Jesus and the Virgin Mary, and they went so far in their zeal and interest in dramatic art, that their ecclesiastical duties had frequently to suffer from it. Thus a Jacobin monk of Troyes (in the year 1490) confessed that he had neglected his office for seven years in order to study and perform the part of Jesus in the Passion play.

Magistrates, also citizens of the higher classes, and lawyers, frequently participated in the performances; nevertheless the petty tradespeople contributed the largest share to the staff. We have seen how in England the different trades shared the divisions of the mysteries between them, and undertook their equipment and performance; such distribution did not take place in other countries, but all classes united in accomplishing the whole work; a barber was not too shy to act together with a nobleman or a magistrate, and we nowhere hear that this caused dissension among the classes.

As a rule women did not appear on the mediæval stage, but children frequently did; they represented angels, young girls, or children's parts, which occurred repeatedly in such plays as treated of the lives of the characters from their birth to their death. The more important female parts were performed by half grown-up youths, and particular care was taken to choose young men who were beardless and good-looking, and whose voices were not yet breaking. For such handsome children of the poorer classes the theatre sometimes became the first step to a prosperous career above their class, beyond which in those times it was otherwise difficult to rise. Thus we read about a barber's apprentice, who reaped great success in Metz at the performance of *The Life and Sufferings of St Barbara* (1485). "At that time," the chronicle says, "there lived in Metz a young barber's apprentice named Lyonard, who was born in Notre Dame d'Aix in Germany, but who for a long time had been living at Metz in the house of Master Hannes, the barber, who performed the part of St Barbara so thoughtfully and reverently that several persons wept for pity; for he showed such fluency of elocution and such polite manners, and his countenance and gestures were so expressive when among his maidens, that it pleased everybody and could not have been better done. And he found so great favour with all, that there was not a nobleman or priest or layman who did not wish to receive this youth into his house to feed and educate him; among whom there was a rich widow . . . 'who wanted to adopt him as her heir.'" [1] But the barber preferred a canon, who sent him to Paris to study; there he took the degree of M.A., and finally was made a canon himself. The following year, however, his reputation as an actor was partly lost, for alas! his voice was breaking! The part he acted at the time was that of St Catherine, "but the people was not quite pleased with it, because the voice of the said Lyonard was somewhat changed already."

On very rare occasions, nevertheless, women are seen

---

[1] *Croniques de Metz.* Huguenin, p. 473. Quoted by Julleville, *op. cit.* ii. 48.

to have acted in the mysteries. Thus, besides the famous barber, Metz possessed another scenic celebrity in the person of an actress, who even appeared in the same parts. We know, at all events, that she performed the part of St Catherine, for the chronicle says : " And the 'person' (*personnaige*) of St Catherine was performed by a young girl, about eighteen years old, who was the daughter of Dediet the glazier, and she did her duty very well indeed, to the pleasure and delight of everybody. Though this girl had 2300 lines in her part, she had them all at her fingers' ends, and this girl did speak so quickly and so pitifully that she made several people cry and pleased everybody. And for this reason the girl made a rich match with a nobleman belonging to the hired troops in Metz, named Henri de Latour, who fell in love with her because of the great pleasure he took in it [in her play]."

Though this case is not unique—at the Passion play in Valenciennes, 1547, five young girls took part in the performance—we must take it for granted that female parts were only exceptionally acted by women. This is so much the more surprising, as women frequently appeared in the historical pantomimes and *tableaux vivants*, which the mediæval towns habitually produced on festive occasions, such as the arrival of Royalties, etc. That it was not bashfulness which prevented women from mounting the stage is seen clearly enough from the riskiness of the situations in which they exhibited themselves at these festivities. Thus, for instance, at the entry of Louis XI. into Paris (31st of August, 1461), for one thing, ladies appeared quite naked as sirens, without apparently scandalising anybody. Most likely the reasons for excluding women from acting in the mysteries must be sought in old custom and tradition. Originally, we know, priests were the only actors, so, in the nature of things, it was out of the question that women should share in the performance. Later, eye and ear had become accustomed to see men act the female parts, and only very seldom was the idea conceived that the reform might be attempted of allowing the other sex to come forward. The custom was not broken with till the time of the Renaissance, and in some countries not till a later period.

The earlier mediæval drama, from the twelfth to the fourteenth century, did not require a very numerous staff. The twenty to thirty persons were comparatively easy to rule, and though the scenic rubrics prove that even in those times the affair was treated with great seriousness, it is not till the time of the great mysteries that we meet with detailed regulations and severe laws respecting the relation of the actor to his part, which bound down the eager amateurs by stringent provisions to complete the tasks they had undertaken and begun.

The mysteries of the fifteenth and sixteenth centuries as a rule required an immense number of performers. About two or three hundred parts, besides supers and musicians, were by no means unusual, and a few come up to five hundred; for instance, the celebrated *Acts of the Apostles* contains no less than 494 speaking parts, distributed in the following way: in Paradise there were 32 persons, in Hell 19; there were 13 apostles, 7 deacons, 43 disciples, 4 cousins of the Virgin

Mary, 5 Marys, 10 widows, 11 other women, 5 maidens, 18 servant girls, 8 emperors, 11 kings, 5 queens, 14 judges, 19 pro-consuls, 44 knights, 23 armour-bearers, 63 Jews in the synagogue, 44 ordinary citizens, 15 philosophers, 5 magicians, 6 bishops, 14 scribes, 9 tyrants (viz., executioners), 8 jailers, 9 messengers, 15 sick persons, 9 beggars and prisoners, 3 seamen, 2 charioteers, and 1 smith.

Great as the common interest and zeal might be supposed to be, it was natural that such an enormous company had to be bound by strict regulations, if order and decent behaviour were to be secured at rehearsals and performance.

A committee of the best men of the town undertook to distribute the parts according to discretion among those who might be considered qualified for acting in a mystery. And every man who was accepted as an actor had to swear on the Gospel that he would submit to the rules of the leading men, and bind himself to accomplish his task to the best of his ability. Sometimes a solemn contract was concluded with severe and detailed penal clauses. It was in the power of the superior to inflict fines for infringement of the rules, and the amount of the fine was fixed in the contract. Thus it was punishable to leave the theatre during the performance—it must be remembered that it lasted several days in succession; it was likewise forbidden to the actors to assemble before, during, or after the performance for the purpose of drinking; they had to be satisfied with the meal provided for them by their superiors, and to eat it on the spot.

We understand that an exceptional zeal, reverence and energy were required to persevere with these studies, which lasted for months, even half a year, where the large parts to be learned amounted to whole books, and where the memory had no prompter to fall back upon. We saw that the young girl in Metz had 2300 verses (lines) to learn by heart; that is about as much as a whole modern play. And certain parts of Christ even amounted to about double the number. A few parts, indeed, were divided between two performers, but this was not done for the sake of lessening the difficulties for each of them. It was for a very different purpose.

We hear that a few years ago a play was presented to our Royal Theatre (in Copenhagen); it was in one act, and treated of the eventful life of Moses from his early infancy in the reed basket on the Nile to his death in old age. The censor did not advise the acceptance of this play, calling attention, in particular, to the great difficulties it presented to the performer of the principal part.

Such difficulties, however, did not discourage the producers of the old ecclesiastical plays. The people of those times, on the contrary, appreciated plays in which the hero began as an infant and ended as an old man, and in such cases several actors were employed for the same character—a boy, a youth, and an old man. Some plays simply indicate when these changes have to take place. Thus in the long collective mystery, *The Old Testament*, in which, after a scene between Abraham and Isaac, there is a note with the remark : " Here little Isaac ends." And further on : "Great Isaac begins."

And the same about Joseph after his arrival in Egypt: "Here ends little Joseph." And a little later: "Great Joseph begins."

It was not only the size of the parts and the many fatiguing rehearsals which rendered the work troublesome ; from a mere physical point of view the performance was at times a great tax on the strength, even dangerous to life. In the Passion plays the impersonator of Christ, in particular, was exposed to considerable injuries, and all the tortured saints had constantly to be prepared for some serious physical injury. It is stated above how authors and spectators agreed in relishing scenes of torture, and though the torturers had the most emphatic instructions always to remember that they were simulating, their professional zeal would sometimes carry them too far, and make them offer the reality instead of the illusion.

The worst dangers regularly fell on the performers of Christ, and we hear of many accidents in connection with this part. The mere act of hanging naked on a cross—in this case, it must be observed, the costume was kept strictly in accordance with historical truth—and, in this attitude, reciting 3400 lines, required a strong constitution and, no less, a great enthusiasm. Nor did all the performers of this part pass safely through the ordeal. In the chronicle of Metz, which has provided us with so much valuable information about the mysteries of those times, we also find accounts of the dangers to which the actors were frequently exposed. Thus we read in a report of the Passion play in 1437 : "The part of our Lord was performed by a priest named M. Nicolle from Neufchâtel in Lorraine, who was at the time vicar of St Victor in Metz. The said priest incurred great danger of life, and thought he was going to die while he hung on the cross, for he was so sick that he would have died if help had not come in time. And it was decided that another priest should be hung up in his stead in order to perform the part of Christ, and this priest was one of the executioners and tyrants in the same play; but, nevertheless, the part was given to somebody else, who performed it on the cross for that day. The next day the vicar of St Victor had recovered his strength, and he acted in the Resurrection and performed his part very bravely."

During the same representation Judas nearly came to a bad end. This mishap is related as follows : " In the said play was also another priest, whose name was M. Jehan de Missey, and he was a chaplain in Mairange, who executed the part of Judas; but as he hung too long, he also fainted and nearly died, for he lost his breath, wherefore he was hastily taken down and carried to another place close by, to be rubbed with vinegar and other things to restore him."

Sometimes these accidents, though of a less serious nature, were disturbing to illusion. In the play, *The Conversion of St Paul*, performed at Basle in the sixteenth century, thunder as well as lightning was produced. The thunder was made "*mit Fassen so voll Steine umgetrieben wurden*" (with barrels full of stones that were rolled about), and this did no harm. But about the flash of lightning, which was to strike Saul on his way and blind him, the report says: " The mayor

of Brunn performed St Paul, and Balthasar Hahn the
Lord in a circular sky, out of which, as a flash of
lightning, a rocket of fire was darted, so that St Paul,
in falling from his horse, had his trousers burned."

On the whole, all this fire, natural and artificial,
which was used in Heaven and—especially—in Hell,
caused a number of accidents, and those who performed
the devils, and had constantly to creep in and out of the
fire-spitting mouth of the dragon, had hot work indeed,
and not unfrequently got an unpleasant foretaste of the
real Hell.   Thus, for instance, it happened to Satan
himself in the St Martin play in Seurre (1496), when
he was going to creep out of his hidden subterranean
entrance, the fire caught his dress on the lower part of
his back, so as to burn him badly ; but he was so speedily
helped, undressed and re-dressed, that, without betraying
anything, he came forward and played his part, and then
retired to his house."   On the following day he apologised
to the public quite wittily, beginning his first speech to
Lucifer with the following little apostrophe :—

> Malle mort te puisse avorter
> Paillart, fils de putain cognu
> Pour à mal faire t'enorter
> Je me suis tout brulé le cul.[1]

However, if the toil and trouble of these performances
were considerable, if great patience and fortitude and
much energy were required before the goal could be
reached, the compensation was great, the joy and pride

[1] Foul death befall you, lewd fellow, whoreson !
To encourage you to do evil, I have entirely burned my hind part.

of the persevering amateurs unbounded, when the great day arrived on which they were to show the result of their work to their wondering and expectant fellow-citizens. It was a transport of pride, not only to those who had the great important parts, which in one day spread their fame many miles round, so that the neighbouring towns would send for them when their turn came to perform a mystery. The secondary performers too lived in a rapture of pride. It must indeed have been inconceivable bliss to an ordinary shoemaker to feel himself an emperor even for a week, wear the most magnificent clothes, a crown on his head, and sparkling ornaments on his body, and be followed by a hundred attendants, wearing his—the humble cobbler's—colours.

To mediæval people who had a childlike passion for gaudy, expensive clothes, the costly splendour of the dresses was not the smallest attraction of these plays. The eagerness to dazzle the eye by splendour and luxury went so far, that even servants, beggars and other insignificant characters in the plays sometimes appeared in costumes, which were almost as expensive as those of the royal personages.

No wonder that this delight in magnificent clothes often degenerated into childish vanity and ridiculous arrogance. We suppose this to have been the case particularly during the later period of the mysteries, when greater attention was paid to outward magnificence than to a devout and exact reproduction of the holy plays. Bonaventure Despériers[1] proves in a little anecdote that

[1] A French Renaissance author, d. 1544.

even among the naïve actors of those times, the type
existed which is seldom wanting at any theatre, that of
the actor who, by virtue of an unshakable faith in his distinguished appearance, considers himself naturally entitled
to represent persons of the highest rank, and very un-
willingly condescends to undertake untitled characters.
In Despériers' account it is a barber who is possessed
by this mania.   He always used to impersonate kings,
princes, or at least very distinguished noblemen.   Now,
in *The Acts of the Apostles*, he was to have the honour
of performing the King of India.   He was already seated
on his throne, holding the sceptre in his hand and " exhibiting as great royal majesty as any barber might."
But the prologue of this same play was to be recited
by Pontalais, the famous farce - player in the time of
Francis I.   Pontalais, who knew the barber's weak
point, recited his humorous introduction, and wound up
by stating about himself, that however humble a person
he might seem to be, the King of India had shaven his
beard hundreds of times.   Here the malicious *farceur*
pointed towards the barber sitting high and mighty on
his throne, who did not know where to hide from the
laughter of the public which understood and appreciated
the joke.

The expensive costumes were generally paid for by
the actor himself.   If this was beyond his means, the
burden was laid on some of his rich fellow-citizens, who
did not perform in the play.   The costumes of all the
supers who formed the retinues of kings, etc., were
borrowed.   The clergy, in particular, were very ready
to lend surplices, hoods, robes, and all kinds of ecclesi-

astical garments, for which there was always a great demand in the mysteries, as they were used not only for the clergy, but also for the Lord Himself, for prophets, high priests, and other historical characters of a religious stamp.

On the whole, it was a fundamental rule, that all plays, in whatever country or time the scene was supposed to be laid, were acted in contemporary mediæval costumes (fig. 6, p. 132), the chief reason of this principle no doubt being, that people did not know anything about the costumes of former times, and had no idea that such knowledge might be acquired. The painters of those times, we see, followed the same principle in their biblical or historical subjects.

So the theatrical costume of this period has no history, or rather its history coincides with that of the general costume. Yet there are some peculiarities, especially in the English costumes, which deserve mention, as they give a fairly good idea of the naïve love of finery which was characteristic of the actors in the mysteries. We are pretty well informed about the English costumes, as a number of account books belonging to the companies, and containing detailed notes about the garments used, have been preserved; however, we should by no means be justified in assuming that similar costumes were used everywhere. We must suppose, on the contrary, that, generally speaking, France exhibited a more developed taste and less primitive simplicity than we find in the English choice of costume. The English dresses are interesting for one thing, because they show how close was the connection be-

tween church imagery and ecclesiastical dramatic art.   It
is not easy to decide which of the two imitated the other,
but so much is certain, that in reading the description of
all the bright variegated dresses with their gilding and
grotesqueness, we seem to see before us the ancient
church-pictures sparkling with gold, and the gaudily
painted wood-carvings.

The costume of Christ was particularly striking.   He
wore a coat of white lamb with long sleeves, ending in
" hands," *i.e.* a pair of white gloves.   By the by, gloves
were worn by nearly all characters.   Christ's coat was
painted — probably, as observed by A. Ebert,[1] with
symbolic signs—and elaborately gilt.   A belt joined it
round the waist.   On his feet he wore red sandals, and
on his head a gilt wig, probably indicating the halo,
which was represented in the same way by painters and
sculptors.   The Apostles wore similar wigs.

Less outward show seems to have been exhibited in
the figure representing the Holy Ghost, who—like the
celebrated antagonists of Falstaff—appeared in buckram;
the Angels, on the other hand, were represented in
beautiful white surplices, with large wings on their
backs (comp. fig. 4).

Among the less elevated characters in the Passion
plays we must mention Herod.   Through the crusades
it had become a popular notion in the Middle Ages that
heathens and Saracens were, and had always been,
identical.   So an attempt was made to give the heathen
prince a Turkish appearance by providing him with a
scimitar and wide oriental breeches.   On the whole, he

---

[1] A. Ebert : *Die englischen Mysterien*, p. 62.

displayed royal magnificence in silk attire, with gilt helmet and a sceptre in his hand.

As ecclesiastical characters the Jewish high priests were robed in the ordinary episcopal attire, in which, as mentioned above, God the Father also appeared.

There was, moreover, a marked distinction of costume between the "white" and the "black" souls who appeared on the day of Judgment. The former were dressed in white like Christ, the latter wore a costume of black and yellow linen, indicating the hellish flames to which they were doomed.[1]

But the most characteristic costumes, and those which differed most from everyday dresses, were those of the devils. Here mediæval fancy cut its wildest capers in the way of grotesqueness, and for centuries to come fixed those images of the evil spirits which nowadays may appear childish, but which, nevertheless, in their principal features are reproduced in most pictorial and theatrical representations. The ordinary equipment of a devil, which no doubt in the main was accepted in all countries where mysteries were performed, consisted of a tight-fitting skin, which covered the whole body except the head, and which was generally made of the shaggy hides of wolves or calves. This skin-coat—especially, we suppose, that of Lucifer, the prince of hell (comp. fig. 4)—was sometimes painted in different places with hideous heads of devils. Sometimes a kind of feather-dress covered the devil's body, or, as in fig. 5, a green painted, reptile-like skin. The

---

[1] A relic of these mystery costumes is found in the penitential garments in which heretics were clothed at the autos-da-fé of the sixteenth century.

devils either had their faces grotesquely painted—which, we suppose, was mostly the case with those who had "speaking" parts — or, where their parts were more pantomimic, they wore different masks, for the most part heads of animals, *e.g.*, rams or goats, or, occasionally, of birds.   As a rule they had big horns of oxen or rams. Their feet ended in long claws of beasts or birds of prey ; hoofs appear less frequently.   In their hand they generally held a cudgel of stuffed cloth for beating the refractory souls ; but a later period, with its taste for fire-work effects, replaced these cudgels by hollow staves filled with combustible explosives, or by burning torches on which was thrown witch-meal (vegetable sulphur). Round their waist were sometimes hanging large cow- or donkey - bells, which made a hellish noise at the slightest movement.[1]

We have still to add that with respect to one guise— where, according to the Bible, *nakedness* is prescribed— the characters are represented with perfect historical truth.   We have seen above that in the Adam play this was not the case.   Here Adam and Eve before their fall were clothed respectively in a red and a white costume,[2] but in later plays the words of the text indicate plainly enough that the situation in question was performed with all the realism that could be desired.[3]

[1] Comp. Rabelais : *Pantagruel*, Book 4, chap. xii.

[2] Comp. p. 9.

[3] Thus in the mystery of *The Old Testament* Adam says : "Je suis honteux de ma nature—Autant je vois ma fragilité—Donc je veux changer couverture—Pour musser mon humanité. (Adoncques doit Adam couvrir son humanité faignant avoir honte). . . . Icy se doit semblablement ver- gogner la femme et se musser de la main." *Myst. d. viel Testament* éd. Rothschild, v. 1242 ff., Quot. by Jullev., *op. cit.* i. 382.

Even Christ before the crucifixion was represented naked, and thus He also hung on the cross. The scene of undressing was even represented with the intention of producing a half comic, half brutal effect. In the frequently mentioned Passion play by Grebans, the scene is performed in the following way :—

ANNAS THE HIGH PRIEST.

We want him to be stripped as naked as an earthworm. And neither for prayers nor entreaties must you allow him to keep, at the top or at the bottom, large, middling or small pieces of garment with which to hide one single spot.

ORILLART.

You want him as he came out of his mother's womb?

JEROBOAM.

Exactly.

After which further on there is this note: " Here they strip Him quite naked."

This strange, realistic scenic effect, which in its mildest form appears ludicrous, but most frequently coarse and indecent, was scarcely regarded as such in those times. It was closely connected with the matter-of-fact way in which the Middle Ages looked upon scenic representations. Their ideas about artistic illusion differed from our own; or, we should say, in matters where we are satisfied with a conventional indication, they wanted the full palpable reality, and in cases where we require a perfect illusion, they contented themselves with nothing at all.   Therefore, in our eyes, mediæval art so frequently appears grotesque where it is meant to be sublime.

V

The Representation—State of Feeling in the Mediæval Town where the Event took Place—Announcement and Expenses—Decadence of the Mysteries — Reformation Plays in Switzerland — The " Passion-Brotherhood" in Paris—Prohibitions and Persecutions.

To a mediæval town the performance of a mystery was an event of immense interest ; everything else was pushed into the background for it.

Before the theatre became an established institution, such an event was rare in the history of a town.   It was a great, expensive, time-swallowing enterprise, which could only be undertaken at long intervals.   As long as the rehearsals lasted, the citizens who acted in the play had to break off part of their professional work. As a rule they received no—or at most a very small— remuneration [1] for their loss of time, as they mostly played for the sake of their own pleasure and at their own risk.

However, honourable and gratifying as it might be to please God and the Holy Virgin by acting in a play, trade would suffer too much by lying fallow for months year after year, and it did not take less than a couple

---

[1] In some curious accounts of English mysteries we find a scale for the salaries allotted to the different parts.   According to this account Pilate receives the highest payment: 4s.   Then follow Herod and Caiaphas each with 3s. 6d.   Christ, strange to say, only gets 2s.; and Judas and the devil, whose importance in England is not nearly so considerable as in France, are paid 1s. 6d each.

of months to prepare a performance which lasted two or three weeks, sometimes more. So each town had to content itself with showing its religious feelings and skill and maintaining its reputation now and then on appropriate occasions, such as a great Church festival, the arrival of a prince, the cessation of a plague or scourge, by a magnificent representation. Some towns performed their religious plays at regular intervals of five, six or ten years, as is still the case in Oberammergau.

The very fact of their rarity was reason enough for the great excitement created by these performances.

Moreover, a great number of the families in the town added each its member as a contingent to the staff of performers. We have seen that in the long plays this staff was very numerous, and, including supers, children and functionaries, might well amount to about a thousand persons. In the less populous towns of the Middle Ages it might easily happen that almost every family contributed a representative to the staff, which naturally added to the personal interest with which the townsmen followed the course of the performance.

Finally, the pleasure was, so to say, compulsory. Even if some quiet citizen should have felt more inclined to stay at home and mind his business, than to go to the play, he was not at liberty to do so. On the day of the performance the magistrate ordered all the shops to be closed, and forbade all noisy work. The streets were empty, the houses locked up, and none but solitary armed watchmen, specially engaged for the occasion to watch over the abandoned dwellings and property of the citizens, were seen walking cheerlessly about; they alone were excluded from the beautiful play.

But on the place of the festival—usually a common or a large market place—the inhabitants moved about in high and festive spirits as long as the performance lasted.   It always took place by daylight, sometimes beginning early in the morning and making a pause at noon to allow the actors a rest; then going on afresh for some hours, till nature again asserted its claims.

The festival attracted multitudes of jugglers and musicians to the town, and when nothing was going on in the theatre, people amused themselves as best they might with singing, dancing and playing till late at night, while strong beer and unadulterated wine refreshed dry throats.   Sometimes the spectators even got their liquors gratis.   When it was a rich nobleman who defrayed the expenses of the play, which happened occasionally, he now and then gratified the public and secured success for his entertainment by providing not only a treat for the mind, but also substantial refreshments for the body. Thus it is written about Gilles de Rais, the more than ill-famed French nobleman, the mediæval Marquis de Sade, afterwards popularly baptised *Bluebeard*, in a complaint composed by his heirs, after he had been put to death as a punishment for his incredible misdeeds, and sent to the king in proof of his extravagance : "Item he provided plays, farces and *morisques* (morris-dances), and at Whitsuntide and Ascension mysteries on high pageants, beneath which were stored as in a cellar mead and hot wine."

However, when the citizens themselves undertook

the performances, neither the play nor the meals were gratis. Considering the great value of money in those times the prices were rather high, and it was a rule that the places in the boxes on the elevated scaffold cost about double of the inferior seats on the benches below. The eventual surplus in the cash-box was divided between the performers, according to the size and importance of the parts, but, of course, there could not always be a surplus. The expenses, as a rule, were very considerable, though the actors themselves had to provide the costumes, and a very large share of the profits went to pay for the large tribunes that were erected here and there for spectators. At the above-mentioned play, *Les Trois Doms*, in Romans in 1509, the expenses amounted to 1737 florins, 2 denars, nearly £2000, whereas the profits did not come to more than £830; but on this occasion the sums spent on the equipment of the play-house had run exceptionally high. Generally, we think, expenses and income balanced pretty well, especially in the large towns which supplied a more numerous audience, and at the long performances, since, of course, the cost of building a theatre for a play lasting a couple of days was nearly the same as for one meant for a representation of twenty-five days, whereas each additional day of performance increased the income.

Though the interest and anticipation were so great that a formal announcement was quite superfluous, it took place nevertheless, and in the most pompous way. Some days before the great event all the performers were summoned by trumpets to meet in a suitable place

in full costume, after which the whole procession started
on its way through the narrow streets. And what a
magnificent procession ! There were gambolling devils,
fools, dazzling princes, beautiful angels, the Lord in shining attire, and all who were able to ride on horseback,
accompanied by sound of trumpets. Wondering multitudes crowded to see them. The artisan left his shop,
the housewife her kitchen, while the young girls gazed
from their windows after the handsome young men, and
the apprentices hailed the sight with loud cheers.

The procession stopped in the market-place, and a
long versified invitation was recited by one of the most
eloquent of the actors. This invitation—*le Cry*, as it
was called in France—recommended the anticipated
festival in long-winded complicated verses, whereupon
the procession moved on to the next halting-place,
repeating the same scene each time.

Sometimes the representations were announced much
earlier, and the procession and cavalcade had the
additional purpose of finding actors for the play. In
that case, of course, the procession could not consist of
the performers in costume, but of other men who were
interested in the play : the committee of citizens, the
starters of the enterprise, authors, etc. We still possess
a description of a procession on horseback started in
December 1540 by the well-known Passion-Fraternity
in Paris—a company of citizens whose object was to
arrange performances of mysteries—in order to find a
staff of actors for their gigantic play, *The Acts of the
Apostles*. This procession was headed by seven
trumpeters ; behind them went the sworn public crier ;

then a troop of armour-bearers on horseback and archers to keep the crowd in order; further a number of military and civil officers; two heralds dressed in black velvet, with sleeves of grey, yellow and blue satin, whose business it was to deliver the versified invitation to enlist as performers in the play; behind them came the two leaders or directors of the mystery, one of them a priest, the other a layman, both decently dressed and well mounted "according to their station"; then the four "undertakers" (what we should call managers) of the play, a butcher, a paperhanger, a lawyer, and a gardener, all on horseback; four officers of justice on mules; and, finally, all the members of the fraternity, "tradespeople and other citizens, in long or short coats, all well mounted according to their rank and ability."

On the day of the performance the whole staff again marched in procession to the theatre, of course, in full costume. In the meantime the spectators took their seats in the auditorium; nobility, clergy, and rich people in the beautifully-draped upper boxes; the common people on the simple wooden benches lower down. On arriving at the stage the procession walked round it once—such was the custom—after which its members retired to the background, each to the place previously assigned to him. Not till all were seated—the spectators on their tribunes, the actors in their boxes—did the performance begin.

As a rule the summer season was chosen for these festivals, for fear of bad weather; nevertheless it happened not infrequently that all were driven home because the proceedings were interrupted by torrents of rain, which washed the paint off the faces of the actors, and drenched the spectators in their open seats. Occasionally the stage and auditorium were covered with awnings, but this was only a doubtful protection against a heavy, strong continuous rain. In such cases the performance was put off till the following Sunday, for Sunday was generally chosen for these representations. The great mysteries were not always acted on a number of days in succession, but sometimes on several successive Sundays.

For at least four centuries the ecclesiastical plays had enjoyed unmixed popularity, but now their time had passed. A new taste began to assert itself, and the tedious old popular plays were no longer looked upon with the same naïve devotion as before. The art of printing spread the knowledge of the classical authors more and more, and people of higher culture, who had become acquainted with a fully developed and formally perfect literature, so entirely different from that of their own day, no longer wished to promote what they had learned to consider as a crude popular entertainment. The Greek and Roman works on the theory of art, which laid down definite rules, also for the form and construction of dramatic works, became generally known; and people arrived at the conclusion that the clumsy, large-limbed mysteries could not be compressed into the tight classical form.

The old popular authors had composed their plays in happy ignorance of Aristotle and his unities. They had found the form which suited themselves and their public, and it had been the greatest delight of many generations to behold these variegated pictures, at which the mind was edified by witnessing the sufferings of Christ and the saints, and comforted by the ever gracious interference of the Virgin Mary. Now suddenly the learned authorities declared that this was all wrong, that it was coarse, barbarous and ludicrous to find pleasure in such plays, ignoring, as they did, the rules, the sacred rules, which—alas!—the learned men scarcely understood themselves. In falling from the higher classes into the hands of artisans, the mysteries lost the solemn dignity which had hitherto kept them from decadence. In fact, they became ludicrous, and therewith lost the soundboard which justified them and had been their real condition of life. Faith in them began to waver, the power of the Church was shaken. The sacred histories were no longer listened to with implicit confidence; they were criticised and scoffed at. What formerly had called forth pity without disturbing enjoyment was now received with scornful laughter. The machinery which was frequently very complicated might, as we have shown above, easily get into disorder; and while, during the good times, the public had considered it a point of honour that all should go well, it now gave vent to malicious sarcasms at the slightest mishap which exposed the performers to ridicule. There were shouts of laughter when a fault in the machinery prevented the Holy Ghost from "descending," or when a flash of lightning burned the trousers of an apostle. The artisans, who were no longer supported by the learned class or the higher clergy, naturally committed many blunders and sins against good taste, and the public, having no longer any share in the responsibility of the actors, went to the play to find amusement, rather than to edify their minds and honour God and our Lady.

However, it was by no means the Reformation, as we might feel inclined to think, that brought the mysteries into discredit.   On the contrary, in the countries where the Reformation prevailed, the ecclesiastical plays survived longer than elsewhere, and to some extent became the starting point of further development.   Nay, in certain places the Reformation produced an independent dramatic literature, which in its form and mode of performance resembled the mysteries, though it contained a strongly polemic element, which, of course, was directed against the pope and his power.   Switzerland possesses a whole literature of such polemical Reformation plays. Especially the towns of Basle and Berne produced fertile dramatic authors, who were inflamed by a common hatred of popery.   Basle, for instance, was the native town of Pamphilius Gengenbach, a most productive author and printer, who, between 1515 and 1522, wrote and printed a number of plays, among which we may point out *Die Todtenfresser* as a violent attack on the Roman Church.   In Berne lived his contemporary, the painter, poet and statesman, Niclaus Manuel (b. 1484), a clever and witty writer, author among other plays of *Vom Papst und seiner Priesterschaft*, *Der Ablasskrämer*, *Die Krankheit der Messe*, the titles of which reveal their tendency clearly enough.[1]

[1] This is not the proper place to enter more closely into the subject of the Swiss Reformation plays, which otherwise possess great literary interest. Readers wishing for more information about them are referred, among other works, to Rud. Genée : *Lehr- und Wanderjahre des deutschen Schauspiels*, and Jak. Bächtold : *Schweizerische Schauspiele des 16ten Jahrhunderts*.

In the Roman Catholic countries, however, the rupture between the Church and the mysteries gradually deepened, whereby indeed the basis of their existence was undermined. Professional actors began to appropriate the sacred subjects; and, partly because these poor strolling mountebanks could not infuse into these sublime dramas the dignity and magnificence which had formerly impressed the people, partly because the clergy now seemed to be superfluous at the representations, the Church deemed it right to oppose itself categorically to the mysteries and their performers. It was scandalised at the same plays, which were formerly acted exclusively for the honour of God; interdicts poured down from magistrates, clergy, pope and king. At first these prohibitions were not taken very seriously, but very soon they succeeded in extinguishing the last remnants of the mysteries, which, as it was, had not much vital power left.

The interdicts aimed in particular at the civic "fraternities." During the later Middle Ages it had become the custom for citizens, artisans and tradespeople, to join in a kind of dramatic club with the object of performing fine and edifying mysteries, always in honour of God, but no less to please themselves and their fellow-citizens. The most celebrated of all these companies was the Parisian Passion-Fraternity, which, on December 4th, 1402, had received "authorisation, privilege and permission to perform and act whatever mystery it pleased, be it the said Passion and Resurrection, or any other about holy men and women." King Charles VI. himself had been present at the performances of the fraternity, and had liked them so well, that his letter conferring the patent was conceived in particularly gracious terms.

As long as the clergy sided with the mysteries, all went well, and in Paris the Passion-Fraternity had gradually established an almost regular theatre, which in "Trinity Hospital" (*l'hôpital de la Trinité*) had its plays represented every Sunday throughout several months, and found great favour and concourse with the population in Paris. But when the higher clergy began to fear that these direct and often tasteless reproductions from the Holy Scriptures, intermixed with apocryphal events and comic episodes, might become a dangerous weapon in the hands of the increasing party of reform, they changed their tune. The royal grace was soon changed into warnings and modifications, which culminated when the Fraternity solicited permission to produce *The Old Testament* in the year 1541.

The petition met with violent opposition in Parliament, and the *procureur général* spoke of the Brothers in anything but a flattering manner, but at the same time in such clear and graphic terms that his plea, partial as it may have been, affords very interesting evidence as to the state of the mysteries at that time, and the decay into which their performance had fallen. The *procureur général* expresses himself in the following harsh terms: "The managers as well as the actors are ignorant people, artisans by profession, who have not even learnt to spell [*sachant ni A, ni B*], who have never been taught or trained to undertake this kind of performance in theatres and public places, and neither possess a fluent tongue nor appropriate language, nor a proper and decent accent, nor any understanding of what they are saying; so that they generally make three words out of one, put a full stop or a pause in the middle of a sentence, a phrase or an incomplete speech, make an exclamation out of an interrogative clause, or by gesture, expression or action contradict what they say, out of which often arise laughter and general disorder in the theatre, so that their play, instead of elevating the minds of the people, becomes a scandal and a mockery."

Then he refers to the performance of *The Acts of the Apostles*, which had taken place in the same year, and describes it in the following way : " These people who are neither learned nor versed in such matters, but are of low estate, such as joiners, stick-makers, upholsterers or fishmongers, have arranged the performance of *The Acts of the Apostles* ; and in order to lengthen the play they have added several apocryphal things, and at the beginning and the end of it have introduced loose farces and pantomimes, and have extended their play to the length of six or seven months, which led and leads to neglect of divine service, indifference in almsgiving and charity, adultery and incessant fornication, scandals, mockery and scorn."

Then he shows how the indecent plays draw people away from church, seducing even the priests : " As long as the said play lasted, the common people neglected matins and sermons at eight or nine o'clock, as well as evening service, in order to go to the play, retain seats and remain till five oclock in the evening ; all preaching stopped, for nobody would have been there to listen to

it.   And on returning from the plays, they made fun of
the performers loudly and publicly in the streets, and
mimicked faults of language which they had heard in the
said play, or bad acting, and they made blasphemous
jokes about the Holy Ghost having refused to descend,
and other such mockery.   And the vicars, in order to
amuse themselves by going to the said play, used to
neglect their evensong or to say it by themselves at
noon, an unusual hour ; even the cantors or chaplains
of the Palace [*Palais de Justice*], as long as the said play
lasted, held their evensong at noon on the days of the
festival, and even went through it in a hurry in order to
get to these plays."

In spite of all his efforts the *procureur général* did
not succeed this time in preventing the performance of
The Old Testament, which took place in the following
year.   But a hard blow had been dealt at the mysteries,
and the final interdict was not long in coming.   The
Passion-Fraternity no longer had its headquarters in
the Trinity Hospital and its surroundings; after being
stationed for some time in the Hôtel de Flandre, they
had now hired the afterwards so famous Hôtel de
Bourgogne, and applied for a fresh licence to perform
mysteries and other plays in the new home.   By a
parliamentary decree of November 17th, 1548, however,
it was communicated to the Fraternity that they were
forbidden to perform in future the "mystery of the
Passion of our Saviour, or other mysteries, on pain of
an arbitrary fine, whereas they [the Brothers] should be
allowed to act other profane mysteries, which are decent
and lawful, without offending or damaging anybody;

and it shall be forbidden by law to all others to act or represent in future any play or mystery, in the city of Paris as well as in its suburbs and surrounding country, except in the name and to the advantage of the said Fraternity."

This interdict dealt the death-blow to the mysteries as far as Paris was concerned. The Passion Brothers, it is true, retained their privilege of acting other secular plays; it was even renewed by three subsequent kings. But the ecclesiastical plays had been their strong point; in the farces they were beaten by the professional actors, and the secular subjects (from legendary lore) which they performed never became very popular. The court and the people began to take more pleasure in professionally trained Italian companies, who now immigrated into France, and whose peculiar characters and merry art, to which we shall return in a later chapter, opened out new prospects to dramatic art. Pressed on all sides, the Passion Brothers finally, towards the close of the sixteenth century, determined to leave off playing, and to make over their licence and quarters to professional companies in exchange for a sum of money and admission to a certain number of boxes.

Abandoned by the clergy, who had no longer any interest in supporting them, but who, on the contrary, turned against them as works of the devil,[1] scorned by

---

[1] There is interesting information on the subject in a work called : "*Remonstrances très-humbles au Roy de France et de Pologne*" (1588), in which the author speaks in the following terms against the Passion Brothers : "There is also another evil committed and tolerated chiefly in your city of Paris on Sundays and holidays . . . viz., the public plays and performances which are exhibited on the said Sundays and holidays by foreign Italians as well as

learned Renaissance authors, who in these formless plays saw nothing but the coarsest barbarism, the mysteries now definitely expired, not only in France, but everywhere.   In Italy Pope Paul III., in 1549, forbade the celebrated representations in the Coliseum.   In England the ecclesiastical plays enjoyed great favour with Henry VIII., who was personally fond of acting; but in the year 1594 we see the Chester plays definitely prohibited. In the south of Germany, too, the performance of religious plays is stopped, and only in a few places in the country the old pious custom survives of representing the sufferings of our Saviour "in figures," as a pale relic of former great days.

by Frenchmen, and, above all, those which are represented in a cesspool and house of Satan, named the Hôtel de Bourgogne, acted by those who unjustly call themselves Passion Brothers of Jesus Christ.   In this place thousands of scandalous meetings are held, to the prejudice of respectability and female chastity, and to the ruin of poor artisans' families, of which the low hall is quite full, and who more than two hours before the play commences pass their time in indecent talk, with cards and dice, in revelry and drinking . . . out of which arise many quarrels and fights."   Quoted by Julleville, *op. cit.* p. 433.

SECULAR PLAYS

I

IT has been mentioned occasionally that side by side with the mediæval ecclesiastical plays there ran a whole series of secular and comic pieces, which did not derive their subjects from the Bible or from the stories of the saints, but scoffed at and moralised over the absurdities and vices of life wherever they were found.

We may suppose that in those times ecclesiastical and secular plays were not so sharply distinguished from each other or classified according to their subjects as the people of modern times are inclined to think. The mysteries, as we know, were full of comic scenes, preceded by way of introduction by the most wanton farces or interrupted by irrelevant merry interludes; on the other hand certain of the so-called secular pieces— the moralities—were frequently more religious than many a mystery, and were not inferior to the ecclesiastical plays in thorough earnestness of purpose.

There is even confusion in the names. What we

should now call a morality may formerly have been named a mystery, and *vice versâ*. In short, little attention was paid to an exact definition, partly for this reason, that in those times much less literary importance was attributed to dramatic works than is the case nowadays. They created immense enthusiasm and attention at the moment of performance, but it did not seem to occur to anybody to consider them worthy of being lasting literary monuments. This is the reason why, in the course of time, so many plays were lost, especially of the short farces, which it was not even thought worth while writing down.[1]

This is one of the reasons why we have more difficulty in tracing the primary forms and origins of the secular than of the ecclesiastical theatre. Not till the fifteenth century does comic dramatic composition receive its real impetus ; at least we do not know of any secular theatre to speak of previous to this period.[2] But, we acknowledge, it is quite possible, even most probable, that there previously existed merry plays and farces, only they have not come down to the knowledge of our own time.

---

[1] Not even the printed plays were preserved. It is a noteworthy fact that our principal knowledge of ancient French farcical literature is due to a printed collection of about 1550, of which only one copy remains, which was found by mere chance in a garret in Berlin, whence it was removed to the British Museum.

[2] A few Dutch farces, probably of the fourteenth century, and preserved in the so-called Hulthem MS., are closely related in form and subject to the French plays of the fifteenth century, and we possess evidence which proves that as early as the fifteenth century it was customary for young people in Holland to assemble at Shrovetide, and, mounted on carts, to perform merry little plays. Comp. W. Creizenach : *Geschichte des neueren Dramas*, i. 401 ff.

One single author of the thirteenth century, whose
two dramatic works are still extant, seems to indicate
this.   The Frenchman, Adam de la Halle, surnamed
"the Hunchback of Arras," has left two merry plays,
written between the years 1262 and 1284, which are as
characteristic in form as in subject, and which, if they
did not stand isolated, would bear witness of an earlier
stage of secular dramatic art differing considerably from
the later period.   As it is, and as neither France nor
any other country possesses any works similar to those
of this early author, Adam de la Halle stands unique
with an interest of his own ; but we cannot from his
works draw the conclusion that there existed a number
of contemporary plays of the same kind, and that his
plays were only specimens of a whole group.

We do not know much about the life of Adam de la
Halle, yet a little more than about most of the other
comic dramatists of the Middle Ages, of whom scarcely
even the names are remembered.   If we can trust what
he says in one of his own pieces, he was the son of
a citizen of Arras (in Flanders), but, according to his
own account, though he received the nickname of "the
Hunchback of Arras," he was not particularly deformed.[1]
He was probably intended for an ecclesiastical career,
for he studied as a clerk in the Abbey of Vaucelles.
But in his early youth he fell in love with a pretty
girl named Marie, and married her.   In his first play,
le Jeu d'Adam, or *Jeu de la Feuillée*, he ridicules his
own love-story with undisguised cynicism : " It was a
beautiful and clear summer day, mild and green, bright

---

[1] " On m'appelle bochue, mais je ne le sui mie."

and fine, with delightful song of little birds. In the high wood, near the brook which flows over the fine gravel, there I caught sight of her, who is now my wife, and who now seems pale and yellow to me. . . . " He describes her as he saw her with the eyes of Cupid, and as he sees her now without love. " Therefore I had better get into my right mind again, before my wife gets pregnant and increases my expenses, for my hunger after her is satisfied." [1] During certain disturbances which threatened his native town he left it, but it seems that he took his wife with him in spite of the satisfied hunger. Afterwards he left his country altogether, went to Naples with Robert the Second of Artois, and remained at the court of this king till his death, which occurred before 1288. In Naples he probably wrote his last play, *le Jeu de Robin et Marion*. Besides these two dramas Adam de la Halle composed a great number of poems, master-songs, rondos and motettos.

His two plays differ very much from each other, and are both very remarkable. The first one, *le Jeu d'Adam*, is a kind of fantastic review, which satirises the state of things—both public and private—in the good town of Arras; it is incoherent in form, without head or tail, a collection of satirical scenes of everyday life in the town, intermixed with fantastic events, in which fairies and other supernatural beings make their appearance. This play perhaps reminds us most of the fantastic-political satires of Aristophanes, to which, however, they are in every way very inferior. *Le Jeu*

---

[1] *Li Jus Adam ou de la Feuille*, published by Monmerqué and Michel, *Théâtre français au moyen âge*, pp. 57 and 61.

d'Adam contains in all eighteen characters, among which are the author himself, Master Adam, his father, Master Henri, who is ridiculed for his avarice, several other citizens of Arras, a begging friar, a physician, etc. The fantastic element is represented among others by the three fairies, Morgue, Maglore and Arsile. There is a kind of allegorical figure whom the author names *le commun*, viz., public opinion. Finally, the *fool* appears in this play, probably for the first time, but in his original character as a real maniac, not merely as a jester. This fool's chatter about everything affords the author an opportunity of extending his satire to the most diverse subjects, political, ecclesiastical and personal.

To summarise the plot of the play is no easy matter, as there is no plot properly speaking, and the scenes follow each other without internal connection. The mere outward frame, if we may say so, is that Adam de la Halle wishes to leave Arras and his wife in order to go and study in Paris, but the happy prospect of having this desire fulfilled is forfeited by his forgetfulness. At a meal given in the open air—*sous la Feuillée*—to which the three above-mentioned fairies are invited, he has forgotten to lay a place for Maglore. In her anger this fairy curses her hosts and expresses her wish that Adam may never leave his wife, but remain with her in Arras.

The second piece written by Adam de la Halle, *le Jeu de Robin et Marion*, is of a very different nature, more concentrated in form, more homogeneous in subject, less original than the first mentioned play, quite destitute of satire and political allusions, but a graceful merry idyl about the old, yet ever young subject: the young country maiden who is tempted by the stately knight, yet remains faithful to her shepherd. The little piece is full of charming songs; *Robin and Marion* has with some reason been called the first comic opera. The old music in its triple time, as also the text, are still enjoyable to modern ears on account of the peculiar grace which distinguishes this pastoral play.

We cannot doubt that both these plays were performed; *le Jeu d'Adam*, we suppose, to a more intimate circle, as the personal satires seem to be too sharp to be intended for the ears of the public. We know that Arras possessed a company of Mastersingers, a *Puy*, as it was called; very likely this was the audience which listened to Adam de la Halle's merry satire; whereas *Robin and Marion* was not composed till after the poet had left his native town to go to Naples, and here, at the court of Robert d'Artois, we must imagine the graceful little opera to have been performed for the first time. The piece indeed deserves to be called an opera, for it contains no less than twenty-six songs with musical accompaniments. Nor did it only find favour in Naples; even in France it became very popular. "Robin and Marion" became the regular names for tender lovers, and for a whole century the play survived in different adaptations—those times did not respect original texts as we do nowadays—as a favourite among scenic performances.

Strange to say, however, none of these plays formed a school, not even the last, which would seem to have been well qualified to do so. Not till much later did pastorals come into fashion again. Mediæval taste meanwhile followed new grooves. People wanted more substantial food than these light pastoral plays, and found it in all kinds of coarse cuckold stories, comical love adventures of clerics, quarrels between lawyers and shop-keepers, who tried to outwit and cheat each other by all kinds of knavish tricks. Such stories, chastising the absurdities and vices of all times and countries, were related all over Europe. Who did not know such characters as ill-tempered, unfaithful wives, foolish hen-pecked and deceived husbands, hypocritical priests, greedy after those things which they feigned to condemn, cunning lawyers and avaricious tradespeople?

And these general subjects and merry anecdotes about everyday events, which always gave amusement, were dramatised and presented on the boards with a directness, a delightful ignorance of their riskiness, which render these Farces, *Fastnachtspiele*, Interludes, whatever we choose to call them, at once so quaint and so attractive to modern readers.

It was by no means the bright and pleasant sides of life which these old farces drew to light. On the con-trary, they passed all the vices in review : falsehood, deceit, adultery, manslaughter, everything, and described them in the crudest matter-of-fact way. But there was in all this a total lack of sentimentality, a kind of coarse *naïveté*, which laughed at everything and seemed to think that, if there were two sides to every question, a serious and a comical, it was the latter people had come to see, and that they meant to enjoy it thoroughly.

Thus, for instance, the deceived husband. No doubt

the condition of an unfaithful wife was as grave in the Middle Ages as it is now, and the deceived husband can scarcely have found his situation more amusing in those times than nowadays.   But on the stage the matter looked very different.   Whereas modern dramatists have analysed this subject with a steady and serious determination and with almost scientific thoroughness, elucidating it from all sides to an interested public, the Middle Ages looked ûpon it exclusively from one point of view.   As a matter of fact, the cuckold was ludicrous.   It was, indeed, impossible to ignore that there were two sides to this question also, but it was thought, perhaps, that the serious side must remain inside the four walls of home, whereas if represented in public it could only appear comical.

And so with regard to the other subjects.   The ludicrous side was held up to ridicule ; sentiment would have been out of place.

We often wonder at the callousness of our great dramatists respecting some of their characters.   We can hardly laugh at Molière's Arnolphe or George Dandin, and we regard Shylock almost entirely in a tragic light, though we feel convinced that this is not the author's intention.   But in spite of their marvellous artistic development, Shakespeare and Molière are much nearer akin to the Middle Ages than to our own time, as far as way of thinking and dramatic conception are concerned ; their lack of sentimentality is thoroughly mediæval.   An oldish man who in his own mind is wiser than everybody else, and who, to avoid being deceived, educates a girl so as to make her a wife according to his own views, is deceived in the usual way—is it a laughable or a sad thing? A grasping and vindictive Jew who is caught in his own snares, and who loses his money as well as his vengeance, is it sad?—no, a capital joke!

Thus and only thus did these subjects appear to the mediæval public; for them the other, the sentimental side did not exist on the stage. This must be constantly borne in mind, if we are not to be repulsed by all the vices accumulated in the old farces and Shrovetide plays.

Nevertheless we have great difficulty in reconciling ourselves to the form which at times is so excessively coarse, that we are at a loss to understand how not only men, but virtuous ladies, could have been present at the performances of these plays. And that they were seems to be beyond doubt. Thus we know for certain that the well-known farce about the miller,[1] whose soul was to be taken to Hell, in which the stupid devil—with reverence be it spoken—got something else in his bag instead of the soul, was performed in Seurre in the year 1496, together with, or, more correctly, before, the performance of the mystery of *Saint Martin*,[2] at which the whole population of the town were present. This farce is by no means one of the very worst, nevertheless it is so coarse that from our modern point of view it is inconceivable that it could be performed together with a religious play before a select audience.

The point of the piece, however, is witty; its dramatic

---

[1] It is ascribed to Andrieux de la Vigne, the author of the mystery of *Saint Martin*. Its subject is taken from one of Rutebeuf's *Fabliaux*.

[2] Comp. above, p. 87.

construction is not bad, and its dialogues and situations despite all their coarseness are droll indeed.   The first scene shows us the miller on his sick-bed, and his wicked wife, who, far from helping him, takes advantage of his weakness to beat him mercilessly every time he says anything that displeases her.   Her husband accuses her of constant infidelity, and at the time being she is in love with the parish priest, who naturally is obnoxious to him.

The priest steals into the house, and he and the miller's wife anticipate in expressions of undisguised coarseness the death of her husband, which will enable them to enjoy their love undisturbed.   Even now they take a small advance on future pleasures, while the husband lies raving and swearing in his bed.

However, to prevent his getting quite beside himself, the priest takes off his robe and appears in the disguise of a relative at the sick-bed.   At first the poor cuckold refuses to be taken in,[1] but the cunning priest ensnares him by a tissue of lies, and finally the miller feels confidence enough to reveal his anxiety about the relations between his wife and the priest, abusing the latter most violently to his face.   The pretended relative is served with wine and meat by the treacherous wife, and herewith the first part of the play ends.

Now we are taken to Hell, where Lucifer is in a rage, abusing his devils for not making mischief enough. The devil Berith, who is neither clever nor experienced,

---

[1] He expresses his distrust in the following drastic way :—

" Sainct Jehan ! s'il est de mon lignaige
C'est du quartier devers le cu ! "

is ordered to find a soul for his master at once, and to take it to the deepest abyss of Hell. But the devil is so ignorant that he does not even know which way a soul leaves the body, and he has to ask Lucifer, his stern master. "It goes the back way," he replies, "and there you must watch for it and seize it." [1]

Berith sets off for the earth in good faith, and the scene is again laid at the miller's house, where the sick man is now lying at the last extremity. He sends for the priest in order to confess his sins, and the pretended relative again changes his dress and returns to the patient in his true character. There he receives the confession of the miller's rather heavily laden conscience.

Meanwhile Berith has appeared too, and has hidden under the bed in order to catch the miller's parting soul at the right moment in a bag which he has brought for this purpose.

After the excitement of the confession the miller feels very ill, and requests his wife and the priest to leave him. Now he gives up his "ghost" in his own way, and the devil gladly catches his soul in the bag and returns to Hell screaming and howling. [2]

Here he exclaims joyfully to Lucifer that he brings him splendid prey, and all the devils assemble to see the soul he has caught. He seizes his bag and empties it proudly into a cauldron. But the effect is most unexpected. All the spirits of Hell recoil in horror from

---

[1] "Elle sort par le fondement
Ne fais le guet qu'au trou du cu."

[2] Il mect le cul dehors du lit, et le diable tend son sac, cependant qu'il chie dedans ; puys s'en va cryant et hurlant.

the abominable smell of this soul,[1] and poor Berith gets
a good flogging for his trouble.   After he has begged
pardon in the proper way, Lucifer ends the play by a
solemn exhortation to all devils never to bring a miller's
soul to Hell, as it is nothing but dirt and filth.[2]

But sometimes the whole amusement of these plays
consists in an accumulation of coarseness and filthy
speech, which does not lead up to any particular point,
but is only used for its own sake; thus, *e.g.*, farces
about tinkers or sweeps, literally sole object of which
consists in obscene allusions to sexual phenomena, with
which the occupations of these two kinds of artisans are
compared.   The German Shrovetide-plays in particular
revel in such filth for its own sake, though, characteristi-
cally enough, it is the activity of the digestive organs—
to use a mild circumlocution—which seems to have interested the Teutonic public, whereas the Gallic nation
seems to have found more relish in sexual subjects.   Thus
the deceived husband appears much less frequently in
Germany than in France, whereas the Germans ridicule
ill-tempered old women much more than the French.

In the other leading European countries we do not
know of any considerable development of the farce

[1] The dialogue runs thus: *Sathan*: Qu'esse là?—*Proserpine*: Que
diable esse cy? ce semble merde toute pure.—*Lucifer*. C'est mou! Je le sens
bien d'icy.   Fy, fy! ostez moy telle ordure, etc.

[2] "Sur payne de hayne assouvye,
Deffens que nully, par envie,
Désormais l'ame ne procure
De munyer estre icy ravie,
Car ce n'est que bran et ordure."

La farce du munyer de qui le diable emporte l'âme en enfer.   Published by
P. L. Jacob in his *Recueil de Farces, Soties et Moralités du XV e siècle,*
Paris, 1859.

during the Middle Ages proper, but Germany as well as
France has provided us with sufficient material to enable
us to form a perfectly distinct image of this popular
branch of art.

Though the French farce[1] and the German Shrovetide-play seem to have developed quite independently of
each other, and to have very few subjects in common,
they are very much alike in their fundamental character,
and to some extent also in their form. They are short
pieces, always versified, but seldom containing more
than a few hundred lines; the best of them are built
on some comic point, which is generally taken from some
merry tale. The German Shrovetide - plays generally
begin with a little prologue requesting silence and ex-
plaining the subject of the piece. As in the mysteries,
the speaker of the prologue is generally called "Precursor" or "Herald," also *Einschreier*. The French as
well as the German farces sometimes end with a short
moral or a few religious verses, which, especially after
indecent scenes, produce a strange effect. Sometimes
the author simply desires the audience to forgive him
if he has been too free in his jokes.

As a rule, however, the French farces are very
superior to the German ones in form as well as in
subject. Among the former we find indeed little pearls
of comic power, and not all of them are made repulsive
by the filth with which the greater part are infected.

---

[1] The origin of the word *farce* is the Latin verb *farcire*, which in the past
participle has *fartus* or *farsus*, in the feminine and the neuter plural
farsa. *Farcire* means to stuff, to fill in, so *farsa* means what was
filled into the ecclesiastical plays. Comp. Julleville: *La comédie et les
mœurs*, p. 51.

Thus we find no indecencies whatever in the most celebrated of the number, the farce of *Pathelin*.   It is
the only one, the speeches of which have become pro-
verbial, and which in different adaptations has preserved
itself on the stage down to this day.   The author of this
little witty play, which is full of genuine Gallic ingenuity
and merry humour, is unknown, like most other farce-
writers ; but that even in its own time it held a unique
position and enjoyed extreme popularity is proved by the
numerous editions in which—unlike other contemporary
plays—it has appeared.[1]   And *Pathelin* alone survived
from the massacre perpetrated by the humanists of the
Renaissance in France on the despised mediæval poets.

Pathelin—as we know—is a poor advocate without
clients.   On the day when we see him appear in the
play he has sworn to provide himself with a new suit of
clothes before sunset, as he is in great need of it.   For
this purpose he goes to the shop of his opposite neighbour, the draper, Guillaume Joceaulme, flatters him,
speaks of his late father, his late aunt, praises his goods,
and finally is persuaded by the draper to buy six ells of
beautiful cloth for as many dollars (fig. 7).   He takes the
cloth with him and invites the draper to come and eat roast
goose at his house, while he goes to fetch the money.

Joceaulme goes to Pathelin, but finds him in bed
and his wife in tears.   Pathelin is raving, and wails
piteously in all the languages of the world—Picardish,
Flemish, Provençal, even Turkish—so that the shop-

---

[1] From the fifteenth century alone there are six printed editions, in the
sixteenth century twenty-four different editions appeared.   Comp. Julleville :
Répertoire du théâtre comique, p. 191 ff.

6

7

6—The Rape of Helen and the Conquest of Troy, performed in mediæval costumes
7—Scenes from the farce of *Pathelin*.   Pathelin bargains with Joceaulme.
Pathelin pleads in court.

keeper, beside himself with horror, makes the sign of the cross, and flies home.

On the way he meets his shepherd, Agnelet, whom he accuses of killing and eating the sheep which are committed to his charge. Agnelet tries to assert his innocence, which nevertheless is rather doubtful, but Joceaulme, who is in a rage already at not having received the money for his cloth, declares that he means to bring an action against him.

So Agnelet thinks the best thing he can do is to put his cause in the hands of Pathelin, and the latter, who is familiar with this kind of doubtful causes, is not without resource, but advises Agnelet to make the judges believe that he is a fool, and to answer nothing but " Bah!" to all their questions. Then he stipulates for an appropriate fee from the honest shepherd, if the matter ends in his favour, and Agnelet, very pleased, promises due payment.

Now the affair goes to law, but when the draper discovers Pathelin, whom he has just seen raving in fever, he is quite put out, and in his confusion makes a muddle of the cloth and the sheep, till finally the judge loses patience and gives him a good scolding.[1] And as Agnelet answers nothing but " Bah!" the judge thinks he must be a poor innocent fool, and acquits him (fig. 7).

Pathelin thinks it is time to get his salary, and reminds Agnelet of his promise in several impressive ways. But all the answer he gets is " Bah!" according to his own instructions. He goes home in a fury,

---

[1] To this scene belong the famous words, " Revenons à ces moutons ' (not "à *nos* moutons," as frequently quoted).

confessing that he has been outwitted by a simple shepherd.

As this play surpasses most other contemporary farces in importance and especially in dramatic construction, it also materially exceeds them in length. As a rule the other plays settle the dramatic complication in a great hurry. *Pathelin* contains about 1600 lines, but —like other mediæval plays—is not divided into acts and scenes. The scenes follow each other without interruption. Though the date of the original play is unknown, we can refer it with considerable certainty to the time shortly before 1470. In the year 1706 it became included in the repertoire of the *Théâtre français* in an adaptation conformed to the taste of the time, by the dramatists Brueys and Palaprat. Adapted and produced by the well-known scholar Ed. Fournier in a shape which approached much closer to the original, it gained a new victory on the modern French stage in the year 1872. Also as a comic opera with music by Bazin, *Pathelin* has appeared on the boards many times.

No other mediæval play has obtained anything like the popularity and longevity of this amusing farce, but no other can be compared to it in dramatic structure and ingenuity. Most of the others have rather the character of anecdotes under the form of dialogues, and none of them would be at all likely to find a place on a modern stage. Each gives a comic situation instead of a developed intrigue. Thus, for example, the well-known farce of *The Washing-tub* (*le cuvier*), which treats of an honest man, Jaquinot, who is dreadfully cowed by his wife and his mother-in-law. He complains most piteously of having too much domestic work to do, so in order to prevent future quarrels, his mother-in-law proposes to put down on a list (*rollet*) all the duties devolving upon him. This is done; his wife dictates him a long list of duties: he shall be the first to rise in the morning, he shall make the bed, look after the child at night, bake bread, etc., etc.; and whenever he ventures to object, he is speedily silenced by the strong women.

At last the list is written, and Jaquinot at once begins performing one of his duties, viz., to help his wife with the washing. But as soon as the couple have commenced wringing the linen, Jaquinot suddenly lets go his hold of it, and his wife falls head foremost into the tub. She screams for help, but Jaquinot calmly pulls out his list and looks closely at it to see if it is one of his duties to help his wife out of the tub. This case is not mentioned at all, and so he keeps answering all her cries for help with these words: "*Cela n'est pas à mon rollet.*"

Meanwhile the mother-in-law arrives, but, she not having strength enough to help her daughter, there is nothing left for the women but to yield and to promise obedience to the husband. On this condition Jaquinot helps her out, but from his final sentence: "*Heureux serai se marché tient,*" we conclude that he has no absolute faith in the future.

Sometimes the farces have a more pronounced moral point, as in the two farces of *The wives who have their husbands remoulded*, and *The husbands who have their wives salted*. The moral is the same in both : married life may be bad and ludicrous enough, but don't attempt to change it, for you will make matters worse.   Perhaps this is shown more distinctly in the first farce.   Two young women have married old men. These husbands are good-natured and allow their wives to rule, and being rich they can give them as many presents as they want, and allow them to go out to as many festivals as they like.   They have everything that can be desired : fine houses, magnificent clothes, beauti- ful ornaments ; all this, however, does not console them for the one unpleasant thing, their husbands are old and weak.   Then a founder (*fondeur*) makes his appearance (the prototype of Ibsen's bell-founder in *Peer Gynt*), and the grumbling wives conceive the idea of asking him to remould their husbands.   The founder consents to do so for a reward of a hundred dollars for each, but before doing it he tries to dissuade them from the experiment. " You should not do it," he says, " for they change their character with their age."   But the wives will not listen to reason ; they have made up their minds to have young husbands ; and as the husbands have no objection either, the founder begins his work.   " Blow on," say the wives, "spare no effort ! "   " But, suppose I get four husbands out of the two ? "   " Never mind, so much the better."   At last the work is done.   The husbands come out of the oven young, handsome and strong men, per- fectly changed.   But the founder was right, their char- acters are altered too.   They have now become imperative and short - spoken ; they command and expect to be obeyed.   They at once ask for the keys, and as their wives hesitate, they are beaten.   In despair the disappointed wives run to the founder for the second time, and implore him to put the men into the oven again to make them old as before. But the founder declares this to be impossible, and sends them home with the following moral : " Keep your husbands, ladies, just as they are, and don't think of remoulding them."

A perfect counterpart of this farce is that of *The husbands who have their wives salted.* Some stupid husbands find their wives too "sweet"—*trop doulces*—and desire a charlatan, maistre Macé, to "salt" them for ten francs each. After the salting all sweetness has left them so completely that they beat their husbands, who in vain beseech Master Macé to take the salt off them again. But his art is exhausted, and the wives must be left as they are.

The farce proper afforded a great variety of characters to the performers. Each class of society was represented in nearly all its types : clerics, physicians, schoolmasters, undergraduates, artisans, peasants, shopkeepers, noblemen, lawyers, women of all ages and descriptions, virtuous, ill-tempered, fast—light caricatures drawn in a few bold lines, which gave no occasion for deep study of character, but allowed the actor to make use of his observations of everyday-life, of gestures and accents which strikingly reminded the spectator of the class to which the character belonged ; in short, variegated superficial pictures of real life.

But we do not meet with the standing types, such as were so common in the Greek and Roman plays, and which appeared again in the Italian comedy, thence passing to the French classical theatre, and its imitations

in other European countries. Though many figures in
the old farces may resemble each other, and scarcely differ
in anything but their names, we see distinctly that the
ruling principle is to copy the characters of real life, and
it never occurs to the authors of those times to establish
a character once for all, to be represented as a fixed type
in all pieces. We do not even meet with a typical fool.
It is true, *le Badin* appears in a number of plays, but
neither frequently enough, nor with sufficiently marked
characteristics to allow us to regard him as a typical
jester.

We must make a reservation with regard to the
peculiar kind of farce which appeared in France under
the name of *Sotties*. The Sotties formed the repertoire
of the special *fool-companies*, and were performed within
their sphere. Many such fool-companies existed in
France under different names, as, *e.g.*, the *Enfants sans-
souci* in Paris, where at Shrovetide they practised their
jokes and performed their merry plays. These fool-
companies will be mentioned more in detail in the
following chapter; here we only indicate the nature of
their repertoire.

By the word *sottie* we now generally understand a
farce with typical fools, as the " Prince of fools," the
" Mother of fools"—*Prince des Sots* and *Mère sotte*—
the heads of the company, and their inferiors, the
ordinary fools of different degrees; and it is often stated
that, while the farce treats ordinary subjects of everyday
life from a merely comical point of view, the sottie is a
kind of political satire which deals with public questions
in a comical way. The language of the time scarcely

made a sharp distinction between sottie and farce, but it is quite certain that in the course of the sixteenth century a political sottie grew up, which did not satirise everything indiscriminately, but aimed directly at certain facts and parties. It was under Louis XII. in particular that the political sottie flourished. The Middle Ages knew nothing of newspapers, political meetings, or similar means of agitation. So it was no bad idea to take the theatre, which attracted so large a public, into the service of political agitation. Of course the persons and institutions that were to be chastised were not portrayed or represented openly on the stage—such a thing would not have been permitted—but the veil of disguised names and puns which covered them was so transparent, that everybody understood what they aimed at. Thus, for instance, when in the year 1503 the Maréchal de Rohan had had a quarrel with Queen Anne, the wife of Louis XII., and had fallen into disgrace, a play was performed in Paris, in which a blacksmith — *maréchal* — is shoeing a donkey — Anne, *âne*—but gets a violent kick which sends him flying far away.

While, as we have said before, the names of most dramatists of this time are forgotten, or do not tell us anything about their bearers, that of the principal author of political sotties, Pierre Gringoire, has preserved its reputation down to our own days, owing to the poetic treatment of which he has twice been the object, first in *Notre Dame de Paris*, the famous novel by Victor Hugo, afterwards in the graceful play by Théodore de Banville, which bears the name of its hero, the poet.

However, the poetic representations have not retained much more than the name of the real Gringoire, who seems to have been anything but a starving dreamer or a fantastic pedant.

The works of Pierre Gringoire were composed during the reign of Louis XII., not Louis XI. He was born in Normandy about the year 1475, so he was twenty-three years old when Louis XII. came to the throne. During the reign of this king the gay brotherhoods, *la Bazoche du Palais* and *les Enfants sans souci*, had their most flourishing period. The king not only made use of these companions for political purposes, but he, as well as Queen Anne de Bretagne, greatly relished these merry sotties.

As a young man Gringoire joined the company of the "Enfants sans souci," in which he was an eager performer, and for which he composed a number of different plays. His first work is a morality which bears the title, *le Château de Labour* (1499). At the age of thirty-five he had attained to the next highest dignity in the brotherhood, becoming *Mère-Sotte*, who was only second to the *Prince des Sots* (fig. 8). This title he frequently used afterwards as a *nom de plume*. (*Les Fantaisies de Mère-Sotte, les Menus Propos de Mère-Sotte*.)

We have reason to believe that Gringoire was an enterprising and practical man, whose ambition was not satisfied with composing and performing gay sotties for his company. He entered into partnership with a carpenter, Jehan Marchant, and became a kind of manager or impresario of the plays which were performed officially at the expense of the town of Paris. The carpenter constructed the theatre, and Gringoire arranged the plays, which were especially performed on the arrival of royal personages. On these occasions, however, only pantomimes and *tableaux vivants* were represented.

Gringoire also composed real mysteries; thus he wrote for the masons' and carpenters' companies in Paris the before-mentioned *Vie de Saint-Louis*.

The king himself employed the author as a political agitator in his struggles against Pope Julius II., and in his satire *la Chasse au cerf des cerfs*,[1] in the morality of *l'Homme obstiné*, and especially in the sottie *le Prince des Sots*, Gringoire really succeeded in exciting the hatred of the lower classes against the king's pontifical antagonist. The *Prince of Fools* was performed, together with the morality, on Shrove Tuesday, 1512, in the Halles of Paris, and made the name of Gringoire famous.

The reign of Francis I. was not altogether favourable to the drama, and least of all to the political sottie, which was the strong point of Gringoire. He also seems to have been superseded by the Italian comic actors, who by this time began to invade Paris. Practical enough to retire at the right moment, he went to Lorraine after having married (in 1518), became king-at-arms to the Duke Antoine, and adopted the name of Vaudemont. Here he devoted his talents to a line of politics entirely differing from that which he had served under Louis XII.; he probably resented the court's preferring foreign professional actors to his own art, in spite of the latter having

---

[1] *Cerf des cerfs* is a pun upon the title of the pope, *servus servorum, le serf des serfs*.

rendered his country several services.   In the service of
his new master he lived a more retired life than before.
And after the year 1527, in which he published his
Notables renseignements, adages et proverbes, no more was
heard of him in literature.   He died at the age of sixty-
three, at the close of 1538 or the beginning of 1539.

The Prince of Fools, Gringoire's principal work, is a
good specimen of its kind.   It has scarcely any action ;
all its importance lies in the perpetual allusions to
political persons and events, which are disguised by
grotesque names and apparent jests.   The principal
characters of this sottie are : the Prince of Fools himself,
who stands for Louis XII. ; he quarrels with *Mère
Sotte*, who appears dressed as "holy Church" ; Pope
Julius II.   A third important character is *la Sotte
Commune*, viz., the People, who is in despair on account
of the quarrel, and wants peace at any cost, "for," she
says, "it is I who have to pay the piper, after all."[1]
At the end of the play *Mère Sotte* is stripped of her
clothes, so that everybody can see who she is, not
holy Church, but only *Mère Sotte*.   And therefore
she is deposed from the throne she has usurped ; in
other words, the only thing to do with Pope Julius II.
is to depose him, for he is unworthy of representing
holy Church.—

In Germany the farce, or as it was called there, the
"Shrovetide Play," had its principal seat in Nuremberg,

[1] "Enfin je paie toujours l'escot."
[2] "Affin que chascun le cas notte
   Ce n'est pas Mère Saincte Eglise
   Qui nous fait guerre ; sans feintise
   Ce n'est que nostre Mère Sotte."

at least most of the plays extant date from this town, which throughout the Middle Ages and the Renaissance was the seat of a flourishing intellectual and industrial life. Old customs were held in honour, and each year at Shrovetide masked crowds of apprentices marched through the streets and sang their songs, or acted their merry little scenes disguised as fools. They also performed dances, and many of the oldest of these German so-called plays rather appear as a kind of introduction to the merry cock-dance or the stately sword-dance, because they are so short, because they have no dramatic point at all, and because they end with an invitation to begin dancing. One of the Shrovetide fools had to announce the arrival of his comrades and the commencement of the play. Such a forerunner was called *der Einschreier* (*le crieur*), and his function and name survived in the shape of prologues even after the plays had ceased to be directly connected with the Shrovetide processions. An "Ausschreier" (out-crier) ended the play, and when the little company had received its reward—a pot of beer or a glass of wine, sometimes even a little gift in money—it marched on to the next street. These Shrovetide processions were called *Schembartlaufen*, and from these entertainments dates the abundance of farces in the literature of Nuremberg.

So far, we must say, there is no marked difference in form and subject between the German and the French

---

[1] The cock-dance, which for a long time held its ground as a favourite entertainment, was originally a rustic dance, in which the performers had to balance a wine-barrel on their head. The best dancer was rewarded by receiving a cock. Comp. Creizenach, *op. cit.* p. 411.

farces. Only, the German ones are very inferior to the
French in artistic composition and ease of language.
Whereas in France the dialogue is quite animated, and
the verses broken in various manners, in German farces
it runs on in regular verses, so that two consecutive lines
rhyme with each other, and are very seldom divided,
one person taking the first rhyme and another the next;
if this happens occasionally, it is pointed out in the
stage - directions, evidently to prevent the actor from
making a mistake. Thus, for instance, in the *Neithart
Play* :—

> " Gott grüesz euch, lieber Herr und liebe frau !
> Helft mir, das ich ain kloster pau !
> Uns hat got zu euch gesant,
> Ich han euch pracht ain ganz convent,
> Die han ich all selber geweihet.
> Get dann ! Wer will werden peicht,
> Der mag wol werden seiner sünden an.
>   (*Der Herzog der erfüllt den Reim und spricht :*)
> Herr Neithart, ir seit ein guoter man," etc.[1]

With regard to the subjects of the farces, we have
already called attention to certain differences which were
connected with the different characters of the two nations.
We may add the observation that in France we do not
by any means meet with the coarse, even hateful mockery
of the peasant class, which is so common in the German

---

[1] God be with you, dear Master and Mistress ! help me that I may build
a convent ; God has sent us to you. I have brought you a whole conven-
tion, and I have consecrated them all. Now then, come everyone who
wants to confess, he can get rid of all his sins. (*The Duke fills up the rhyme
and says :*) " Mr Neithart, you are a good man."

farces. A great many of these plays have no other
object than to represent peasants as dirty, coarse and
cowardly animals, and the peasant girls as sensual and
cynical creatures. It is a favourite joke to treat rustic
weddings and wooings where the young girl is described
as anything but a virgin, and her physical advantages
and defects are discussed by parents and bridegroom
with an openness which leaves nothing to be desired,
where the confessor "credences" the bride, and where
the wedding gifts consist of old trousers, hats, kettles,
and similar treasures.

The hatred of the rustic class which we find in these
ancient authors, all of whom were probably townspeople,[1]
finds a particularly drastic expression in the *Neithart
Play*, the longest of all German Shrovetide-plays, as it
exceeds two thousand verses. The plot of this play is
very slender, but the whole composition evidently serves
as a frame for a number of dances, graceful roundelays
performed by noble maidens, grotesque rural dances,
stilt-dances, etc.

Immediately after the prologue the pipers begin to
play and the "duchess" and ladies to dance; then, as a
kind of parody the coarse peasants perform a dance,
headed by their leader, Engelmair. The action keeps
swaying the whole time without much transition between
these two extremes : the ducal court and the company of
peasants. It is spring, the beautiful month of May is at
hand, and the duchess is longing to see the first violet.

---

[1] The authors of the great majority of Shrovetide-plays are unknown.
Only the names of two Nuremberg poets have come down to us, those of the
iron-founder and gun-maker, Hans Rosenplüt, of the middle of the fifteenth
century, and the barber and mastersinger, Hans Folz, of its close.

Neithart, the young knight, goes out in search of it and is at once successful. He places his hat over it to enable him to find it again, and with a gay song he goes home to fetch the duchess and her ladies.

But no sooner has Neithart gone than one of the peasants, Enzlman, lifts up the hat, picks the violet, and deposits another less sweet-smelling souvenir in its place.[1]

Now the duchess returns with her attendants, headed by Neithart, and orders the company to dance round the violet.

> Mit pfeifen und mit schalmaien
> Sullen wir darumb raien,
> Wir wellen auf den freudenplan
> Den lieben sumer schon emphan.
> Was ich sprich, das main ich ganz.
> Schicht nach den spilleuten und macht den tanz.[2]

Then they dance, after which the duchess lifts up the hat to see the delicious spring-flower. She recoils in disgust from what she sees, and in great anger goes away with her maidens, after making a thundering speech to the innocent Neithart.

The latter, who stood speechless while the great lady was present, now breaks out into a rage, and

---

[1] This is done quite openly on the stage. The stage-directions have this note : *Und Enzlman der nimbt den huot auf und pricht den Veiol ab und thuot ein Dreck an des Veiol stat und dekt in vider mit dem huot zu.*

[2] With pipes and shalms
We will dance round it,
We will on this festive spot
Receive the dear summer.
What I say I certainly mean.
Send for the musicians and begin to dance.

swears terrible vengeance on the person who has played
him this trick. It soon comes to light that the coarse
joke is due to the peasants, and Neithart undertakes a
regular crusade against them. The remainder of the
piece shows the various torments which Neithart and
his companions inflict upon the miserable peasants;
they make them prisoners, cut off one leg and replace
it by tying on a wooden one; they make them drink
to excess, and during their state of intoxication which
lasts three days—though on the stage only a minute—
Neithart dresses them out as monks and banters them
without mercy.

At last the devils join the party, with Lucifer at
their head, and excite the peasants to quarrel, which
ends in a great fight with sharp weapons. In the end
Neithart is praised and rewarded by the duke for his
great zeal against the peasants.

It is doubtful whether the *Neithart-play*, like
most other Shrovetide-plays of that time, dates from
Nuremberg; neither its home nor its author is known.
But Nuremberg, at any rate, for a long time to come,
maintained its supremacy in German dramatic poetry;
we may even say, not till now did the latter burst into
full bloom, owing to the remarkable man, who in the
course of the sixteenth century imprinted his stamp
on German dramatic art. Though neither the time
nor the mind of Hans Sachs were mediæval, we must
say that his Shrovetide and other plays are so distinctly
continuations of the works of Rosenplüt and Folz, that
he naturally finds his place in connection with these
predecessors.

He was indeed a younger contemporary of Hans Folz, and Sachs mentions particularly this *durchleuchtig deutsche poet* as one of the select twelve mastersingers in the *Singschule*, among which we also find Six Beckmesser and others who have been immortalised by Richard Wagner. Hans Sachs was born in the year 1494. He was the son of a tailor, but was apprenticed to a shoemaker. On his professional journeys through the country, he combined with shoemaking the art of master-singing, which was eagerly cultivated by the trade-companies in all parts, especially in South Germany and the Rhine-lands; and on his return to Nuremberg he threw himself with glowing enthusiasm into the art of master-song as well as of other poetry and dramatic production, at the same time continuing his trade.

He had travelled far and wide, had visited Frankfurt, Würzburg, Cologne, Munich, Vienna, Lübeck, and many other places, and everywhere he had learned something new, not only about boots and shoes, but especially about poetry, so that when at the age of twenty-two he again settled down in Nuremberg, he was able to stand up as the reformer of the German drama, while Luther, whom he joined as an ardent admirer, became the reformer of the Church.

His life was long—he died on the 19th of January 1576, at the age of eighty-two (fig. 9)—and from beginning to end his productive power was marvellous. There were years in which he wrote as many as eighteen plays, *e.g.*, in 1556 alone eight tragedies and ten comedies; and he left in all 198 dramatic works, 59 tragedies,

8

9

8—Pierre Gringoire as "Mother Fool" (with his motto in the border).
9—A portrait of Hans Sachs in his 81st year (from a print).

65 comedies, 64 shrovetide-plays, and 10 dramatic works, which he only calls "plays." Besides these he composed an immense number of fables, epic poems, and of master-songs more than 4000![1]

It goes without saying that all these works could not be pearls, and that he could not begin by being a mature artist. His first works, some Shrovetide-plays, are not very superior to those of his predecessors, and only in so far inaugurate a new era, as they introduce a more decent tone, and are not steeped in filth, as was invariably the case with the old comedies. Not till later did he acquire the concise form and the genuine dramatic humour in his dialogues which render him so superior to contemporary dramatists. There can be no question that his Shrovetide-plays hold supreme rank, while his "tragedies" and "comedies" stand between the Middle Ages and the Renaissance. These terms were borrowed from the Renaissance, though he does not seem to have been quite clear with respect to their meaning. The decisive question to him was whether the play ended with somebody's death or not; in the former case he called it a tragedy, in the latter a comedy. But he is not consistent even in this point. For instance, he calls his drama of *Judith* a "Comedi," but even in the prologue he changes his mind, and makes the "Ehrenhold" (herald) say :—

> ". . . Sind wir gebeten hieher kommen
> Und haben alhie fürgenommen

---

[1] Probably he did not consider his master-songs worthy of being preserved, for in the collection of his works (3 vols. in folio, Augsburg 1558-1561), edited by himself, he did not include them.

Zu halten ein geistlich comedi,
Doch schier vast gleich einer tragedi." [1]

But in subject and construction these works are still
entirely mediæval. In the higher drama he is wont to
represent the action in the form of dialogues, which
succeed each other without being properly connected,
either in meaning or outward form, just as was the
fashion in the mediæval plays. It is true, his tragedies
and comedies—at all events those of his later period—
are divided into *acts*, according to French and Italian
Renaissance fashion, but this division is merely external.
The act, as a rule, does not form a unity in itself as to
time and action, but is frequently broken by long intervals of time, and the action is interrupted arbitrarily
where the author thought it convenient to make a rest.
However, the division into acts—the number of which
was not limited to a maximum of five, but might rise as
high as ten—necessitated that at the close of each act the
author had to find a pretext for making all his characters
leave the stage. For the play which now, at least partly,
was performed indoors, no longer required all the persons
represented to remain on the stage throughout the dura-
tion of the piece. On the other hand, there was no front
curtain to mark the close of the acts. Consequently the
performers had each time to be removed from the stage,
leaving it empty for a few minutes, a custom which was
and still is adopted in the French classical comedies and

[1] " We have been asked to come here,
And have here undertaken
To perform an ecclesiastical comedy,
Though it is almost like a tragedy."

tragedies performed in the *Théâtre français.* Then, of course, the performers had also to enter on the stage at the beginning of each act, and were not previously arranged in groups as in our own time. The pretexts for making the actors go off were often very naïve, such as for instance in the otherwise tolerably regular comedy in five acts about Persones, the wife of Alexander Magnus, who "rides on the philosophum Aristotelem," in which the two reasoners of the play suddenly, at the close of the third act, interrupt their conversation about court matters by these words :—

> Komm, zum Frühmal man jetzt trommet
> Der Hunger hat mich lang gefret,[1]

upon which both go out. Or in *Die schön Magelona,* a comedy in seven acts, in which Sir Peter, after a touching love scene with Princess Magelona, unexpectedly tears himself out of her arms, exclaiming :—

> Hört! hört! man thut zu Tisch blasen,
> Ich muss gehn eilend hin mein Strassen,
> Bei dem wöll wir's jetzt bleiben lassen,[2]

and after these—to say the least of it—prosaic parting words the lovers leave the stage.

And as the form balances between the old and the new, so do the subjects. Hans Sachs gets his subjects everywhere. He treats the old Biblical motives, such as *The Passion, The Sacrifice of Isaac, The Childhood*

---

[1] Come, the drum calls us to breakfast,
Hunger has long tormented me.

[2] Hear! hear! the trumpet calls us to dinner,
I must go away in a hurry,
So now, this must be enough.

of Moses, etc.; he takes up mediæval legends such as *Tristan and Isolde, Siegfried the Horny, Oliver and Artus*, etc.   But he also introduces a multitude of classical subjects, such as *Clytemnestra, Alcestis, The Destruction of Troy, Ulysses, Perseus and Andromeda*, and many others.   But these classical themes, for which the influence of the Renaissance had given him a taste, were treated entirely in the mediæval style, and owing to his ignorance of the sources, and his working at third or fourth hand, the plays which he himself considered as faithful imitations from Greek and Latin, abounded in ridiculous mistakes and anachronisms; in fact, they were imbued with the spirit and views of the Nuremberg petty tradesman, which contrasted comically with the sonorous old historical names.

It is in the Shrovetide-play that Hans Sachs appears as the great master and reformer.   Here he is not hampered by new rules and ancient models.   His wealth of humour flows on freely without ever degenerating into coarseness.   He takes his subjects from real life, speaks the language he has heard with his own ears, and which suits the characters he paints.   At the same time, the knowledge, which he had acquired for the sake of the great and serious plays, proves useful to him in the light productions; the harmony between subject and style which, in spite of all his labour, he failed to obtain in the former, appears quite naturally in the latter. Whereas the old German Shrovetide-plays before the time of Hans Sachs are quite formless, and, in spite of amusing details, difficult to classify even as primitive dramatic works, we find in the best of these plays by

Hans Sachs a solidity of construction, a life and consistency in the dialogue, which would allow of their performance on a modern stage.

To quote an example, let us peruse the Shrovetide-play about *The Wandering Scholar and Exorcist*.[1] The subject has been frequently treated; in ancient times after Hans Sachs by his successor, the Nuremberg barrister and notary, Jakob Ayrer (d. 1605). In Denmark Hans Andersen has derived some of his ideas for the story *Big and Little Claus* from this play. In Hans Sachs we must say the nature of the subject is not quite so innocent as in Andersen's tale, though he avoids coarseness and pictures of amorous situations, where earlier authors of Shrovetide-plays would no doubt have yielded to the temptation.

In Sachs the play has four characters—the lame and hunchbacked parson, the wandering scholar, the farmer and his wife. Here, as in the other Shrovetide-plays by Sachs, there is no division into acts and scenes. The piece begins with the appearance of the farmer's wife who comes in alone soliloquizing. We learn that her husband is out working in the wood, and is not expected home till the evening. Now she has an ardent desire to see the parson, who, in spite of his physical defects, is the friend her heart has chosen, and she wishes that he would profit by the opportunity and call upon her. In the midst of her reflections about the taunts of her neighbours and the jealousy of her husband, she discovers the parson, who has sneaked round the barn in

---

[1] *Der fahrend Schüler mit dem Teufelbannen*, ein Fastnachtspiel mit vier Personen.

order to avoid gossip.   The farmer's wife is delighted,
and offers him fresh sausages made from the newly-
killed sow, a cup of wine, and white bread.   The parson
accepts the tempting offer, but urges her to be quick,
as he is afraid that her husband may return.   She goes
to fetch the food, and her friend remains alone.   Meanwhile he expresses his fear of the husband, and his
wonder why he himself dares brave the scandal of being
caught in the act by a peasant.

> " Ich bin zwar mit einem Narrn besessen,
>   Dass ich weit lauf nach Huren aus,
>   Hab doch selbst eine in dem Haus," [1]

he says philosophically.

Now the woman reappears with sausages, wine and
bread, and they are just going to enjoy the feast when
sounds of a cow-bell are heard outside.   A moment
after the young traveller enters, one of these wandering
students, who beg their way in order, as they say, to
collect some money to help them to study for holy orders.
Here also the begging student asks for a gift, in the
following words :—

> " O Mutter, gieb dein milde Steur
>   Mir armen fahrende Schüler heur
>   Denn ich sammle mit diesen Dingen
>   Dass ich mein erste Mess mög singen." [2]

---

[1] "I must be possessed by a devil of folly,
    To run so far afield after women,
    When I've got one in my own house."

[2] "Oh, mother, give your little share
    To a poor travelling scholar to-day,
    For I collect such gifts
    That I may sing my first mass."

But the parson turns him out sharply with these words:—

" Du sammelst leicht zu einem Schalk.
Hebst dich hinaus, du Lasterbalg." [1]

The student goes on begging, but the priest and the woman load him with abuse, and knock and kick him out of doors. But before disappearing he warns them and promises that he will make them repent of their hard-heartedness. In a speech aside he informs us of his intention to hide himself in the house, and to take a thorough revenge on the two when the farmer comes back.

Now after having locked the door the parson finds himself alone with the woman. They are just going to partake of the delicacies when there is a violent knock at the door. The woman looks out, and, to her great fright, discovers her husband who has returned. Wine and sausages are concealed in a hurry, the priest hides himself in an oven, and the woman promises to help him to escape as soon as her husband has gone to sleep.

Then she opens the door to her husband, who has returned so soon from the wood, as he has broken both his axes. He asks for bacon and sausages, but his wife tells him there is nothing left; everything is eaten or given away. While they talk the cow-bell rings again, announcing the return of the begging scholar. The wife, in a great fright, runs to meet him, and tries to get rid of him in a hurry, offering him a trifle, but he approaches her husband and asks hospitality for the

[1] " You may easily collect enough for a rogue,
Be off at once, you rascal."

night.   This being granted, he at once imposes silence on the unfaithful wife by whispering in her ear, " Hold your tongue, little mother, and I will hold mine!"

Next the peasant inquires what his occupation is, and the scholar replies that he and his equals walk from high school to high school teaching necromancy. They know many other crafts besides, they can cure sore eyes and toothache, lay on hands, and render invulnerable, tell fortunes, dig treasures, and ride on goats at night.   "I have also heard," the peasant says, "that you scholars can exorcise the devil."—"So we can indeed," the student answers; "we can exorcise him, and make him do what we like; we can even order him to bring sausages, wine and wheat-cake."—"My dear man," the peasant exclaims, "I confess there is nothing in the world I should like better than to see a real devil."—"Well, look at your wife!"—"No, joke apart, suppose you let us have a look at the devil." —The cunning student promises, though the thing is very dangerous, but, to begin with, he orders husband and wife to go upstairs backward to the loft, while he summons the devil, and to remain there till he calls them.   Then they must descend backwards again, and they will see the devil.

The couple do as they are told; but as soon as they are out of the door, the student gets hold of the priest, threatens to betray him to the husband, and puts him into such a state of terror, that he not only gives him all his money, but also consents to play the devil in the following drastic way: he is to strip himself to the skin, and to paint his body as black as a raven, then

to put on an old horse-hide which is found in the
stable. He is moreover told to come in at a given
signal, and to growl like a wild bear. But he must
not forget to bring the sausages, wine and cake with
him. If he promises to do all this, he shall be allowed
to leave the house in peace. The shivering priest
promises all, and goes away to put on the disguise.

Now the artful student calls back the couple, who
descend backwards from the loft, and sit on tenter-
hooks, each absorbed in his or her own thoughts.
The scholar draws a magic circle with his sword, and
solemnly exorcises the devil three times. At last he
appears in his whole diabolical apparel, and brings
the sausages, wine and cake. The peasant is nearly
stricken dead with horror, and remains speechless till
the spectre is gone; even then he cannot recover from
his terror. He had no idea that the devil was so
ugly, nay, deformed. He was just like the hunch-
backed parson, even lame like him. At last the
student calms him by means of an amulet which he
hangs round his neck, and the peasant goes to bed
after giving the exorcist a florin for his trouble.
Now the woman and the student are alone. After
trembling with a fright very different from that of her
husband, she begins to breathe more freely. But she
is not allowed to escape till the student has squeezed
as much money out of her as out of the priest. Finally
he possesses himself of the wine and sausages, and
loaded with his rich prey, he winds up with reciting
the epilogue and moral of the play.

I have described this little Shrovetide-play in

detail, because I think it gives a clear idea of the progress in scenic technique which we find in Hans Sachs. This progress reveals itself for one thing in the natural and consistent observation of the unity of place. To a modern reader this may seem a matter of course, but in those times it was by no means so. A Shrovetide-play of an earlier period would have allowed the action to move about at random, now on the road with the traveller, now in the wood with the peasant, with his wife in the room, with the couple in the loft, etc. I do not mean to say, that each of these localities would have been represented, or that the author would have had any idea that they ought to be; only it would not have been clear to him that all the scenes of the play might most easily be laid in one place, and he would not have taken the trouble to arrange them in such a way that it should appear natural for them to be thus performed. The theatre of Hans Sachs certainly had to do without any help from decorative painting, yet there is not the slightest doubt that the action takes place from beginning to end in the same room of the farmer's house, and the surrounding localities present themselves to our minds as distinctly as if they had been reproduced by a clever modern technician. While, as we know, it is often very difficult to determine where the scenes of an eighteenth century play are supposed to pass, and what image stood before the poet's mind when he composed them, Hans Sachs leaves no doubt whatever on this point. He may be naïve and ignorant, but his scenic imagination is as sharp as that of any dramatist, and in spite of his immense productiveness, each of his plays is worked out with a minute care, which beats many of his later colleagues.

This progress is not so unimportant as a layman might presume. In fact it leads in the direction of modern scenic art, which presents life in images as well as in words, creating a pictorial as well as a poetic illusion. In power of poetic expression also Hans Sachs takes a great step in advance. The dialogue is much more consistent in its construction; the speeches fall on each other with much more logical and psychological necessity; we seem to hear a real conversation, not a succession of incoherent descriptions, lyrical exclamations or heterogeneous efforts at witticism. The delineation of character also becomes more distinct, though on this point we still feel great deficiencies. We cannot say that each character speaks his own particular language, and that Sachs possesses the power of giving expression to the inward character through strongly personal and individual speech. This dramatic gift still belongs to the future. Nevertheless he is very superior to his predecessors in the art of distinguishing his characters from each other, of giving to each his psychological, if not linguistically characterised, stamp.

In other respects, too, which even more immediately concerned dramatic art, the excellent old Nuremberg shoemaker was a reformer. He was not only an exceptionally productive author, but also an eager and clever actor and theatrical manager.

There was no permanent theatre in Nuremberg yet, though the contrary has been stated. In ancient handbooks, such as the *History of German dramatic art*, by Eduard Devrient—an excellent work for the time at which it came out—we read that the first theatre in Germany was built in the year 1550[1] by the company of Mastersingers in Nuremberg.

This, however, is incorrect. Hans Sachs and the mastersingers were amateur actors like their mediæval predecessors. In the course of time theatrical performances had been withdrawn from the open street and public square and confined within the four walls of a church, a convent yard or an inn, and the nature of the plays had contributed to bring about this change. But we cannot conclude from these facts that the mastersingers possessed a permanent theatre. Though the dramatic performances became more regular and frequent, they retained their amateur stamp, and constantly changed their locality. After the Reformation the Nuremberg mastersingers were allowed to use the Church of Martha for their performances, and they remained in possession of this privilege for about a century, up to the year 1614,[2] when it was withdrawn. Sometimes, however, the town council had reason to repent of its liberality to the amateur actors, as it happened occasionally, that eager playgoers entered into the church during the afternoon service in order to secure seats for the play.

When the mastersingers were allowed the use of the Dominican convent, Hans Sachs was peremptorily enjoined to prevent the public from entering before the sermon was finished. The admission fee was fixed; it was not to exceed two kreuzer. They were not permitted to play more than twice a week, and that not all the year round, but only in the season during

[1] Ed. Devrient : *Geschichte der deutschen Schauspielkunst*, i. p. 114.
[2] R. Genée : *Lehr- und Wanderjahre*, etc., p. 126 f.

which plays were generally performed, *i.e.* as a rule from Epiphany to Lent.

However, secular localities were also used by Hans Sachs and his company during this period, and we may suppose that in these places they were less restrained. In the register of the town hall references are made in particular to the three inns: "The Golden Star," "The Golden Swan," and the "Heilsbronner Hof," as having been most generally used. The last-mentioned, especially, is said to have been very suitable for a theatre, its yard being long and narrow, so that a platform could easily be raised at one end of it, while there was plenty of room for spectators, partly in the remainder of the yard, partly on the surrounding balconies and in the windows.

So here it was—in inns, church and convent—that Hans Sachs directed his companions and rehearsed his plays—merry and sad ones—with them. There can scarcely have been much scenic decoration, at least not in any illusive or picturesque way. In an anonymous play, *The History of Susanna*, of about 1534, the garden in which the action is supposed to take place is thus described in the prologue :—

> Dieser Gart ist gar hübsch und schön
> Von Kräutern und viel Bäumen grün,
> Welchen, so euch zu sehn gelüst,
> Gar scharfe Brillen ihr haben müszt.[1]

[1] This garden indeed is handsome and fine
Green with herbs and many trees,
For which, if you wish to see it,
You must have strong spectacles on.

We see, moreover, from the stage-directions—which are a good barometer for judging of the author's knowledge of the stage—with how much care and understanding Hans Sachs prepared the performance of his plays. His predecessors contented themselves with giving vague hints as to the movements, entrances, exits, gestures, etc., which were to accompany the action on the stage, while Sachs, as a rule, gives precise instruction on these points. He explains not only *when*, but *how* the actors have to come in and go out, whether quickly or slowly, in a sad or a cheerful way, as, for instance, in the tragedy *von der strengen Lieb' Herrn Tristrant mit der schönen Königin Isalden*," where King Mark has discovered the guilty love of Tristrant and Isolde; Tristrant "goes away sad" and Isolde "likewise and slowly," but the king goes out "in anger." He prescribes fixed expressions for grief and despair, prayer, mockery, joy, etc. Thus, at the death of Antony, Cleopatra shall "tear her head-dress, scratch her face, and weep bitterly with grief." Solon, on learning the death of his son, shall join his hands above his head, and shall cry out and shed tears. In the comedy of *The innocent Empress in Rome* (the same subject as Shakespeare's *Winter's Tale*) the repentant slanderer Alphonsus "falls on his knees and lifts up his hands to the empress, imploring her pardon, after which she raises him up and forgives him." When the "patient and obedient Margravine Griselda" receives the message that her young son is to be taken away from her and killed, "she looks at her child, kisses it, makes the sign of the cross over it, and then gives it to the yeoman." But when, shortly after, he goes away with the boy, "she looks longingly after him."

Such little observations reveal a very delicate dramatic sense, and show, even without being considered in relation to the undeveloped state of dramatic art at the time, a high standpoint of scenic intelligence. Even to modern readers, who frequently meet with overloaded descriptions of stage and characters, these simple indications appear striking and exhaustive. If, moreover, we take into account the time and *milieu* of Hans Sachs, we must bow down in admiration before this man, this born aristocrat of art, who in the rudest of trades, without the slightest ostentation, in his leisure hours, so to say between two pairs of boots, worked up his art day by day to a height which it had never reached before, nor was to reach for ages after his time.

For it is a remarkable fact that, in spite of the great and general favour in which he stood, Sachs did not become so important to German dramatic art as there was every reason to expect he would.

Hans Sachs and his companions, his predecessors and closest successors were amateurs, worthy tradesmen and artisans, who occupied themselves with dramatic art as a refreshing and edifying pastime. About his company we read the following statements in a local description[1] dating from the eighteenth century. "It is true, the oldest actors, even those of the time of Hans Sachs, were all simple people of humble condition, wall-painters, slaters, brushmakers, etc., most of

---

[1] A treatise by W. (Will) in *Historisch-diplomatisches Magazin für das Vaterland und angrenzende Gegenden.* Vol. i., Nuremberg, 1781, p. 206.

them mastersingers. Nevertheless we learn that a number of them performed their parts admirably. A certain Häublein was a master in the tragic parts, and made all the spectators weep. Teisinger was grave, and very clever in representing the Emperor of the Turks, or even the devil. Perscha, a young man and a brushmaker, performed a maiden so well that no woman could have done it better."

But soon after the time of Hans Sachs, a professional class of actors began to grow up in Germany; in the beginning their condition was very bad, and they had to fight too hard for bread and popularity to allow of their relations with good taste and good literature to become very intimate.

In a later chapter we shall return to the German dramatic companies and their repertoire; in this place we will only accentuate the fact that Hans Sachs must be considered rather as the climax of the entire German mediæval amateur art, than as the creator of a new period.

II

Moralities—Their Relation to the Character-play—"The Castle of Firmness" — "Wise and Unwise" — "Condemnation of Banquets" — Costumes in the Moralities.

BEFORE leaving the secular repertoire of this age, we have still to mention a species of plays which gained great popularity in the later Middle Ages and the beginning of the Renaissance, viz., the *moralities*.

By a " morality " we understand a play, the characters of which are personified abstractions. The morality is the classical character-play *in ovo*. The object of the character-play is to depict and to chastise a vice or a defect, such as hypocrisy, misanthropy, meddlesomeness, arrogance, or whatever it may be. Some person is invested with this particular vice, and placed in situations which set off the defect most conspicuously, after which he is chastised or converted as the case may be.

The morality proceeds in a simpler way. Its object is also to represent a vice, a virtue, a defect ; in short, some quality which it exposes, punishes or corrects. But it does not take the trouble to individualise such qualities. Instead of representing a Harpagon who is avaricious, a Tartuffe who is a hypocrite, an Alceste who is a misanthrope, the morality takes the abstract quality itself and presents it on the stage. We do not see a gluttonous man like Apicius in Holberg, but *gluttony* itself, not a snobbish Pourceaugnac, but *snobbishness* itself. And the virtues are placed in opposition to the vices. Pride is combated by humility, gluttony by temperance, just as the gentle, reasonable Philinte is placed by the side of the hot-tempered misanthrope Alceste.

The gap between the moralities and the character-plays perhaps would not have been so great as it now appears, if there had been men of genius like Molière and Holberg among the authors of the former. We may well ask : are Harpagon and Tartuffe anything but abstractions — vices with a personal name, to which an ingenious combination of details gives the appearance of individuals, but which after all show us but the one side of the man through which his vice reveals itself?

Meanwhile, we find no works of lasting value among the old moralities, though this species of drama enjoyed rather more consideration and not less popularity than the rest of secular literature. To our taste these colourless personified abstractions on the stage seem very inferior in interest to the lively and variegated farcical characters, and we cannot help wondering that this peculiar variety of drama preserved its vitality so long.

On the whole, abstraction and allegory were in great favour during the Middle Ages. Perhaps it was to a great extent owing to the monster-allegory *The Romance of the Rose* that this style spread all over Europe. The purely allegorical plays, however, do not appear on the boards till the fifteenth century, but thenceforth they flourish very abundantly, especially in France, their native country, and in England, where these *moral plays* became more popular than any other variety. The half-allegorical names with which we meet as late as the nineteenth century—Surface, Candour, Backbite, Sneerwell, etc., in Sheridan's *School for Scandal*—still bear witness of the hold which the moralities had taken on English taste. In German and Danish plays, too, it has been a general custom—no doubt under English influence—to let the name briefly express the prevailing fault or virtue of the character ; we need only recall such popular names as : *Vielgeschrey, Leerbeutel, Zierlich,* etc., etc.

In our section about the Indian theatre we mentioned a remarkable play of the close of the eleventh century : *The Rise of the Moon of Knowledge,* in which King

Error and King Wisdom war against each other. Though there is no evidence to prove that the moralities of the fifteenth and sixteenth centuries stood in any connection with the old Indian play, the two are indeed essentially alike. There is the same struggle between vices and virtues. As a rule it is a human being—the principal character of the play—whose life is described from birth to death, and about whom the good and the evil powers fight incessantly, till at last the virtues are victorious and the vices duly punished.

Thus, for instance, in the English morality *The Castle of Perseverance*, where the hero, Humanum genus, viz., Mankind, begins life by following the advice of his evil angel: to put off practising virtue till he gets old, and to spend the golden years of youth in worldly pleasure. The young man is taken to Mundus (the world, worldliness), who gives him three companions on his way: Stultitia, Voluptas and Detractio: Folly, Voluptuousness and Contempt.

Detractio introduces him to Avaritia, and through her he makes acquaintance with the other six deadly sins, among which Luxuria (Lust) is the one most to his taste, and becomes his mistress.

But now the powers of good set to work. Led by his guardian spirit, the corrupt youth makes the acquaintance of Confessio, with whom at first he will have nothing to do, and whom he puts off till a later time. Poenitentia, however, prevails upon him to trust in Confessio, who places him in the "Castle of Perseverance," where he will be better able than anywhere else to avoid the vices. The castle is besieged by all the seven deadly sins at once, but the virtues defend themselves bravely and repel the attack.

Meanwhile Humanum genus has grown old, and the sins attack him in a different way.   Avaritia, the one among the deadly sins which is most likely to find a willing ear, sneaks up to the wall of the castle, and by all kinds of tricks succeeds in drawing out Humanum genus.   Now he is entirely in the power of sin, and does not even derive pleasure from the wealth he has accumulated by the help of Avaritia, for the boy Garcio wants to appropriate it entirely for his own benefit. Moreover, Death is approaching, and wants to exercise his power over this tempest-tossed man.   In the hour of need Anima, the soul, calls Misericordia, Mercy, to her assistance.   But in vain ; the evil angel has already taken hold of Humanum genus and is going to carry him to Hell on his back.   But suddenly Mercy and Peace make their appearance, and obtain mercy from God for the poor sinner.   Peace drags the human soul from the evil angel, and Mercy carries it before the throne of God (fig. 10).

There are many other moral plays of the same style. The whole species is rather monotonous, and generally moves within the same frame and has the same abstractions for principal characters.   It frequently bears a strong religious stamp, and, so to say, forms a transition between the ecclesiastical and the secular play.   Even in those times these qualifications were mixed up.   Thus one of the oldest and most pronounced French moralities, *Bien-Avisé and Mal-Avisé*, is called a mystery in the original MS., though in form and subject it corresponds

10—Man between his good and his bad angel, the devil and death.   Scene from
a morality.

entirely with the moralities.   The story of this piece is
of a similar kind to that of *The Castle of Perseverance*,
except that the French morality has two heroes instead
of one: *Bien-Avisé* and *Mal-Avisé* (Wise and Unwise).
From two opposite sides Wise and Unwise meet.   They
walk together for a while, but soon Wise is led by
Reason to Faith, who gives him a lantern "made with
twelve windows, in which are to be seen all the articles
of faith and a burning candle; and in handing the
lantern to him she says:[1] Take care not to lose this
torch, this light."   Faith sends him to Contrition, but
she desires him to go to Confession.   On his way he
meets Humility, who advises him to strip himself of his
gorgeous clothes and long pointed shoes (*souliers à
grans poulaines*, which were considered by the moralists
of the time as a particular sign of extravagance).
Thus Wise marches on the road of salvation urged by
Free-Will.

But Unwise does not choose to go the same way.
"Then let us go to the left," Free-Will says; and,
carried away by Idleness and Revolt, he arrives at a
tavern, where he revels and gambles in company with
Folly and Debauchery.   These nice companions finally
rob him of all his property, after which they leave him
alone.

Meanwhile Wise remains some time with Confession, who recommends him to go to Blissful-End
(*Bonne-Fin*).   Occupation leads him to Repentance, who
recommends Penitence to him, after which she sends

---

[1] The vices and virtues appearing in the play are of feminine gender, and
are consequently represented as women.

him to Content. This figure appears before him quite naked, and also asks him to lay aside everything he has taken from his neighbour.

Unwise, who is beside himself with grief at his misfortune, throws himself into the arms of Despair, and beseeches her to take him to Bad-End (*Male-Fin*). Then come Poverty, Bad-luck and Theft, accompanied by the vices who formerly seduced and robbed him. The whole company crowd round the unhappy Unwise, bind him and lead him amid loud cries to Disgrace. At last he is taken to the terrible Bad-End, whose looks are thus described in a stage-direction: "Mark, Bad-End shall have large breasts like a sow, and she shall have a host of little devils following her as pigs follow their mother."

Wise steadily follows the path of virtue, which, after long sojourns with Chastity, Abstinence, Obedience, Diligence, Patience and Wisdom, leads him to Glory. The latter allows him to look at Fortune and her wheel. Fortune herself shows the spectators a double face, the one smiling, the other terrible. Her wheel, which she keeps constantly turning, is a splendid toy, to which four men are attached. The first is named Regnabo (I shall reign), the second Regno (I reign), the third Regnavi (I have reigned), and the fourth Sum-sine-regno (I am without a kingdom). These four keep falling from the summit of fortune down to its deepest pit, thus symbolising in a visible manner the instability of power (fig. 11).

We are again taken back to Unwise, who is still in the hands of Bad-End. Bad-End asks whether he

11—The Wheel of Fortune.

repents of the way he has hitherto followed. But the hardened soul protests that he feels no repentance. Then he is killed by Bad-End, and the devils crowd round him in order to seize his soul and take it to Hell. The place of damnation in this case is not represented in the usual way, but, we read in the stage-directions, as the kitchen in a great lord's house, with devils as waiters. From inside are heard the wailings of the damned souls. Here Unwise, together with Regno and Regnabo, who have also gone to Hell, are now supplied with a truly diabolical supper, which is served on a black table with a fiery red cloth. The dishes are of blazing flames, and, as a final effect, they are upset on the guests, and set fire to them.

In contrast with this infernal tableau, we see Wise's pure soul being carried to Heaven by Good-End; here he is received by the angels, who also give a good reception to Regnavi and Sum-sine-regno, who by their contrition have obtained mercy from God and from the author.

It is obvious from the style of their subjects that the moralities could not help being very monotonous, and even if occasionally an author as, *e.g.*, Nicolas de la Chesnaye, found new subjects and other abstractions than the usual ones, the whole species was bound to suffer from a deplorable lack of variety and life. The said la Chesnaye conceived the idea of employing the morality in the service of what we should call total abstinence. He names his play *Condemnation of Banquets*, and it was published among a number of tracts, all of which recommend sobriety, and warn against gluttony and drunkenness. It is a tolerably long morality, containing 3650 lines and 39 characters, among which we may mention: Dinner, Supper, Banquet, Good Society, Gluttony, Greediness, I drink your health, I pledge you again, Apoplexy, Paralysis, Colic, Dropsy, Experience, Help, Clyster, Pill, Bleeding, Diet, etc., etc.

In spite of the queer, tract-like subject, there is a sort of dramatic life in it. We are first introduced to a gay company, consisting of Gluttony, Pastime, Watering Mouth, Good Company, I drink your health, I pledge you, Habit, guests invited by Dinner and enjoying his meal. All well so far; but outside the windows some uncanny fellows are on the look-out, meditating evil against the merry company; they are the diseases : Apoplexy, Paralysis, Epilepsy, Pleurisy, Quinsy, Dropsy, Jaundice, Gravel and Gout, who show their hideous deformed faces, and are so strangely decked out that "it is difficult to distinguish whether they are men or women," as the stage-direction tells us.

These gloomy disturbers of the peace make common cause with Supper and Banquet, by whom afterwards the revellers are invited, and they make up their minds to attack the party during the meal.

The banquet of Dinner is over, and without delay the guests march off to Supper, where revelling begins afresh. But during the meal the diseases, which have been lying in wait all the time, attack the unsuspecting comrades, give them a good drubbing, and drive them away limping and wailing. This serious warning, however, is without effect. The pains are soon forgotten, and the revellers, remembering that they have an invitation from Banquet, set off, and eating and drinking begins afresh.

After a sort of dietetic sermon inserted here and delivered by a Doctor, who also serves as Prologue to the play, we notice that Banquet secretly opens the door to the diseases, who fall on their prey with renewed fury; this time they do not mean to let them off with a flogging, they want to kill them outright. The four worst revellers, Gluttony, Greediness, I drink your health, and I pledge you, are defeated and strangled by the terrible foes. Pastime, Good Company and Habit escape with their lives, and Good Company thinks he cannot do better than to apply to Dame Experience in order to gain his cause against the treacherous Banquet.

The good lady immediately sends her servants Help, Sobriety, Clyster, Pill, Bleeding, Diet and Remedy, with order to imprison Banquet and Supper.

They are seized, and Dame Experience establishes a kind of jury consisting of Hippocrates, Galenus, Avicenna and Averrhoes—four celebrated physicians— and asks them to be judges in the cause. Supper gets off rather easily. To prevent him from serving meals too quickly, he is to wear leaden cuffs; he is ordered, moreover, to keep himself at six miles' distance from Dinner. But Banquet is sentenced to be hanged. Face to face with death he repents, confesses his sins, and acknowledges that he has never served anybody but the physicians, whom for this reason he desires to pray for him. It is Diet who carries out the sentence against Banquet.

The above-quoted details clearly show what sort of tasks the moralities laid upon the actors. These were not characters of real life, like those of the farces; not a realistic, but rather a symbolistic art was required. In a few striking, perhaps exaggerated, outlines, the actor had to impart personal life to the abstract ideas, if they were at all to be represented as and by human beings on the stage. It would not do to individualise too strongly, as this would efface the generally accepted typical character of the part; on the other hand, he had to represent a human being, not merely an abstraction. So the task was a difficult one, and we can scarcely suppose that the amateur actor of those times was equal to it. But the importance of the moralities to dramatic art consists essentially in the fact that they prepared the way for the great art of representing character. The mystery lays the principal stress on the sublime, on religious feeling, without aiming at particular development of individual character; the farce throws a comic light on all its characters, and represents them indiscriminately as avaricious, hypocritical, stupid, or cunning, just as they are most likely to call forth laughter; the moralities are the first to catch hold of the prominent features of the human character, and expose each of them to contemplation, thus laying the foundation of future great pictures of character. They afford opportunities to the actor of studying how gluttony, hypocrisy, lewdness, slander and other vices reveal themselves physically; he must learn the appearance, gestures, language, etc., of the glutton, the hypocrite, the slanderer; this forces him into new grooves of art, which lead to other ends than those hitherto pursued. In so far we understand the interest which the Middle Ages and the Renaissance—for these plays held their ground far into the Renaissance period—took in the moralities. They exhibited human character from a new point of view; classified, not according to rank or condition, but according to vices and virtues; and the satisfaction felt by the spectators in seeing vice punished was all the greater, because the moral and satire were held within such general limits, that they seldom hit a particular individual, and nobody felt himself directly aimed at by the lash.

However, the moralities contained other characters besides mere abstractions.[1] To begin with, they borrowed from the mysteries angels, devils, Satan, etc., and the whole scenic apparatus—at least in the Middle Ages proper—was probably the same as in the purely ecclesiastical plays. But we also meet with ordinary doctors, priests, apothecaries, etc. Then there is also the fool, likewise borrowed from the mysteries, though a little different in character. In the English moralities, where he appears much more frequently than in those of other nations, he has a character of his own. The fool in the English moral plays generally goes by the name of the Vice, still we also meet him under more special names, *e.g.*, Iniquity and Fraud, or as Sin, Ambidexter, Shift. He was provided with donkey's ears and a wand, and

---

[1] I do not take into consideration the plays which are called moralities, though they do not contain the personified abstractions which otherwise characterise the species, as, *e.g.*, the French morality of *The Emperor who killed his Nephew*, a play which in subject closely resembles the aforementioned miracles, and which has nothing whatever in common with a morality properly so called.

amused the naïve spectators by his jests and capers. It was a favourite joke, for instance, to see him "nimble as a monkey, jump up on the devil's back, and have a ride on him, beating him with his wooden sword so as to make him howl."[1]

In French moralities also, Vice and Sin are sometimes personified, but there they are not in the same way identical with the jester as in the English plays. For example, in *The Malady of Christendom*, by Matthieu Malingre, we meet a *Péché* (Sin), whose costume, as prescribed by the author, is "in front a secular dress, at the back a devil's costume."

The moralities, which had no occasion for exhibiting such magnificence as is seen in the great mysteries, nevertheless paid great attention to fine and ingenious costumes, which might both rejoice the eye by their beauty, and impress the mind by their symbolic meaning. In the above-quoted play, *The Malady of Christendom*, we find a brief description of the costumes. Thus Faith is dressed in a beautiful white robe, Hope in violet, Charity in scarlet, Good Work is attired like an honest merchant, Christendom like a respectable lady (*en honneste dame*), Hypocrisy like a nun, Inspiration like an angel, etc.

In length the moralities generally come between the mysteries and the farces. In the sixteenth century certain rules were laid down as to the length of farces and moralities. The latter were not to exceed a thousand verses; the maximum for the farce was five hundred. But these rules did not exist in the fifteenth

[1] Harsenet : *Declaration of Popish Impostures.*

century, and we find moralities of six thousand, eight
thousand, even more than twenty thousand verses. To
judge from the multitude of extant printed editions of
moralities, which far exceeds that of the mysteries and
farces, we must conclude that they occupied a higher
literary rank. In modern times, it is true, they have
been degraded, being ranked beneath the other dramatic
species. Nevertheless, we can still find interest in
reading these queer outcomes of mediæval fancy, and
in the best of them we find amusing observations as
well as acute reflections.

III

Comic Actors in the Middle Ages—Fool-companies—The "Enfants sans
souci"—Costume of the Fools—Pontalais and Jean Serre—The
Bazoche—The School-comedy—French Professional Farcers.

ABOUT the scenic arrangement for the secular repertoire
we know next to nothing. This is owing, for one thing,
to its simplicity; it had no conspicuous features which
called for descriptions, such as give us an idea of the
stage on which ecclesiastical dramas were performed.
The short, gay farces did not require any decorations,
complicated scenery, mechanical contrivances, or magnificent display. All they required was, that the words
could be heard and the movements seen; so they could
be performed anywhere; in a hall, on a platform, in the
open air, in a market place, or in a street.

While the moralities require some display of
equipment, it is essentially the same as that of the
mysteries. It is the apparatus of Heaven with God

and the angels, and Hell with its messengers. So the ordinary mystery-stage was admirably adapted for the moralities, and it was actually used for these representations. We nowhere hear of a special stage for moralities, but several proofs testify to the fact, that moralities were performed on the same sort of stages as the mysteries.

The same may be said of the farces. It has been previously mentioned, that it was a general custom to play a farce before or after a mystery, so of course it must have been on the same stage. Nor have we any reason to suppose that the scenic decorations were changed on these occasions. This would have been too much trouble to take for such a little *hors d'œuvre*, which, as a rule, did not last more than about half-an-hour. And on the clear space in front of the background decoration, where all the performers of the mystery were seated in their "boxes," enjoying the merry jokes till it was their turn to appear, the farce-players had more than sufficient scope for their unpretending pieces.

However, though, as a matter of fact, the farces were frequently performed together with the mysteries on the same stage, we are not justified in concluding that this was their original home, nor that they belonged to an ecclesiastical play, as soup and dessert belong to a dinner. The comic plays had also a stage, and especially actors, of their own.

Whereas the performance of a mystery enlisted all classes in its ranks, and was, so to say, a municipal, almost a national undertaking, the farces found their actors within a narrower sphere. It was suitable neither for priests nor for noblemen or officers to appear in the licentious plays, which in subject and tone passed beyond the utmost limit of decency; priests were forbidden by law to act in farces. Even to a sedate citizen it was rather a dubious affair to share in these coarse jokes. And even if his dignity could be sacrificed, it did not follow that he had sufficient talent or sense of humour. For so it is, and always has been—deficiency of talent is more easily concealed by the serious than by the comic mask. Dulness and seriousness are often confounded by the public; a yawn may bring tears to the eyes. But you cannot cheat anybody out of the good drollery he expects of a farce, and a grimace without talent will never do.

So it was natural that in the Middle Ages comic art should find its performers and its proper home within narrower circles. We do not mean to say that professional actors undertook this peculiar class of art, as such a class did not as yet exist. Strolling players, jugglers, minstrels, *Spielleute*, whatever their names might be, these vagabond creatures, half acrobats, half musicians and singers, might occasionally include a kind of play in their repertoire, little humorous introductions to their other performances—*parades*—in which the clever head of the company talked nonsense for the amusement of gazing peasants and rustic squires. Nor is it inconceivable—especially in the later Middle Ages —that they got hold of real plays, or helped in the great dramatic performances.

Yet it is not here that we must seek for the real comic companies, not even for their ancestors. The secular comic plays originated and were performed in the merry fool-companies, of which the Middle Ages possessed a multitude.

It has been recently stated how the Shrovetide-fools in Nuremberg walked from door to door reciting their more or less merry dialogues, and receiving the customary gift from the master of the house. As a rule it was artisans' apprentices, or sometimes scholars, who diverted themselves in this way during the gay Shrovetide, where they made up for many days of hardship and gained an extra penny, or at least a good drink gratis. We saw how the Shrovetide-plays were included in the repertoire of the mastersingers' company. This society, however, was by no means a fool-company, no more than the kindred societies in France, which go by the name of *Puys*. It was grave, sedate citizens who assembled at these academies of the art of poetry, who discussed sacred as well as profane subjects, composed verses according to complicated rules, and only at Shrovetide kicked over the traces with merry farces.

But, in addition to these societies, the Middle Ages possessed a number of companies or brotherhoods, whose only business it was to ridicule and in various ways to satirise persons and institutions to which they had to submit in daily life. The origin of these merry brotherhoods is clothed in darkness. It cannot be ascertained whether—as many authorities suppose—they arose from the "clerical fool-festivals," at which the subordinate clerks and church officials once a year were allowed to parody the whole church service, where the church became a ball-room, the altar a bar, the mass nonsensical Latin interspersed with spicy jokes, where the clerks played at nine-pins on the rood-loft, and the choir boys preached ludicrous sermons from the pulpit; or whether they are not much more likely to date from pre-Christian popular customs and merry companies, who carried on their heathen mummeries in immemorial times. However this may be, the merry brotherhoods flourished throughout the Middle Ages; especially in France, in Paris as well as in the provinces.

Acting was not the only object of the fool-companies. As a rule they had a perfectly organised constitution. They were ruled by a Fool-king, and had functionaries of different rank. At certain seasons they had great processions, which perpetrated all kinds of practical jokes, sparing neither high nor low. Thus it was a very queer but popular custom with these fool-companies to punish husbands who were known to be beaten by their wives, or occasionally—though less frequently— husbands who beat their wives, by compelling them to ride through the town sitting backwards on a donkey and holding its tail. Sometimes—probably when they could not get hold of the culprit—they contented themselves with taking his neighbour and forcing him to undergo the disgraceful ride. In this case the rider had to keep crying: "It is not I who am the fool, it is my neighbour!"

At times, however, the satire aimed much higher, and was exceedingly bold. Thus in the year 1541, *Les Connards*,[1] a very well-known company in its time,

[1] Or *Cornards*, thus called from the two horns (*cornes*) or ears which they wore on their fool's cap.

and one of the largest and most important of all,
whose headquarters was Rouen, gave a performance, where, among other things, Henry VIII.,
Charles V., Paul III. and a fool played at ball with
the globe, "and all of them ill-treated the poor world
to such a degree that it had to suffer much at their
hands."

The most celebrated of all fool-companies was the
previously-mentioned *Enfants sans souci*,[1] which played
an important part in the merry life of ancient Paris.
Tradition traces its origin back to the close of the
fourteenth century; remains of it survived as far down
as the early part of the seventeenth century.

It is possible that the members of this company
were originally, as stated,[2] young, well-to-do men of
good family, who, heedless of the world and its cares,
made fun of everything and everybody; but, no doubt,
in the course of time the character of the company
altered to a certain extent, and its members soon
became the forerunners of professional actors, performing festive entertainments and merry preludes to
dramatic representations.

The existence of this company was indeed founded
on a sort of principle : the whole world was mad, and
all men were fools; in everyday life this fact was concealed, but in the company of the *Enfants sans souci*
it was acknowledged.   Therefore all the members were
fools (*des Sots*);[3] they were governed by a Prince of

---

[1] Comp. above, p. 138 ff.
[2] Parfaict : *Hist. du Théâtre Franç.*, ii. p. 177.
[3] In the language of the time *sot* and *fou* are synonymous.

12, 13—Mediæval fool costumes.

Fools, and on appearing in public all wore the established fool's costume.

This principle gave the fools an immense liberty of speech, for to the fool everything was permitted; and we cannot doubt that at their Shrovetide — especially Shrove - Tuesday — festivals "the Children without care" told their fellow-citizens many home truths.

The fool-costume had its traditional form. Its most characteristic feature was its tight-fitting hood with the long donkey ears; sometimes it had a comb of large bells at the top (comp. fig. 12); frequently the flaps of the coat ended in bells too. The long tight trousers were variegated, the remainder of the dress generally in two or three colours. The favourite tints were saffron and light green. Green meant youth, spirit, hope, vigour; saffron meant gaiety, as the smell of saffron was supposed to be particularly animating.[1]

As a token of his dignity the Prince of Fools carried a magnificent staff, a kind of sceptre, which no doubt was frequently much more expensive than the one seen in fig. 12. From the fool-company, *La Mère Folle*, in Dijon, a counterpart of *Les Enfants sans souci*, we possess an illustration of a very fine, elaborately and artistically worked fool's staff of 1482, on which we see a fool with a bottle and glass in his hand arising from a luxuriant vine from behind the foliage of which other laughing fools' heads peep out.[2]

---

[1] Julleville : *Les Comédiens en France au moyen âge*, p. 148.

[2] An illustration of this staff is found in Paul Lacroix : *Sciences et lettres au moyen âge et à l'époque de la Renaissance*, 2nd ed. Paris, 1879.

We have already mentioned the repertoire of the "Children without care," the Sotties, which were either merry preludes to the principal performances, or plays with a political tendency.   The typical fool did not acquire the importance to the theatre which we should have expected ; the mad fools of the Middle Ages were soon superseded by the type of the Italian comedies of masks, which afforded greater variety, and at any rate won higher favour with the public.[1]   In the Middle Ages, however, the fool played a very important part, not merely in the fool-plays, but also, as we have seen, in the serious mysteries, in which the fool's part was put into the hands of a particularly clever—though not yet a professional—actor.

For the actors of the fool-companies still continued to be and to be considered as amateurs, and used to have a means of livelihood besides dramatic art, though the latter procured them an income and took up most of their time.

We have seen how Gringoire divided his time between theatrical work and literary political agitation, a kind of journalistic business which was placed at the disposal of any princes who chose to pay for it.   His contemporary and companion, Pontalais, or, as his real name was, Jehan de l'Espine, was more of a real actor, the most popular comic performer of his time, the

---

[1] In England, no doubt, the fool remained much longer on the stage than in most other countries.   But the English fool is not quite the same as the *Sot* or *Fou* of the fool-companies.   He is more of the so-called court fool, influenced by the Italian Arlecchino, and, as a rule, is more closely connected with the action of the play than the fool of the Middle Ages.

prototype of a strolling actor, who travelled round the country, composed, arranged and performed his merry plays, acted as fool in the mysteries, and was paid for it. He is also known by his surname of Songecreux, which, however, we suppose, was mostly used as a pseudonym.

The hunch-backed figure of Pontalais, invested with the insignia of the Prince of Fools, seated on a magnificent throne, holding his court and administering justice among his mad subjects,[1] was a spectacle of majestic folly, which deeply impressed the contemporary public; and—as frequently happens in similar cases—Pontalais became a kind of comic legendary hero, to whom all witty anecdotes were attributed. However, his great popularity rendered him insolent, and tempted him to insult blameless persons of distinction, by which he got into various difficulties. It was bad enough once, when at court, where he enjoyed consideration, he went up to a cardinal, who was hunch-backed like himself, leaned his own hump against that of the high prelate, and said: "You and I, Monseigneur, prove that it is not true to say two mountains can never meet."[2] But worse luck befell him in the year 1516, when, by order of the king, Francis I., he was thrown into prison with two of his companions. At that time it had become the custom

---

[1] De Pontallays, roy et prince des sotz,
Là il estoit garny de ses supostz,
Hault elevé en chaire magnifique
Enluminé, visaige déifique
Tenant sa court, corrigeant les forfaictz.

[2] It is Parfaict who is responsible for this anecdote, which is reported in *Hist. du Théâtre Franç.*, ii. 226.

for the *Enfants sans souci*, when on the stage, to wear masks representing certain well‑known persons, and Pontalais had been foolhardy enough to give the Mother-of-fools the features of the queen-dowager. For this *lèse-majesté* he had to atone by spending three months in the prison of Blois, and evidently for a long time afterwards he did not feel safe in Paris, for he began a series of excursions to the provinces, where he created the same enthusiasm as in the capital. However, he was restored to favour at the court of Francis I., and even obtained a kind of public office in 1530, being made "Undertaker of public festivals." [1] The year of his death is unknown.

Among the other "Children without care" some may indeed have gained a name as "fool-actors," but of the great majority we only know that they belonged to this class, nothing else. Only about one of them we possess a little more information ; his name was Jean Serre, and he was the companion and rival in fame of Pontalais. The poet, Clement Marot, who in his early youth was one of the "Children" and a zealous actor, wrote a long epitaph on Jean Serre, which gives us a good idea of this excellent farce‑player's costume and appearance. We are told that he excelled in acting drunkards and fools, whereas it was wholly denied him to represent a sensible man, "for nature had only endowed him with the face of a fool or a drunkard." But "when he appeared on the stage with a dirty shirt, with his forehead, cheeks and nostrils covered all over with flour, a

[1] Comp. Julleville : *les Comédiens*, etc., p. 177.

baby's hood on his head, and a high triumphal cap [1] decorated with capon feathers, I will answer for it, that with all this, and seeing his naïve grace, people were not less pleased than if they had been in Elysium." [2]

From this description we gather that Jean Serre did not wear the ordinary fool's costume with donkey-ears, bells, etc. And perhaps we may conclude that he did not limit himself to appearing in the sotties of the "Children without care," but cultivated the farce in general. It is supposed that the Fool-society and its prince stood under the supremacy of another contemporary brotherhood, *la Bazoche*,[3] a company of young lawyers, clerks and assistants to attorneys, solicitors, judges and parliamentary councillors, which, as tradition says, was founded as early as 1303 for mutual support and amusement.

The Bazoche was constituted like a kingdom. The president was its king, who had his chancellor, his vice-chancellor, his *maître des requêtes*, his referendary, and his "lord chamberlain," just like the old French kings. As a society the Bazoche enjoyed no slight consideration in Paris, and found a strong support in the time of Philippe le Bel by being acknowledged as an independent community, a privilege which—genuine or not—was respected by the law courts.

---

[1] The statement that Jean Serre wore a baby's hood (*béguin d'enfant*), and a high cap with feathers on his head means that, like Pierrot or Harlequin, he wore a tight-fitting kind of scull-cap to hide his hair beneath his ordinary hat. Such head-covers were worn by babies in the sixteenth century.

[2] The whole epitaph is reprinted in *Hist. du Théâtre Franç.*, ii. 245 ff., and in Julleville: "*les Comédiens*," etc., 181 ff.

[3] *Bazoche* is the ancient French popular form of the Greek *basilica*, by which name the royal Palace of Justice in Paris was often designed.

Three times a year the Bazoche held public perform-ances ; on the Thursday before or after the Epiphany, which in the Middle Ages was always a season of gaiety ; on the first, or one of the first days in May—when the Maypole was fetched from the wood and planted in the yard of the *Palais de Justice*, and in the beginning of July, when the great and solemn *Montre* (procession, parade) took place.

In the large hall of the Palace of Justice stood a huge marble table,[1] which nearly took up the whole breadth of the hall and was a splendid piece of furniture, hewn out of one gigantic block of marble, and originally used by the French kings for serving meals to foreign monarchs. On this royal table the Bazochians, with the king's permission, performed their moralities and farces, when they were not acted in the open air; and this stage must have been very suitable indeed, especially for the farces, which required no scenery.

Farces and moralities formed the repertoire of the Bazoche, whether they were performed in the open air or inside the palace walls ; but about the special pieces which they acted we lack information. It may be sup-posed, however, that farces like *Pathelin*, which is full of law-suits and legal subtleties, originated in the social gatherings of the clerks of justice.

At a time when no permanent theatre existed, the Bazoche contained the first elements of an official dramatic institution paid by the State, as it received certain sums out of the royal exchequer to defray the

---

[1] This famous marble table was destroyed by fire in the night between the 5th and 6th March, 1618.

expenses incurred by the society in arranging festivals and performances in honour of the royal family. In exchange they were bound to play and dance on such occasions as the magistrate might find appropriate. On the whole the magistrate had the merry lawyers under his thumb. The plays were under a strict censorship, and the actor who transgressed the proper limit—which probably was not very narrow—suffered corporal punishment.[1]

That flogging was indeed used as a punishment in cases where actors or authors had sinned against the laws of censure is shown, *e.g.*, in an incident of the time of Francis I. During the first years of his reign, in particular, this king did not relish the free language of the farce-players, and though he liked to amuse himself, he did not like others to be amused at his expense. A poor dramatic author and actor, M. Cruche, who was a priest into the bargain, found this out to his cost. A joke in one of his plays contained a disrespectful allusion to a lady, who at the time was the king's mistress. She was a married woman, daughter of a parliamentary councillor, whose name was Lecocq, wherefore Mr Cruche in his play called her a hen, and declared that she carried something about her which was sufficient to kill ten men. This joke displeased the king, and he sent half a score of noblemen to look at the farce, in which the clerical author acted in person. But when he appeared Mr Cruche was seized, "stripped to the skin, flogged marvellously with stirrup-leather, and reduced to a miserable condition. At last a sack was held ready into which they were going to put him, after which

---

[1] Comp. Parfaict : *Hist. du Théâtre Franç.*, ii. 99, note 6.

he was to have been thrown out of the window, and finally into the river. And this would have been done, if the poor man had not cried very loud, pointing to the tonsure which was on his head; and these things, as was confessed, were done by order of the king." [1]

Both the Bazoche and the "Children without care" found numerous imitators in the provinces, and these societies became the real supporters of the secular play. It is a noteworthy fact also, that schools and universities everywhere in Europe eagerly cultivated dramatic art, and the *school-comedies* obtained an importance which extended somewhat beyond the narrower circle for which they were destined. This importance was due in particular to the reckless audacity with which they entered into the burning social and political questions of the time, a boldness which is the more striking to us, as the school-comedy of our own time—though it has not gone out of fashion—is the tamest, most harmless thing imaginable.

In those days the schoolmasters wrote plays themselves, and were no more afraid of spicing their dramatic works with exceedingly strong jokes, than of directing the sharpest attacks against the highest authorities. The school-comedies were not considered as a mere amusement, but also as a means of education, and there may be some reason for regarding them in that light, though modern pedagogues would hardly acknowledge the repertoire of these school-comedies to be commendable exercises in elocution.

[1] *Journal d'un bourgeois de Paris*, publ. by Lalanne, p. 13 f.

14—Scene from an old French farce (after a print by Jean de Gourmont).

We are scarcely mistaken in assuming that a certain number of the best mediæval farces owe their origin to performers of school and university plays. Especially the farce of *Maistre Mimin*, who speaks Latin to his rustic parents, and forgets his mother-tongue at the university, till he is cured at last by learning the language of love from his bride. Maistre Mimin was one of the most popular farces in the Middle Ages, and the type appears in more plays than this one. It was succeeded by the Italian typical pedant, to whom we shall return in a later chapter.

We do not think that the school-comedy contributed much to the formation of a permanent class of professional actors. The gay fool-companies did far more towards it. Men like Pontalais and Jean Serr were almost like professionals, and in the latter part of the sixteenth century we suddenly find a whole class of actors springing into existence, and satisfying the requirements of the time; we scarcely know whence the actors came, and who they were.

We have seen how, towards the close of the century, the "Passion-Fraternity" became tired of resisting the new taste, and made over their privilege and their theatre in the *Hôtel de Bourgogne* to professional actors,[1] and that the latter competed successfully with the Italian companies, which were acting at the same time in the *Petit Bourbon* Theatre. The authors of the time give us hardly any information about the method of acting of the earliest farce-performers; a few names at most, a eulogistic remark in an epitaph, the eternal antithesis

[1] Comp. above, p. 116 f.

about tears and smiles, which seems inseparable from all memorial words on comic actors; but no characteristic details whatever, not an allusion to their specialty, their costume, or the like.

It has been more practically useful to me to study the pictures, dating from this time of transition, which have been within my reach.   Here I think I can trace a marked difference between the methods of the early period (viz., the time when the farces were still performed by semi-amateurs), of the earlier professional actors, and of the later well-known and (some of them) celebrated farce-players.

Let us compare the illustrations in figs. 14, 15, 16 and 17.   The first represents a scene in a farce from an engraving by Jean de Gourmont, who lived in the middle of the sixteenth century.   The verse underneath does not give any information about the performers, and the actors do not differ from the spectators either in costume or appearance : they are everyday types in everyday situations.   We see two women quarrelling, and a number of men, grouped without any order, interfere in the quarrel.   It is difficult to see what kind of people they are, except a king in the background, of whom, however, nobody seems to take any notice.   The stage is a wooden platform without any other decoration than a back curtain.

With fig. 15 we enter into the domain of professional actors.   The picture is a reproduction of a rare engraving by H. Liefrinck,[1] whose works date from the time between

___

[1] This picture, as well as the two following ones, is taken from a curious collection of theatrical illustrations, which from ancient times has been in

15—Scene from a farce played by professional actors (from a print by Liefrinck).

1540-1580. We see in the centre an old married man, whose young wife is decorating his head with a peculiar ornament. The old man's dress and mask remind us in several ways of the Italian Pantalone type. He wears a close-fitting dress, long tights of tricot, a loose, wide mantle, and a long pointed beard, all like Pantalone. The figure to the right is evidently the typical servant or jester, and in spite of his queer antiquated costume, which no doubt must partly be laid to the account of the draughtsman, he possesses a good deal of the Italian Zanni type. He is masked. The young woman, no doubt, is an actress, while the old women seem to be disguised men. The young man with the large sword is strongly influenced by the Italian Capitano type. The stage has the same simple equipment as that of the preceding picture: a wooden platform and a background of hangings, but there is much more art and calculation in the arrangement of the figures.

Fig. 16 is no doubt a great rarity, though Copenhagen possesses two copies of it, one in the Royal Library, and one in its Collection of Engravings. At least I have nowhere seen a reproduction or description of it. Only two of the four actors it represents are known as yet, and with regard to one of them only do we know for certain what special parts he performed. The picture is by Huret, and has a versified, though not

the possession of our (Copenhagen) Royal Library. The collection consists almost exclusively of portraits of old French and Italian farce-players, and scenes from their repertoires, a series of engravings, arranged and collected (according to the manuscript title-pages) by a royal French *Maître de Chapelle* named Sieur Fossard. The kind help of the Chief Librarian, Mr Bruun, has enabled me to supply the present book with several reproductions from this unique and most interesting work.

very poetical, inscription at the bottom, which runs thus :—

> Michau, Boniface, Alison,
> Et Philipin qui les seconde,
> Se mocquent avecque raison
> Des impertinences du monde.
>
> Michau ne plaist pas moins aux yeux
> Qu'il est agréable aux oreilles,
> Boniface le serieux
> Ne raconte que des merveilles.
>
> Alison se fait admirer,
> Philipin raille sans mesdire
> Et tous ensemble font pleurer
> Mais j'entends à force de rire.[1]

The names of two of these actors were previously known, those of Boniface and Alison, viz., Nos. 2 and 3 in our illustration.   Both names are frequently mentioned in the history of the French theatre, especially that of Alison.   We know that he was one of the earliest actors at the Hôtel de Burgogne, and that he performed female parts, *soubrettes* and ludicrous old

[1] Michau, Boniface, Alison
And Philipin who seconds them
Justly mock the follies of the world.

Michau is no less pleasant to the eyes
Than agreeable to the ears,
Boniface, the grave, tells nothing but marvels.

Alison wins admiration,
Philipin mocks without slandering,
And they all call forth tears, but, mark !—tears of laughter.

Michau.   *Dr Boniface.*

16—Ancient farce-players (from a print by Huret).

women, and also nurses in the serious plays. " The lack
of actresses, and the free language which the authors put
into the mouths of the servant girls, had necessitated the
introduction of this character." [1] About the appearance
and costume of this character the engraving before us
gives us the first information. It is amusing to see how
distinctly the man reveals himself under the female
costume. Boniface was known to have acted at the
same theatre at the close of the sixteenth century, and
his speciality is supposed to have been that of the comic
doctor. This supposition is confirmed by our picture,
which shows Boniface as a distinct imitator of the
Italian Dottore Graziano, the learned pedant, who will
be described more in detail in the following paragraph.
Both these actors played with masked faces, according
to Italian fashion.

The real names of these two actors are unknown ;
the names of Boniface and Alison of course belonged to
the characters they represented.

I have searched in vain for the slightest information
about Philipin and Michau, though they are sure to
have been tolerably popular, as they were found worthy
of being portrayed in a large engraving and praised in
rhymed verse. However, it is not difficult to determine
their speciality. Michau—No. 1 in the engraving—is
evidently an imitator of the Italian Pantalone, the
ludicrous old man, the " hanger-on " of the Doctor, and,
as such, the precursor of the later famous Gaultier
Garguille. His having been " agreeable to the ear,"

---

[1] P. D. Lemazurier : *Galerie historique des acteurs du théâtre français,
depuis* 1600 *jusqu'à nos jours.* Paris, 1810, i. 23.

probably means that, like his above-mentioned predecessor, he was a good singer.   Like Pantalone he wears
a black mask, and has long, straight hair.   Philipin
is unquestionably the typical servant, the jester who
" mocks without slandering," also an imitator of the Italian
Zanni, and a forerunner of Turlupin.   In a play dating
from about 1600, *la Comédie des Proverbes*, which is
ascribed to Adrien de Montluc, the humorous servant
is called Philipin, and the maid Alison.[1]

With fig. 17 we enter into well-known territory.   The
illustration is from a print by Abraham Bosse.   It represents the fairly well furnished stage of the Hôtel de
Burgogne with its most distinguished farce-players, and
at the bottom it has the following versified inscription :—

Que ce théâtre est magnifique !
Que ces acteurs sont inuentifs !
Et qu'ils ont de preseruatifs
Contre l'humeur melancolique !

Icy d'une posture drolle
Ils nazardent le mauvais temps
Et charment tous les Escouttans,
Auec une seule parolle.

Icy l'ingenieux Guillaume
Contrefaisant l'homme de Cour
Se plaist à gourmander l'Amour
Troussé comme un joueur de paume.

[1] Comp. *Parfaict*, iv. 215 ff.

Alison.   *Philipin.*

16*a*—Ancient farce-players (from a print by Huret).

Icy d'une façon hagarde
Turlupin veut faire l'Escroq ;
Et l'Espaignol de peur du choq
Fuit le Français qui le regarde.

Mais le vrai Gaultier les surpasse,
Et malgré la rigueur du sort,
Il nous fait rire après sa mort,
Au souuenir de sa grimace.[1]

The three characters of farce here-mentioned, Guillaume, Turlupin and Gaultier, the pride of the stage of the Hôtel de Bourgogne, and the declared favourites of the public, were the actors Robert Guérin, Henri Legrand and Hugues Guéru.

Judging by the poem the last-mentioned must have

[1] How magnificent is this stage,
How inventive are these actors !
And what preservative against melancholy !

There they stand in a droll posture
Deriding the bad times,
And charm all the listeners
With a single word.

Here the ingenious Guillaume,
Mimicking a courtier,
Tucked up like a tennis-player,
Amuses himself with abusing Love.

Here Turlupin in his awkward way
Tries to pick a pocket,
And the Spaniard, for fear of the shock,
Flies from the Frenchman who is looking at him.

But the true Gaultier surpasses them,
And in spite of the rigour of fate,
He makes us laugh after his death
At the recollection of his grimace.

been the best; other memorial verses particularly commend Robert Guérin (Gros-Guillaume); however this may be, all three were extremely popular, and a whole legend has attached itself to their names.

They were, runs the account, three merry baker's apprentices, who did not like the constraint of their occupation, and therefore took it into their heads to become actors. Each of them created a character for himself, which suited his nature; Hugues Guéru became the typical cut and dried old man; Robert Guérin, who was fat and round like a sausage, became the pithy arguer, and the nimble, graceful Legrand chose the gay valet for his type. They hired a tennis-court near the old Porte Saint Jacques in Paris, and there established their theatre. The decorations were roughly painted on canvas, and the performances took place at noon and at night. But the actors of the Hôtel de Bourgogne complained to Cardinal Richelieu of these jugglers, who trespassed upon their rights; and the Cardinal, who took great interest in theatrical matters, summoned the three farce-players, and ordered them to perform one of their improvised pieces before him. They complied with his request, and Richelieu enjoyed their play so much that, instead of forbidding them to appear in future, he compelled the actors of the Hôtel de Bourgogne to include the three merry fellows in their company. And here they continued acting till their old age. Inseparable on the stage, they are said to have been so also in private life, even in death. For, so we are told, in his eightieth year, Gros-Guillaume was thrown into prison, because he had made fun of a magistrate, and there he died over-

17—A farce performance at the Hôtel de Bourgogne: Gros-Guillaume, Gaultier Garguille and Turlupin (after a print by Abraham Bosse).

come with terror and with the hardships of prison life. But the two others were so deeply affected by the death of their companion that they died in the same week.

Thus far the legend,[1] which has this in common with other legends, that it is more romantic and less probable than the facts. We will try to unravel what is positively known about the three comic actors.

It is quite true, the eldest of them was Robert Guérin. He was already famous in the time of King Henry the Fourth, whom he amused by ridiculing the Gascon courtiers before their own faces. No doubt he was the most original of the three, at any rate the most French, the one least influenced by the Italians.

His mere outward appearance was unique. Fat as a barrel—hence his stage-name Gros-Guillaume—a monstrous fleshy body, he further accentuated his fatness by tying up his stomach between two tight belts, one of them close beneath the arm-pits, the other low down about the hips. His costume was a loose half-long blouse, white, and very low at the neck. His face was powdered with flour, and one of his comic effects consisted in puffing up his fat cheeks and sending the meal flying into the faces of his fellow-actors. On his head he wore a tight-fitting skull-cap, and on the top of it a little stiff cap, which sat like a button on the huge head.[2] Under his chin was attached a piece of white lambskin representing a beard, and he wore striped

---

[1] It is Lemazurier who in his *Galerie*, etc., relates it in the above form after having connected the reports found in different authorities. Lemazurier himself, however, doubts whether it is perfectly trustworthy.

[2] The shape of the cap is badly shown in our illustration (fig 17); in other portraits of Gros-Guillaume it appears distinctly.

trousers which, being too short, further displayed his ludicrous lack of figure. In the numerous extant portraits of him,[1] his face expresses the peculiar calm Falstaff-like impudence, which frequently distinguishes very fat humorous people. His private character is described by a somewhat younger contemporary in the following way: "He was always a great drunkard, low-minded and cringing to his superiors. He was coarse in his talk, and in order to cheer himself up he had to tipple or to drink beakers in some gloomy tavern with his friend, the shoemaker." He was constantly suffering from the stone, and frequently, when he was going to appear on the stage, his attacks were so violent that he screamed with pain. Yet he controlled himself in spite of his sufferings, "and with his despondent face and his eyes full of tears, he amused the audience quite as much, as if nothing had been the matter with him."[2]

Though we may find points of contact with earlier farce-players in the costume and parts of Gros-Guillaume —I have been particularly struck by his resemblance to the above-mentioned Jean Serre—it is evident that this grotesque, fat specimen of a farce-player stands somewhat apart, and is hardly at all influenced by the all-pervading Italian manner.

The same cannot be said of his two companions. Gaultier Garguille, or Hugues Guéru (his private name), was the diametrical opposite of Gros-Guillaume. He was tall, lean as a rake, with legs like stilts, and exceed-

---

[1] In the above-mentioned collection in the Royal Library there are no less than four, two of which are very large.

[2] Sauval : *Histoire et Recherches des Antiquités de la Ville de Paris,* iii. 38.

ingly light and nimble, and thus his movements produced the same comic effect as the abrupt gestures of a puppet. His costume consisted of a black close-fitting garment with red sleeves, short trousers and long stockings, both black ; buttons and button-holes were half red half black ; to his belt were attached a bag and—as shown in the illustration—the portable writing materials common in those days, and a stiletto ; in his hand he held a stick and a pair of spectacles ; on his feet were slippers, according to the written accounts, but laced shoes, according to the illustration ; his face was covered by a black mask with moustachios ; his wig was of long straight grey hair, and on his head he wore a flat black cap.

His whole appearance produced an irresistibly comical impression on the public, especially, we suppose, by its glaring contrast to that of Gros-Guillaume. This intentional opposition of extremes accounts in part for the great success of the two comic actors.

In his private life, too, Hugues Guéru was distinguished from his colleague by his sobriety and economy. Though he was a man of modest condition and circumstances, and though very plain in his dress and whole appearance, he was pleasant and amusing to his friends. He was active in his profession, and led a quiet domestic life with his father - in - law, the well - known juggler Tabarin [1] (Jean Salomon). In the year 1598 he made his first appearance in a company, which acted in the Hôtel d'Argent in Marais, and it was probably not till

---

[1] Tabarin was the partner of the quack and miracle-doctor, Mondor. He sold his ointments and drugs on the Pont-Neuf, and by way of advertisement they performed little farces or *parades*, in which Tabarin was the comic valet. These mountebank performances were very popular.

1615 that he came to the Hôtel de Bourgogne. He died in 1633, a year before Gros - Guillaume. The romantic account of the death of the three actors in one week is a pure fiction. Hugues Guéru also acted both in tragedy and in comedy proper—in those times farce was in great part improvised, according to Italian fashion—and in those plays he went by the name of Fléchelle, whereas Robert Guérin, who confined himself to comedy, had adopted the poetical name of La Fleur. He was a very clever actor all round. Sauval, whom we quoted above, writes of him : " This man, so ludicrous in farce, nevertheless occasionally played the king in the serious plays, and did not badly represent this grave, majestic character, covered by the mask and dressing-gown (*robe de chambre*) worn by all stage-kings in those times ; for the mask concealed his large pimpled face, and the dressing-gown his legs and thin body. So under the mask he was a man of general utility." [1]

One of the specialities that gained him celebrity in farce was his manner of delivering his songs which generally ended the evening performances ; and many were the people, Sauval tells us, who went to the Hôtel de Bourgogne for the sole purpose of hearing " *les chansons de Gaultier Garguille*."

These songs—not all of which were composed by himself, for many were old popular songs [2]—exist in several printed editions, and were, as we may suppose, of a very frivolous nature, in fact something like the

---

[1] Sauval : *op. cit.* iii. 37.
[2] Comp. Levertin : *Fars og Farsórer*, 133 f.

modern French *chansonette,* founded on a smart and
catchy little refrain, which secured rapid popularity.
Let us quote a sample :—

> Jean cette nuit, comme m'a dit ma mère
> Doit m'assaillir, mais je ne le crains guère,
> > Si
> Ma mère n'en est pas morte
> Je n'en mourrai pas aussi.

> Je ne suis pas de ces folles badines
> Qui font venir à l'aide leurs voisines :
> > Si
> Ma mère n'en est pas morte,
> Je n'en mourrai pas aussi.

Sometimes the refrain was nothing but a senseless
combination of rhyming words, such as we know from
the modern Parisian *scie.* Thus for instance :—

> Navet n'avet point de vin
> Navet n'avet point de vin
> Et son valet en avet ;
> Et pourquoy n'en avet Navet
> Et pourquoy n'en avet Navet
> Puisque son valet en avet.

The farce-character represented by Hugues Guéru,
under the name of Gaultier Garguille, was no invention
of his own. It was proved at a very early date that the
ludicrous, love-sick old fellow was borrowed from the
Italian Pantalone. The costume was chiefly derived
from the same source ; the black and red tight-fitting

dress, the mask, the slippers, etc.[1]   But, so far as we
know, it has not been previously stated that Pantalone
was not the direct prototype of Gaultier Garguille ; he
had a French precursor in the afore-mentioned Michau.
If we cast a glance at the two characters Michau and
Gaultier, we shall see that they not only resemble each
other, but are almost identical.   The costume and entire
outward appearance, to the minutest details—*e.g.*, the
objects hanging at the belt—are a faithful copy of
Michau ; so we see that, as early as the time of Gaultier,
this type was a traditional character of French farce,
which had received its Italian impress at an earlier period.

As to the third member of the trio, Turlupin, there
is less to be said.   The character he presented was in
every way a copy from the Italian, still more so than his
forerunner Philipin.   This, indeed, was already pointed
out by his contemporary, Sauval.   " The costume which
he wore in farce," he writes, " was the same as that
of Briguella, who was so often admired in the Petit
Bourbon Theatre.[2]   They resembled each other in
everything . . . were of a similar stature and face,
both played Zanni,[3] and wore the same kind of mask :
in short, no other difference could be discovered than
such as experts in pictures may find between an excellent original and an excellent copy."[4]

The most characteristic feature of the Turlupin
costume is the large felt hat, forming two points in

[1] Comp. the description of the Pantaloon type in the chapters on the
Italian masque.

[2] Here it was—as we have already stated—that the Italian companies
acted.

[3] The merry valet in the Italian *Commedia dell' arte* ; see the next chapter.

[4] Sauval, iii. 36.

front. We find it in nearly all representations by Callot of the old Italian jesters, some specimens of whom will be shown in the next chapter. The striped dress, which was worn already by Philipin, became very popular in France, and is still used as the traditional costume of Scapin and other valets in Molière.

Turlupin's private name was Henri Legrand. He was born in 1587, and was attached to the Hôtel de Bourgogne during his whole theatrical career till his death about 1637. Here he acted in the higher drama under the name of Belleville. Sauval particularly commends his spirited and lively acting in farce, which lacked nothing but a little naïveté; he was also good in comedy, though in this branch others were better. With regard to his private life, we hear that he was a member of a military commission,[1] which proves that he enjoyed more consideration than was usual with actors at this period.

The illustration of the three famous comedians contains three figures more, an actress and two male persons; the one to the left is evidently the young lover who conspires with Turlupin to steal from the old Gaultier Garguille, while the other is a third well-known Italian mask in French guise, the famous Captain Matamore, Rodomont, Fracasse, or whatever his name may be in this play, for his names are as innumerable as his feats. It is not known who acted this character in the Hôtel de Bourgogne at that time. About this character we shall give more information in the following chapter.

[1] Jal: *Dictionnaire critique.* Art: *Henri Legrand.*

Besides the farce - players represented in these pictures, we know the names and specialities of several others; of Agnan, for instance, no doubt one of the earliest professional farce-players of the Hôtel de Bourgogne; like Gros-Guillaume, he powdered his face with flour. Valeran le Comte, who played lovers, also belonged to the earlier period; his acting, with one of the earliest known actresses, Marie Vernier, called Mlle la Porte, is commended by contemporary writers.

Among actors who performed female parts in the style of Alison, we may mention Dame Gigogne, Périne, who acted with Gaultier Garguille, and somewhat later Dame Ragonde, whose name I have not met with before, but of whom there exist some tolerably large prints, which show a figure somewhat different from that of Alison. In the earliest illustrations she wears a black half-mask, which only covers nose and forehead; in a later one she appears as a kind of elderly coquette, gaudily dressed and with large patches on her face. The private names of these actors are unknown.

Among farce-players of the later generation may be mentioned Bertrand Hardouin and Deslauriers, both of whom began as mountebanks in the service of travelling miracle-doctors and operators. The former had indeed studied medicine, and was of good family. He came to the Hôtel de Bourgogne after the death of Gaultier Garguille, and here he created the type of Guillat-Gorju, a ludicrous pedant, not a lawyer like the Italian Dottore, but a physician, and as such a forerunner of Molière's splendid coxcombs of this faculty.

His character became very popular, and is represented in several large engravings, which show him in the traditional black costume with a black mask, large crooked nose and whisker-like bristling beard.

Deslauriers, whose stage-name was Bruscambille, retained more of his character of quack even after he had become a regular farce-player. At the Hôtel de Bourgogne his speciality was the recitation of humorous monologues, nominally as an introduction to the performances. These monologues, which were of his own composition, lie before me in print in several little collections under such titles as : " Bruscambille's Fancies," " New and amusing ideas by Bruscambille," etc. They are full of ridiculous, sometimes most bewildering nonsense, for the most part highly seasoned with coarseness. There are learned dissertations "In favour of spitting," " On fleas," " On the advantage of having horns," etc., etc. This kind of nonsensical monologue has always enjoyed popularity in France. Even during the Middle Ages the *Sermons joyeux* were very fashionable, and in our own days one of the cleverest actors of the *Théâtre Français* has won his fame almost exclusively by reciting nonsense quite as meaningless, but artfully arranged.[1]

To summarise the development of farcical comedy as it reveals itself in the four illustrations reproduced here :—

During the time of genuine Amateurism a simple, natural, but uncultivated and unsystematic mode of representation. No grouping of the actors, no style in the costumes, no professional tricks, no culture

---

[1] Comp., *e.g.*, the monologues in Coquelin *cadet's* repertoire : "The earthworm in love," "On Coffin-bearers," etc., etc.

of gestures and attitudes, no fixed comic types, no female performers (fig. 14).

Then comes the turn of professional actors. The difference strikes us at once. The players are arranged in well calculated groups, a typical jester is introduced, whose costume is unreal and fantastic, a first touch of imitation of the Italian, which appears distinctly in the central figure of Liefrinck's illustration (fig. 15). In spite of the pedantic lack of humour in the execution of the engraving, we can clearly distinguish the principal features of Pantalone; compare the genuine Venetian Pantalone (fig. 22). The young woman, moreover, is evidently represented by an actress, whereas the old women no doubt are masked men.

Henceforth the Italian method gets completely the upper hand. We meet with a Michau, a Gaultier Garguille, who is nothing but a gallified Pantalone, a Philipin, a Turlupin—the counterpart of Arlecchino or Brighella—a Dr Boniface—the French likeness of Dr Baloardo or Dr Graziano—an Alison—the reproduction of Colombina or Pasquella, etc., etc. The costumes become grotesque, unreal, fantastic; the faces are concealed by black, brown, or white masks; attitudes and gestures become systematic and calculated; all kinds of tricks are used : hiding-places, jumping out of windows and doors, somersaults and balancing feats (fig. 17).

By this time the national French art of farce-playing is practically dead. The last relics of the simple mediæval amateur art are superseded by the brilliant professional art of later times.

To convey an idea of this art is the object of the following chapters.

THEATRICAL ART
DURING THE RENAISSANCE

THE ITALIAN COMEDY OF ART AND THE
PROFESSIONAL ACTORS

I

Nature and Origin of the Comedy of Art—Improvisation—How a *Commedia dell' Arte* is studied and performed—Lazzi and Repertoires—Advantages and Shortcomings of Improvisation.

By the Italian Comedy of Art—*Commedia dell'Arte*— we understand neither the literary reform, which was a consequence of the enthusiastic study of ancient classic dramatists, nor the renascence of literature itself, in which Italy went equally ahead, and which exercised such a decisive influence on the repertoires of all European theatres.

The expression "Comedy of Art" refers to the execution, not to the subject of the plays. By this time the performers had become professional "artists," and as such they were distinct from the artless mediæval amateurs, who played comedy to honour God and to please themselves. *Commedia dell'Arte* is the first stage of professional dramatic art.

We possess no information, and are never likely to attain historical certainty, as to the date at which a professional class of actors first constituted itself in Italy, nor how it arose ; whether by a transition from the most persevering amateur actors of mysteries and farces, or by a development from the class of strolling jugglers, acrobats, musicians and singers, or by an amalgamation of both these elements.

The actor Luigi-Riccoboni,[1] whose history of Italian Comedy is remarkably good for that time, traces the Comedy of Art as far back as the eighth century, and attributes its origin to the ancient *atellana*. We do not think he is right in his former statement, and he can prove neither the former nor the latter. A great deal has been written about the connection of the *Commedia dell' Arte* with the ancient Latin typical masks, and its descent from them ; and we have alluded to it in our chapter on Roman dramatic art. But the matter is not really cleared up, and the correctness of the hypothesis has never been proved. Much may be said in favour of the suggestion that some of the old characters survived in popular customs, games, Shrove-Tuesday sports, etc., and in after times were reintroduced on the stage. However this may be, a continuous scenic development is entirely out of the question.

Here, where we are concerned with the *Commedia dell' Arte* chiefly as a particular form of professional dramatic art, we will pass by the question of its origin, however interesting it may be, and take up the subject itself in the state and at the period in which we first meet with it.

But, first of all, what was this Comedy of Art, and in what did it differ from other comedy, so that it had necessarily to be performed by professionals ? Comedy of art means improvised comedy, unwritten drama, in which only the indispensable course of the play, the

[1] *Histoire du Théâtre italien*, Paris, 1730.

outline of the action, was constructed and written down by the author, while the dialogue, jokes, outbursts of feeling, characterisation, soliloquies, everything in fact, were left to the actor.   Herein lay its importance, and this was what gave it the peculiar stamp of professional comedy.

The author, who in this case as a rule was identical with the manager, chose a subject, adapted it, fixed the characters and their mutual relations, invented certain situations and *jeux de théâtre*, or adapted old ones to the new subject, arranged the material into introduction, plot and dénouement, divided the action into acts and scenes, put down which characters were to appear in each scene, how long they were to remain, and what they were to do and to speak about—and there the play was finished.

Or rather, there it began.   For this " canvas," as the French call it—the technical term is *scenario*—was now to be embroidered, and this was the business of the actors.   They had to find the proper words to make the tears flow or the laughter ring ; they had to catch the sallies of their fellow-actors on the wing, and return them with a prompt repartee.   The dialogue must go like a merry game of ball or spirited sword-play, with ease and without a pause.   A man who knew the business well, the popular harlequin Evarista Gherardi, says : " To be a good Italian actor means to be a man who possesses a rich store of knowledge, who plays more from fancy than from memory, who, while he plays, invents all he says ; who seconds his colleague on the stage, that is, matches his words and actions so well with those of his comrade, that he enters at once on all the movements to which the other invites him, and in such a way as to make everybody believe that all has been settled beforehand." [1]

We can well understand that amateurs were insufficient for these tasks. Every dilettante may, without training, and with or without talent, learn any written part by heart, and play it more or less badly, according to his capacities; at least so that the course of the performance is not much disturbed or delayed. But not so with the Italian *Commedia dell' Arte*: there talent alone was not enough; professional training and perfect schooling were indispensable if the play was not to collapse.

Of course, this does not mean that some totally unfamiliar subject was read to the actors, which they had to remember in outline, and then to act. A certain tradition could not help being formed; with a number of stock plays to be learned, and certain set phrases to be used on given occasions, certain accepted questions and replies which passed from generation to generation, —in short there was a complete technique, a mechanism, which was even much more indispensable in this special branch than in non-improvised dramatic art.

The old Italian actors who, as genuine children of the Renaissance, cultivated art in their trade and trade in their art, were also fond of using the pen. A great many of the leading actors were authors as well,

---

[1] *Le Théâtre italien de Gherardi ou le Recueil gen. de toutes les comed. et scènes Françoises jouées par les Comediens Ital.* Paris, 1717. Avertissement i. f.

not merely of comedies, but of works of various kinds. Fortunately several of them have published reflections on their own art, by which they have enabled us to form a tolerably correct idea of the way in which a *Commedia dell' Arte* or a *soggetto*,[1] as it was also called, was performed.

We read how the manager or the most experienced actor assembles the company and reads out the scenario to them. He further explains to each performer the character he has to represent, and his relations to the other characters, and describes the locality in which the scene is laid ; and as this is generally a street in some town, he gives a detailed description of the houses in which the different persons live. " He shall say : the comedy which is to be acted is . . . the persons are . . . . Then he shall mention the houses . . . indicating them in this way : first those on the right hand side . . . then those to the left . . . then in the background (*di man dritta*). . . . Then he shall relate the contents. . . ."[2] The actors are enjoined to notice well where the scene is laid, so that one of them may not speak of Rome, where another has just mentioned Naples, or that he who comes from Spain may not say that he comes from Germany. They shall also pay close attention to the houses, and know where their own house is, so that they do not run into the wrong house, which always looks ridiculous. Nor is it well if a father cannot remember the name of his son, or a lover that of the beloved one.

[1] *Soggetto* = subject.
[2] Andrea Perucci : *Dell' Arte Rappresentativa premeditata ed all' improviso*, Napoli, 1699.—Adolfo Bartoli, in the introduction to his *Scenari inediti*, gives some tolerably large extracts from this book.

These, of course, are the worst elementary faults which can be committed.

When the manager, as we should call him—the technical term is *il guido maestro*, or *il corago*[1]—has got so far, he develops the course of the intrigue, explains to each what he has got to say, and how to say it, where he shall use such or such a metaphor or hyperbole, where he must be ironical or jocular. He arranges the entrances and exits, tells each performer how long his soliloquy or dumb-show may last, and gives directions about what is known as *Lazzi*.

"We call *Lazzi*," Riccoboni says, "that which Harlequins or the other masked actors do in the middle of a scene to interrupt it either by expressing fear or by making jokes which have no connection with the subject of the play, and to which they are constantly obliged to resort; so it is these super-fluities, suggested to the actor by his own genius on the spur of the moment, which the Italian comic actors call *Lazzi*."[2] The purpose of these *lazzi* was chiefly to keep the audience on the alert, while something important was supposed to be going on behind the scenes to fill up the dull parts of the action, and to wind up the act in a lively way. According to Riccoboni, *lazzi* is the Lombardic pronunciation of the word *lacci*, which means ribbon. With his *lazzi* the actor joins the parts of the action where the original connection between them is loose; he binds them together either with knots of his own invention, or with such as have been settled once for all by tradition.

[1] Also *il concertatore*.   [2] Riccoboni, i. 65.

This part of the entertainment always falls of course to the share of the comic actor, especially the valet. These improvised jokes which, as Riccoboni says, generally have nothing to do with the action proper, sometimes form a little action by themselves, as in the following scene, in which the comic character, the land-lord Burattino, is taken in by two thieves. He has just been out fetching provisions, and comes home with a basket full of food. But before putting away the things he wants to take a bit himself, he sits down in the middle of the stage with his basket and prepares to eat But at that very moment two thieves arrive; they greet him very politely, and without more ado sit down one on each side of him. One of them begins a lively conversation, telling him about his beautiful native land, Cocagne, where everyone grows fat on delicious and copious meals. While Burattino is all attention, the other fellow eats part of his food ; when he is satisfied, it is his turn to talk, and now Burattino listens with open mouth to his marvellous stories. He expatiates on the wickedness of stealing, and assures Burattino that thieves will be most severely punished in this world and in the next. Mean-while his companion has not starved himself either, but has finished off what was left in the basket. After this the two fellows rise and take leave of their victim with many compliments. Burattino, half stunned by their overwhelming loquacity, at last comes to his senses, and is going to enjoy his meal, when he finds the basket empty, and goes away weeping.[1]

[1] Scenarii by Flaminio Scala, Giornata 3. *La fortunata Isabella*, close of act i.

Sometimes the comic actor relieves an otherwise dull scene by some droll dumb-show, as, for instance, when Harlequin, while his masters discuss serious matters, pretends to catch a fly in the air, pull off its wings and eat the body, or to have his hat full of cherries, which he eats, and throws the stones at his companions.[1] In another scene we witness the grief of Harlequin, Pierrot and Burattino at an accident which has happened to Pierrot's wife. They express their affliction while eating a large dish of macaroni, and while they swallow the food the tears stream down their cheeks.

Sometimes the *lazzi* were acrobatic feats, in which the actors exhibited their physical dexterity. For most of the distinguished actors in the *Commedia dell' Arte* were splendid gymnasts, like their successors, the modern clowns. The famous Scaramouche (Tiberio Fiorilli) was still able in his eighty-third year to box his fellow-actor's ear with his foot, and in *Don Giovanni* it was traditional for the servant—Trivelino or Harlequin was his name in the Italian version of the play—to express his outraged feelings by a somersault, when his master ordered him to drink to the statue of the commander. A well-known comic actor of the eighteenth century, Tommaso Antonio Visentini, attained such a pitch of dexterity that he turned the somersault with a full glass in his hand, and fell on his feet without spilling a drop of wine.

The examples quoted above show that the *lazzi* were only in so far improvised that the actors had not their speeches dictated to them. It was left to the inspiration of the popular humorist to find some laughable subject

[1] Riccoboni, i. 68.

to represent, but most likely the thing was settled at the rehearsals; at all events the actor studied and prepared the scene at home.   In the written scenarios which we know, the only indications given are generally as follows : *fanno lazzi, Dottore lazzi,* or a little more definitely specified for instance : *Cola lazzi di gelosia* ; *Stoppino lazzi di non accorgersi*[1] (*Cola lazzi* of jealousy ; *Stoppino lazzi* of not noticing it).   Sometimes we see from the scenarios that a *lazzo* has been used previously, as it is alluded to as something generally known.   Thus in *Il finto Principe,* "the pretended Prince," in which every act concludes with a *lazzo.*   The final scene of the first act runs thus :—

Scene X.

Cola [the chief comic principal character], Jews and an impostor.   Cola, with the necklace, says he wants to sell it ; presently an impostor makes *lazzi* with Cola, who asks him if he wishes the necklace to be sold ; the impostor calls the Jews ; the circumcision *lazzo* is performed ; first act ends.

Here we meet with a well-known, but not very decent joke, which had once found favour, and was therefore repeated when an opportunity offered.

But it was not only for the *lazzi* that knowledge of tradition and professional training were required.   Each actor had his *Repertorio* or *Zibaldone,* as it was called, that is, a collection of the most appropriate phrases, descriptions, exclamations, expressions of love, curses, clever sayings, in short : what was called in their technical

[1] *Li tre becchi,* "the three cuckolds," publ. by Ad. Bartoli.

language *concetti*; and out of this *repertorio*, which was safely stored in his memory, the actor of the *Commedia dell' Arte* chose all he wanted on a given occasion, so that a skilled performer was never in danger of breaking down on the stage. Thus the lover had his *concetti*, containing suitable expressions for " mutual love," " jealousy," " contempt," " friendship," " parting," etc. He, as well as the other " Tuscan characters "—those that did not speak dialect like the comic parts—had a whole stock of soliloquies and " exits " (*uscite*), well labelled and arranged according to their meaning and use. There was " the soliloquy with metaphors," " the self-reproach with choice images, which gives a transition to joy," " the despair of the deceived lover with choice images and transition to energy " ; " there was the first exit of the happy lover," [1] " the jilted lover's first exit," [2] and, to wind up the speeches, there were little versified " terminations," called *Chiusetti*, which, if well delivered, secured the actor a good exit with ample applause. There were *chiusetti* of " hope," " parting," " friendship," and many others.

The father had his " counsels to address," " admonitions " and " curses " to his son, among which the curses

---

[1] *Uscita* = " sortie," exit, the modern technical term for the speech with which a person leaves the stage.

[2] The latter begins in the following way : " My heart, art thou of flesh ? My bosom, hast thou sense ? Have you power of judgment, oh my thoughts ?   Hast thou reason, oh my soul ?—If, my heart, thou art of flesh, why dost thou not extinguish a fire which is of no use ; if, my bosom, thou hast sense, why dost thou not pull out the arrows which render thy wounds incurable by any balm but that of contempt ; if you can judge, oh my thoughts, why think you not of detesting the one who hates you ? if thou hast reason, my soul, why dost thou not use thy free will to flee from a tyrannical woman ? " etc., etc

in particular were interlarded with the most grotesque and exaggerated expressions.[1] The doctor had his "encouragements to application," his "general advice," his "nonsensical tirade" (*tirata della Giostra*), an immensely long and complicated rigmarole, full of mutilated names, scraps of Latin and burlesque nonsense. The *capitano*, too (the swaggering soldier), had his fixed bravados (*bravure*), such as the "Calabrian greeting to the lady, with bravado," and others.

Furnished with his *repertorio*, with a well-trained physique and a thorough knowledge of the language and its dialects, the Italian actor might think of serving his apprenticeship in the difficult craft. But much was still left to be done before he became a master, not to speak of reaching the summit in his art. We must not think that these apparently merry, light-minded fellows, these Arlecchinos, Pedrolinos, Pantaloni and Scaramucci, in their variegated costumes, and with their ludicrous grimaces, did not take their art seriously. The Italian actors won fame wherever they went, at court as well as among the people. But their fame laid them under obligations, and they recognised their duty. When we read the writings of the ancient actors about their profession, the pride they feel in their art reveals itself in every line. They see and acknowledge the defects of the improvised comedy, but they expatiate on its advantages, and, indeed, succeed in making them clear, so as to inspire the reader with love for and interest in this ancient and peculiar branch of dramatic art.

[1] No doubt these stereotyped forms had a great influence on the style of contemporary and subsequent comic authors. In Molière the influence is very evident.

Let us listen to Riccoboni's competent and clear description. "After having shown the origin and development of the Italian improvised comedy, I hope the reader will excuse me for expressing my opinion about this kind of play, which is peculiar to Italy. Nobody can deny that it has a charm of its own, of which the written play can never boast. Improvisation gives opportunities for variety in playing, so that though we see the same canvas each time, it is nevertheless a different play. The actor who improvises, acts with more animation and in a more natural way than he who performs a part he has learned by heart. People feel better, and consequently say better, what they invent than what they borrow from others by means of the memory. But these advantages are purchased at the price of many difficulties; clever actors are required, moreover actors of equal talent; for the drawback of improvisation is, that the art of even the best actor absolutely depends on his fellow-performer; if he has to act with a colleague who does not reply exactly at the right moment, or who interrupts him in the wrong place, his words miss part of their effect, or his spirit is gone. To an actor who depends on improvisation, it is not sufficient to have face, memory, voice, even sentiment; if he is to distinguish himself, he must possess a lively and fertile imagination, a great facility of expression, he must master all the subtleties of language, possess all the knowledge which is required for the different situations in which his part places him."[1]

There can be no doubt that the Italian nation is

[1] Riccoboni: *Hist. du Théâtre italien*, i. 61 f.

particularly gifted in improvisation, and no other people has produced an improvised dramatic art worth mentioning beside that of the Italians.   Nevertheless, even the leading actors acknowledge that the prospects of their art were often very bad.   It was so difficult, and so absolutely required inborn talent, that there was frequent lack of sufficiently clever performers.   So the less gifted players had to rely on their traditional *repertorio*, which they knew by heart, and on all those tirades, monologues, and professional tricks, which went by the common term of *Robe generiche, lieux communs*.   But then, of course, the charm was gone.   "This way of carrying on the dialogue will not do," says Riccoboni, "for it frequently happens that the beautiful sentences are applied so inappropriately that they are quite out of harmony with what the actor has just said, and become senseless.   This inconvenience entails another : the actor who can say nothing but what he has learned by heart, and who does not understand what he is talking about, when, after a scene in which he has displayed the most beautiful thoughts which are due to his part, not to his own fancy, and in which he has moved his audience to tears by borrowed splendour, he has left his beloved one or his friend, and is obliged to improvise with his servant, whose *lazzi* and *jeux de théâtre* require an improvised reply, so that he cannot use his commonplaces, he stands bewildered and reveals his true nature ; and this same actor, who in the preceding scene had attracted the attention of the public by his noble, magnificent speech, now uses such platitudes, such coarse language, that he becomes intolerable to the same audience which a moment before bestowed its applause on him. This, you see, is the reverse of the Italian improvised comedy, which has had a continuous existence during the forty years in which I have known the theatre."[1]

We are bound to believe that, in spite of its largely mechanical character, in spite of the defects which came to light when the performance was not in the hands of really talented actors, and of the frequent dulness of the scenarios, this special art must have possessed a particular attraction, a fantastic and romantic character of its own. We cannot help believing it when we see the immense success of *Commedia dell' Arte*, not only in Italy, but in all parts of civilized Europe. In France, Spain, Austria, Germany, England, all over Europe, fluttered the gaudy butterfly, carrying off pollen from the courts, and unfolding its brilliant wings in the favour of kings and emperors.

And to a certain extent we understand its charm when we see the clever drawings by Jacques Callot (figs. 18 and 19), which were inspired by these actors; read the memoirs of Carlo Gozzi, or peruse the large illustrated work by Maurice Sand, or the grotesque *Fantasiestücke* by E. T. A. Hoffmann—works which, each in its way, have been influenced by the peculiar spell of the Italian masques.

This magic attraction was due in part, perhaps, to the queer unreal costumes, but in part also to the fact, that this "Comedy of Art" was, consciously or unconsciously, an attempt to relieve dramatic art from all constraint, to cultivate it as a pure, independent, and self-sufficient

[1] Riccoboni, i. 63 f.

18

19

18—Scene from an Italian masque (after Callot's *I balli di Sfessania*).
19—Italian masques (after the same).

art; and, the attempt being to a certain extent successful, it was so much the more surprising and attractive,
as hitherto dramatic art had only been known as im-
perfect amateur art.

So the Italian *Commedia dell' Arte* is an extremely
important link in the history of dramatic art.   Indeed,
it inaugurates a new era, and I do not think that the
influence it has exercised in all civilised countries has
been sufficiently appreciated.   In the following chapters
we will look a little more closely at its artistic value, and
try to follow it on some of its excursions.

II

Character-drawing and Plot in the *Commedia dell' Arte*—The Obscene
    Element—The Serious Subjects—*Don Giovanni* as an Improvised
    Comedy—The Standing Characters—Pantalone, the Dottore and the
    Capitano, Pedrolino and Arlecchino, Pulcinella—The Unmasked
    Types—The Male and the Female Lover and the Maid-servant.

THE material of the Italian Comedy of Art as we know
it, that is, from the sixteenth century onward, is essentially
based on intrigue and on comic situations.   The subject
of the intrigue is the universal love-affair: two young
people in love with each other, the fathers putting
obstacles in their way, and the servants helping them by
all kinds of intricate means.   The improvised comedy
borrowed this subject from the contemporary written
comedy, which again had taken it from Plautus and
Terence.   To the same sources are due the ever-
recurring scenes of recognition, which in the last act
solved the complicated plot in an easy way: the son,
who in his childhood was kidnapped by "the Turks,"

has spent his youth in slavery, but by a wonderful chance has succeeded in escaping, and at last returns to the home of his childhood; the young girl, who has been torn from her parents in a shipwreck, and lives unknown in great poverty in the very town in which her mourning but wealthy father happens to arrive. He recognises his lamented and dearly beloved daughter by a necklace, with which not even the most urgent need could induce her to part.

The plotting valets and maids, who follow their masters like shadows, are direct descendants of the Greek or Roman slave. In the same way the aged father, the loving couple, the "capitano" or swaggering officer, the procuress or match-making widow, and the parasite have their prototypes in the ancient classic comedy, and recur in the written plays of the seventeenth and eighteenth centuries. In Molière as well as in Holberg, and in many second- and third-rate authors, we find the complete formulas of an Italian *Commedia dell' Arte*. If such plays as *Le dépit amoureux*, *Les Fourberies de Scapin*, or *L'Avare* were written like one of the ancient scenarios and with Italian names, we should not be able to distinguish them from a genuine "canvas." [1]

There is no individual character - drawing in the scenarios. The same characters appear in all plays, though under different names, and beyond the general statements that one is old and ludicrous, another young and in love, one stupid, another cunning, and so forth, it

[1] As an example we add in the Appendix a literal translation of a genuine scenario. The Italian original is to be found in the *Scenari inediti della Commedia dell' Arte*, edited by Bartoli. Firenze, 1880.

is impossible to find any characterisation or individual feature in the scenarios. This does not imply that no characterisation was given on the stage. On the contrary, we suppose that it was the task of the actors to supply their characters with as many individual features as possible. Besides the *History of the Italian Theatre*, which we have quoted above, Riccoboni also wrote a versified guide for actors, in which he constantly recommends them to let truth and nature be their first concern.[1]

No doubt it can only be said in a relative sense that the actors of the Comedy of Art imparted an individual stamp to their characters. The same actors nearly always performed the same kind of parts. A Harlequin, a Pantalone, or Dottore seldom played anything but that one part during his whole life, and he so entirely identified himself with it, that in many cases he was only known by his stage name; however, this did not prevent his imparting a particular stamp to his Pantalone or his Harlequin—a stamp borrowed from nature, and separating this particular character from all earlier Harlequins or Pantalones, so that, in spite of the whole stereotyped inheritance of tradition, he had a life and a character of his own.

[1] " La principale, e necessaria parte
  Dell Comico è di far chiaro vedere
  Che da la Verità non si disparte.
  Cosi facendo, quasi persuadere
  Potrai che non sia falso quel che è finto."
" Il naturale ogn' ora ci dispensa
  Quel chiaro lume, che buon senso ha nome,
  Che è buono in Casa, in Piazza, in Scena, a Mensa."

.   .   .   .

Luigi Riccoboni : *Dell' Arte Rappresentativa*,
Capitoli sei, London, 1728, pp. 17 and 46.

This may be said also of the situations. They recurred from piece to piece, with inconsiderable changes; each with the same mistakes, the same fights, the same night-scenes—where one person is taken for another in the darkness, the same misunderstandings— where father and son are in love with the same girl, each speaking from his own point of view,[1] etc. Besides the *lazzi* which, as we have mentioned, were introduced into the comedies, there were a great number of constantly-recurring situations of this kind, which, though they were not considered as *lazzi* since they formed part of the action and were indicated in the scenario, yet had a time-honoured claim to call forth laughter.

Among the means which were always sure to produce merriment, there were also the obscene situations. We have seen that the Middle Ages were anything but prudish in their comedy, but it must be said that the Comedy of Art did not lag far behind. The circumcision *lazzo* mentioned in the previous chapter, points in this direction. But most of the earliest scenarios—no less than the written literary plays—are to a great extent simply based on lascivious and equivocal, or frequently quite unequivocal scenes and situations. The thing was carried to such an extreme of shamelessness that women — who by the professional actors were allowed to perform the female parts—appeared perfectly naked, merely for the sake of creating excitement and laughter. We know this from the few writers who declaimed against indecencies of this kind; the majority of them did not object to it at all. Thus one of the

---

[1] Scenes of this kind were called *Scene equivoche*. Comp. Appendix.

20—The three little Scaramouches (from a print by Bonnart).

antagonists, Domenico Ottonelli, relates that "in a public theatre the actors represented an indecent attempt of an impudent lover to break into the presence of the coveted woman, who fled with him, letting herself out of an open window, and trying in vain to hide her naked-ness with a large white sheet, so that she stood there like a shameless creature." [1]   In another place he writes about a play, in which a woman, who was to simulate madness, appeared half undressed in transparent gar-ments.

Another writer says: [2] "Who among the ancients would have dared to represent a perfectly naked Europa on the stage? When would it have been tolerated in ancient times that a woman should appear on the stage hiding a man beneath her clothes? [3] Yet all these indecencies have been seen of late on the stages of Florence." The famous actor, Nicolo Barbieri, creator of the Beltrame character, to whom we shall return later on, acknowledges this, though he himself was an accom-plice. He tells us how such opportunities as saving a man or a woman out of a shipwreck or a fire, afforded pretexts for representing them half naked, or in torn and perfectly transparent clothes.

Occasionally, however, such indecencies scandalised

[1] Ottonelli: *Della Christiana Moderatione del Theatro*, Fiorenza, 1646, i. 37.   Quoted by Bartoli, *op. cit.* XC., Note 3.

[2] *Trattato contra alle Commedie lascive*, a manuscript of the seventeenth century, also quoted by Bartoli.   We must say, however, that the author is mistaken in commending antiquity at the expense of his own time.   For it cannot be said that decency was a distinguishing mark of antique comedy. The Roman mimes, on the contrary, took pleasure in exhibiting naked women.   Comp. Vol. I., fig. 62, of the present work.

[3] Comp. fig. 20.   The joke in question was no doubt a favourite trick on the Italian stage

even the public.   Ottonelli writes that once, in the year
1635, when he was in the theatre, "there was an actor
who, in order to call forth roars of laughter, made a
gesture of such unsurpassed indecency, that all, even the
most light-minded, were so ashamed that they drooped
their eyes."   In another instance matters went to such
an extremity that an actor in Palermo was condemned
to the gallows on account of his obscenity.

We may be sure that the things these actors did
must have been incredibly bad, for, as a rule, people
were not very particular, and coarseness of all kinds—
especially in sexual matters—seems to have been a quite
indispensable ingredient, at any rate of comic plays.
The age which could enjoy the stories of Boccaccio and
of the otherwise virtuous Queen Marguerite, the *Gallant
Ladies* of Brantôme and the comedies of Aretino,
certainly could not feel itself outraged by the jokes
invented by the masked comedians of art.   Nevertheless
it seems that the seventeenth and eighteenth centuries
brought some improvement on the licentious tone, and
Nicolo Barbieri expressly blames his predecessors on
account of their lasciviousness,[1] and maintains that the
actors of his own time are exempt from such indecencies.
We do not think he is quite right in his assertion, though
it may be supposed that the refined companies which
acted in the presence of Louis XIV. and his court, of
the Emperor Mathias and other highly distinguished
persons, avoided the worst indiscretions, whereas we

---

[1] A large number of the masked figures represented by Callot are
phallophori (comp. figs. 18 and 19), not only those who are supposed to
be acrobats and jugglers, but also some of the masks which are evidently
representations of actors, such as those representing old men.

may take it for granted that they were kept alive in the inferior popular companies which visited the small Italian towns.

The earliest collection of scenarios we know was published at Venice in 1611 [1] by the manager Flaminio Scala, known by his professional name of Flavio.   This collection, consisting of fifty pieces, contains, as we see from the title-page, not only comedies, but also pastorals and tragedies.   This shows that the improvised comedy did not confine itself to the lighter "play of intrigue" with its stationary types, but also undertook more elevated subjects.   Yet, in the collection of Scala, the comic plays hold a decided majority: among the fifty pieces there are forty comedies of three acts; one only is designated as a tragedy (*la Forsennata Principessa, tragedia*), the remainder are called *opera regia* or *reale*, that is, royal work; *opera heroica*, heroic work; and *opera mista*, mixed work, in which the comic and the tragic species are blended.

These scenarios with "elevated" subjects were the queerest farrago of absurd events attributed to historical persons, of sorcery, sentimental pathos, harlequinades and mechanical tricks.   The usual characters of the *Commedia dell' Arte* were mixed up in the drollest way with mythological and historical characters, and the scene was laid in the most extraordinary countries.   We make the acquaintance of an Egyptian princess named

---

[1] *Il teatro delle favole rappresentative overo la ricreatione comica, boscareccia e tragica, divisa in cinquanta giornate composte da Flaminio Scala detto Flavio comico* [*comico* does not mean comic actor, but actor in general] *del sereniss. sig. duca di Mantua.   In Venetia. Appresso Gio. Batt. Pulciani,* 1611.

Isabella; and Orestes, the king of Sparta, and Oronte, the king of Athens, have in their service such people as Burattino, Pedrolino, and Arlecchino. Shipwrecks, naval battles, fires, metamorphosed animals, all kinds of fire-spitting magic, alternating with touching love-scenes and comic *lazzi;* the whole compound fore-shadowing the era of the later "magic opera" (fig. 21),[1] the German *Haupt- und Staatsaction*, and our modern spectacular drama.

Sometimes, however, more reasonable subjects were chosen, and not all scenarios were so bad as those of Flaminio Scala, who indeed is severely censured by other Italian actors and dramatists.[2] The contemporary Spanish drama, for instance, which was just then in its prime, exercised its influence; sometimes even the contents of Spanish plays were borrowed and converted into scenarios. The subject of *Don Giovanni*, among others, was performed as an improvised comedy. *Il Convitato di pietra* ("the Stone-guest"), an imitation of the Spanish original by Gabriele Tellez,[3] was one of the greatest successes of the Italian comedians *dell' arte*.

The original scenario no longer exists, but the celebrated harlequin Domenico Biancolelli, who played Don Giovanni's valet, left a number of notes, after

---

[1] Fig. 21 represents a scene from an Italian magic play, *La Baguette de Vulcain*, by Regnard and Dufresny, performed for the first time on January 10, 1693.

[2] "La construction de ses Fables est très-foible, et même j'oserai dire mauvaise, mais surtout la plus grande partie en est très scandaleuse."— Riccoboni i. 40.

[3] Also known by his pen-name, *Tirso de Molina*. The title of his play was *El burlador de Sevilla*. The Don Giovanni type is met with probably for the first time in *El dinero es quien hace hombre*.

21-- Scene from a magic play, "La Baguette de Vulcain" (after a contemporary print).

which the Italian canvas has been reconstructed in a very plausible mannner.   This reconstruction[1] is very interesting to read, because the adaptation of the well-known subject furnishes a standard for appreciating the method which these people followed in their work.

The drama begins with a conversation between the king and the valet of Don Giovanni.   [Originally he was called Trivelino, afterwards Harlequin ; then again Trivelino after the different performers.]   The king is revolted at the debauchery of the young nobleman. "Your Majesty must have a little patience," Harlequin says to him ; "young men change their habits when they get older.   We must hope that my young master will become more reasonable and sedate when he has a few more years behind him."   The king consoles himself with this hope, and to change the conversation he desires Harlequin to tell him a nice story.   The valet takes a chair, sits down familiarly beside the king, and begins telling the story about Queen Johanna.   The tale is suddenly interrupted by a sound, and Harlequin hurries off.

Change of Scene.   A Street.

Enter Harlequin, wrapped in a black mantle and holding out a long Spanish sword, to the point of which is fixed a lighted lantern.   He says : "If all knives were only one knife, ugh, what a knife !   If all trees were only one tree, ugh, what a tree !   If all men were only one man, ugh, what a man !   If this big man took this big

---

[1] Undertaken by Castil-Blaze (" Molière—musicien ").   We quote it here from L. Moland : *Molière et la Comédie italienne*, p. 192 ff.

knife and dealt a blow at this big tree, ugh, what a blow!"

This remarkable introduction has no connection whatever with the following scene; it is a perfect parallel to Sganarel's well-known eulogy of snuff in Molière.

Meanwhile Don Giovanni enters. Harlequin, who does not recognise him in the dark, trembles with fright and drops the lantern, which goes out. On hearing the sound of the falling lantern, Don Giovanni draws his sword. Harlequin lies down on his back, holding his sword straight up, so that his adversary keeps hitting it with his blows, and the clashing of the swords is heard. This scene, when well performed, was always a great success. At last Harlequin drops his sword and says: "I am killed." Don Giovanni, who now finds out who it is, and is sorry to have wounded him, asks if he is really dead. "If it be true that you are Don Giovanni," Harlequin replies, "I am still alive; but if not, I am quite dead."

Duke Ottavio enters, accompanied by his confidant, Pantalone, and they talk about their affairs.

While the Duke and Don Giovanni exchange compliments, Harlequin places himself by the side of Pantalone, and makes a deep bow each time Pantalone looks his way. Pantalone crosses to the other side to escape all this politeness. Harlequin follows and repeats the same *lazzo*. He waves his mantle, and coming close to Pantalone in making this movement, he hits him in the stomach and makes him fall. Harlequin falls on the top of him. They rise. Harlequin blows his nose in

Pantalone's pocket-handkerchief; the latter sees it, and strikes the impudent servant; Harlequin returns the blow.

Meanwhile Ottavio has told Don Giovanni that he is about to marry his dearly beloved Donna Anna; he is going to pay her a visit that very night. Don Juan, on hearing this, proposes to change mantles with him; he is going to some adventure, he says; Ottavio consents. Harlequin changes mantles with Pantalone.

When alone with Harlequin, Don Giovanni confides to him that he has only changed mantles with Ottavio in order to deceive Donna Anna. Harlequin tries to dissuade him from this design, and reminds him of the wrath of Heaven. Don Giovanni answers by striking him, and orders Harlequin to follow him.

After some more scenes, Don Giovanni places Harlequin on guard before the house of the Commander, and himself goes inside to meet his daughter, Donna Anna. Don Giovanni comes rushing out of the house again, pursued by the old Commander with drawn sword. They fight. The Commander is wounded, and dies after some agony. Harlequin; *lazzi* of terror; he tries to run away, stumbles over the Commander's body, and runs out.

Enter Donna Anna, who asks vengeance of the king. Ten thousand dollars and pardon for four brigands are promised the discoverer of the murderer.

Harlequin makes his reflections on this reward. Don Giovanni, who does not trust him, draws his sword and threatens to kill him if he ventures to speak. Harlequin swears inviolable silence. " But if you were put on the rack ? "—" Nothing can shake me."—" We

shall see." Now Don Giovanni begins talking like a
barigello, a police-officer, and pretends to submit the
valet to a painful examination. Harlequin confesses at
once. Don Giovanni flies into a rage, increases his
threats, and wants to change clothes with Harlequin for
safety's sake. Harlequin refuses, resists, and runs
away.

Pantalone, who is sure that Harlequin knows who
has killed the Commander, tempts him strongly with the
reward promised to the informer. "If I were only sure
of the reward," Harlequin says, "I would tell you the
name of the man." After some joking, however, he
repeats that he does not know who it is. "But,"
Pantalone says, "now suppose I were the king, and I
examined you.—How do you do, Harlequin?"—"I am
your Majesty's servant."—"Do you know who is the
murderer?"—"Yes, your Majesty."—"Then say who it
is, and you shall have the reward promised, and pardon
for four of your good friends."—Harlequin replies: "It
is—it is—it is Pantalone."—"Go to the devil, you
impudent liar!"—"Can't you see that it is a clever way
of making you earn five thousand dollars? I report you
to the king; I accuse you of having killed the Commander; I get the five thousand dollars, and we share
them between us."

The *sbirros* are hunting for Don Giovanni: they
offer his valet a purse to betray his hiding-place.
Harlequin accepts the purse, and gives them false
information.

Second Act.

We see a young girl, Rosalba, fishing on the sea-shore. Don Giovanni comes swimming; Rosalba stretches out her hand to the shipwrecked man to help him out of the water. Now Harlequin is seen standing in a barrel on the waves, and holding up his lantern. He comes close to the shore, turns a somersault, and comes down on his feet on the stage. He wrings his shirt and exclaims: "Give me some wine, wine, wine! I have had enough of water.' He thanks Neptune for his deliverance. Now he discovers Don Giovanni who lies unconscious in the arms of the pretty girl, and he says: "If I were wrecked again, I should like to take refuge in such a harbour." He wears a belt of puffed-up pigs' bladders; he falls on his back, and bursts one of the bladders. "Well," he says, "we are firing cannon to celebrate our deliverance."

Don Giovanni tries to seduce the beautiful Rosalba. At last he says: "If I don't become your husband I wish I may be killed by a stone-man, eh, Harlequin?" Then he goes away with the young girl. Harlequin looks after them and says: "Poor girl! I pity you for trusting my master's promises. He is so dissolute, that if ever he goes to Hell, as he is sure to do, he will try to seduce even Proserpine. If he had remained longer in the sea he would have made love to the whales."

Don Giovanni comes back to the wood with the fisher-girl, who says to him: "You have promised to marry me, and I trust that you will keep your promise." —"It cannot be," Don Giovanni replies; "ask my confidant, he is an honest man, and he will tell you my reasons." With these words he leaves her. Rosalba is in despair. By way of consolation Harlequin shows her a list of all the women who are in the same condition as she. It is a long parchment, which he unrolls, holding one end and flinging the other out towards the audience, saying : " Please, gentlemen, look it over, and see if, by chance, you do not find the name of your wife or of some relation." Then he adds the name of Rosalba at the bottom of the list, and the young girl in despair throws herself into the sea.

A troop of country people in festive attire appear on the stage dancing. A young peasant and a peasant girl are in love with each other, but make believe that they are quarrelling, hoping to force their aunt to make them marry each other. They are successful, and the wedding is about to take place, when Don Giovanni and Harlequin appear and join in the dance and conversation. Don Giovanni says to the bridegroom : " I congratulate you, Signor Cornelio." [1]—" That is not my name," the peasant replies. " If it is not now, it soon will be," is the joking remark of Don Giovanni. He does, indeed, elope with the bride. Harlequin disappears with the girl he has chosen, and follows his master.

(*Change of Scene.*) We see the tomb of the Commander—a splendid mausoleum. Don Giovanni reads the epitaph which is engraved on the pedestal. He feigns terror on reading a menace that he himself will be punished by a flash of lightning. Harlequin also reads, and trembles with fear that he will get his share of the

[1] *Corno* means " horn."

punishment. He blames his master for his conduct; Don Giovanni makes believe that he repents; he begins praying, prompted by Harlequin, but ends by kicking him and mocking the Commander's statue. At last he orders the valet to go and invite the statue to supper. Harlequin obeys, laughing at the ridiculous order, but comes back horror-stricken, for the statue has nodded its head in acceptance of the invitation. Don Giovanni refuses to believe it; he goes himself and repeats the invitation, but is terrified when the statue not only nods but distinctly answers " Yes."

Third Act.

Harlequin again preaches morality to his master and fills him with instructive fables, one of which is drawn from Homer, and is found in his treatise, *To Prevent Frogs from Catching Cold*. The last one seems to impress Don Giovanni; the prayer-scene is repeated, and ends, like the former one, with Harlequin being kicked, upon which Don Giovanni orders him to serve supper at once. This done, Don Giovanni sits down to eat. Then follow a number of *lazzi*, which can hardly be supposed to have been performed all in one evening, but among which the performers of Harlequin had to choose. First he rushes in, announcing that the kitchen is on fire. Everybody runs away to help in putting it out, and meanwhile Harlequin calmly sits down at the table and eats as much as he can swallow, till Don Giovanni comes back. Then he angles for a roast fowl with his fishing-rod. One of the other servants discovers it, and snatches it away from him. Harlequin boxes the ear of another servant who has done nothing. He runs up to the sideboard, takes a plate, wipes it on his hind-part, and offers it to his master. He dresses the salad in the following way :—First a pint of vinegar, then four cellars full of salt, an abundance of mustard ; then he pours the oil from a lamp into the mixture, at last he throws in the lamp itself, and stirs it all with his wand and his feet.

There is a knock at the door. A servant runs out, but comes back horror-stricken and knocks Harlequin over. Harlequin takes a roast fowl in one hand and a candlestick in the other, and goes out to see who it is. He comes back a moment after dumbfounded with fright, and knocks over four servants. He shows by signs that it is the man who did *so* (nodding his head) who is there.

Don Giovanni takes a candlestick on the table and goes out to meet his guest. Harlequin hides himself. Don Giovanni conducts the statue to the hall with much ceremony : " If I had thought that you would come and dine with me, my guest, I should have emptied Seville of bread, Arcadia of meat, Sicily of fish, Phoenicia of fowl, Naples of fruit, Spain of gold, England of silver, Babylon of carpets, Bologna of silk, Flanders of peas, Arabia of perfumes, in order to offer you a table magnificent enough and worthy of your exalted position. Now please accept what I can offer you with a good heart and a liberal hand."

Harlequin has to come out of his hiding-place to sing, and drink the health of one of Don Giovanni's favourites. His master whispers to him to mention Donna Anna, the Commander's daughter. Harlequin fills his glass and does as he is bidden. The statue bends its head in answer. Harlequin is struck with terror, and turns a somersault with the full glass in his hand.[1]

Fourth Act.

The Commander's sepulchral chamber. All is dark and gloomy. Don Giovanni, who in his turn has been invited to dinner by the statue, arrives with Harlequin. The latter looks round and says: "The charwoman of this house must be dead; it looks very black here." The statue desires Don Giovanni to sit down to table and eat. Don Giovanni gets hold of a serpent on a dish and says: "I will eat, even if you offer me all the serpents of Hell!" Now gloomy dirges are heard from behind the scenes, the statue rises, thunder rolls, the earth opens, hell-fire blazes, and the stone-man drags the wicked seducer to the gaping pit, in which he disappears. Harlequin cries after him in despair: "My reward! shall I have to send the bailiff to Hell to fetch my wages?" At last the King arrives, and Harlequin falls on his knees before him and exclaims: "O King! you know that my master has gone to Hell, where you and the other great lords will also go some day. So do think of what has happened here."

The last part shows Don Giovanni in Hell, where he is tormented and repents. This part of the play was in written verse, whereas the remainder was improvised in prose. In the Italian the conclusion is quite pathetic. Don Giovanni tries to soften the evil spirits, and asks

[1] Comp. p. 218.

them when his sufferings will end, and the spirits respond in chorus : " Never !"

DON GIOVANNI.

Placatevi d' Averno
Tormentatori eterni,
E dite per pietade
Quando terminaran questi miei guai.

CORO.

Mai ![1]

We will not here enter more in detail on the history of the Don Giovanni subject. The comedy of Molière and the opera of Mozart, the two adaptations which have given it world-wide fame, are known to everybody. But besides these, there are numerous versions in Italian, French, and German, as a tragedy, a comedy, an opera, and a pantomime. To us the main interest of its connection with the Comedy of Art lies in the fact that it shows how the typical mask of Harlequin (or Trivelino) and his *lazzi* supersede the action proper, almost reducing it to a frame for the actor's devices. And this is indeed consistent ; for it is in the nature of the *Commedia dell' Arte* to rely for its effects, not on the originality of the subject or on its comic or tragic character, but almost exclusively on the acting of its typical masks. The scenarios were merely opportunities for showing the favourite old characters in a new light.

---

[1] *Don Giovanni :* Be propitious, ye eternal torturers of Hell, and in pity tell me when shall these my pains have an end ? *Chorus :* Never !

It is time to look a little more closely at these standing types, and to see how they were represented.

The pillars of the comedy—if neither the principal nor the most brilliant or amusing of the characters— those who generally headed the list of the persons represented, were the fathers, the old men.   The most famous again among these, the one whose head was indeed surrounded by a halo, and, moreover, as a rule, supplied with an additional decoration, was Pantalone.   Originally he comes from Venice, speaks the Venetian dialect, and is dressed like a Venetian shopkeeper.   He is good-natured, loquacious, credulous, and something of a fool—a *buon diavolo* who is always taken in by his son, daughter, servant, in short by every one with whom he comes into contact.   He is the constant butt of the comic valet's jokes and wanton *lazzi*, and though he flies into a rage at once, in the end he generally forgives all the tricks that have been played upon him.   Besides, he has vices of his own : he is fond of the tavern, and, in spite of his age, a great wencher, which constantly places him in ridiculous situations, for instance where he appears as the rival of his own son.   His *scene amorose* are always of a very popular comic effect.   He is frequently a widower, and constantly a-wooing.   If he is married, his wife is sure to take ample compensation for his excesses. He is a direct descendant of the *senex*, the old man in the Roman comedy, and the "fathers" in Molière (Oronte, Géronte) are close relations of his.

His outward appearance has a more individual stamp.   The most characteristic part of his dress is the long trousers which bear his name (comp. fig. 22).

These, as well as his short jacket, are of red cloth.   But the large mantle with sleeves (a sort of dressing-gown worn by Venetian shopkeepers) is black.   He wears yellow leather slippers, and a red skull-cap on his white hair.   The upper part of his face is covered by a dark brown half-mask, and long after beards had gone out of fashion, so late as the eighteenth century, he wore a long pointed beard and turned-up moustache.

The whole costume is a precise copy of the ordinary shopkeeper's dress as it was worn during the Venetian Renaissance, and we do not suppose that it underwent any change, either in the sixteenth or the seventeenth century.   At the beginning of the eighteenth century, however, the characteristic long pantaloons disappeared, and were replaced by wide knickerbockers and long stockings,[1] and finally, at the end of the eighteenth century, and in our own time, Pantalone wears the ordinary Cassander or Jeronimus costume, with powdered wig and without beard.[2]

The name of Pantalone, however, was not permanent.   In the seventeenth and eighteenth centuries it had almost entirely disappeared from the scenarios.   Gherardi has not a single Pantalone in his repertoire, and in the scenarios published by Bartoli there are only two.[3]   The common names of the old man are Ubaldo, Pandolfo, Oronte, Géronte, Cassandro, etc.

His character also somewhat changed in the course of time.   Pantalone occasionally appears as a dignified

[1] Comp. Riccoboni, ii. p. 310 and illustr. pl. 4.
[2] Comp. Maurice Sand : *Masques et Bouffons*, ii. 21, and the picture of Cassander, pl. 29.
[3] In *I Tappeti, ovvero Colafronio geloso*, and *Il Dottor Bacchetone*.

father, a sensible, honest man, but severe with his children.   This variety, however, is rare during the first flourishing period of the *Commedia dell' Arte*, and in his relations with the cunning valets the ludicrous character is maintained throughout.   But his closeness in money matters becomes a prominent feature, and affords opportunities for many comic scenes between the servant and the old man, in which they vie with each other in sly villainies.   Maurice Sand relates several such episodes, one of which, in particular, is of really comical effect.

It occurs in a play by Giovanni Bonicelli, in which Pantalone appears as an apothecary.   He and his friend the Doctor, a learned lawyer, quarrel about the importance of their trades.   Finally they come to blows. But when at home they wish to be reconciled.

The Doctor takes the first step, and sends his servant Harlequin with a basket containing two partridges to his old friend.   Pantalone is touched, and tips Harlequin a quarter of a ducat.   The servant overwhelms him with gratitude and runs out, but comes back a moment after, and tells him that in running so fast he has split his trousers.

Pantalone is in a liberal mood, and gives him another quarter of a ducat, saying : " Mark well, my son, it is no loan ; I give it you as your property."   Harlequin again covers Pantalone with blessings, goes away, and comes back for the second time.   He is in debt to the tailor, and this hard-hearted miser threatens that if he does not pay half a ducat, the first time they meet he will knock off his charming little hat.   Now Harlequin does not suppose that Mr Pantalone would allow the servant of his dear friend, the Doctor, to suffer such disgrace.

Pantalone is touched again, but now Harlequin returns for the third time, asking for help to pay his mother's needlewoman, who threatens to keep the material of a dress which she was to make, as his mother cannot afford to pay her.

Pantalone gives him the remainder of the ducat, but this time declares it to be a loan.   Harlequin promises to remember this, and goes away for good.

Pantalone opens the basket, but instead of the partridges he finds a large goat's head with both its horns.

He calls back Harlequin.   " Look here," he says, " I am sadly afraid I have given you counterfeit coin. Give me back all four quarter-ducats, and I will give you a good ducat in exchange."

Harlequin, who is clever at cheating others but has no keen scent for a trick played on himself, returns the money in good faith.   Pantalone puts it into his pocket, then he flings the goat's head after Harlequin, desiring him to accept this likeness of his father, and to take good care never to come into his sight again.

The Doctor, whom we meet in this scene as the friend of Pantalone, is the second typical old man.   His home is in Bologna, the most celebrated university town in Italy, where many learned doctors made their lights shine.   He was naturally a rich prey for the comic actor, and *il Dottore* became an exceedingly popular comic figure.   His character resembles that of Pantalone in so far as he is equally fond of the fair sex (though even with less right), close in money matters, and easily taken in on every occasion.   But his salient feature is his constant talking on learned matters, in season and out of season.   Occasionally he possesses real knowledge, but he makes himself ridiculous by pouring out his Latin and his learned phrases in the wrong place and to the wrong people.   At other times he is perfectly cracked and talks mere nonsense, as, *e.g.*, where he makes the Graces cut the thread of human life, and the Parcæ assist at the toilet of Venus.   In both cases, Riccoboni justly observes, the actor who played the part had to possess some knowledge himself.   " The former [viz., those who represented the Doctor as a man of real learning] were obliged to know something, so that they might not risk saying anything wrong in earnest.   The others were under the same obligation, but they had, moreover, to possess talent ; for I feel convinced that it requires more intelligence to apply a sentence wrongly than in its proper sense."   " After all," he adds, " so far as dramatic art is concerned, this part is not difficult to play; it requires little acting, and neither physical grace nor swiftness of thought." [1]

Il Dottore is generally a lawyer, seldom a physician, sometimes a mixture of an astrologer, a grammarian, a philosopher, and a wit.   His name, as a rule, is Graziano, and he is generally the father of one of the young persons in the play.   Later we meet him also under the names of Prudentio, Baloardo, Messer Rovina or Hippocrasso.   Dr Diafoirus in Molière's *Malade imaginaire* is an imitation of this type.   The

[1] Riccoboni, ii. 313.

costume of Doctor Graziano was all black with a long wide mantle, a broad unstarched white linen collar, and a large turban-like cap (comp. fig. 23); in his belt he carried a white pocket-handkerchief and a curved knife; a black half-mask covered his forehead and nose; his cheeks were painted a deep wine-colour.[1]   In later times the character became more burlesque, and so did the costume, though it continued to be black and white; but the cap was replaced by a black felt hat with an enormous brim.[2]

A kinsman of the doctor's is the Pedant.   This character, which in the course of time became more and more grotesque, probably originated in the literary comedy, though it also appears as a general type in the oldest scenarios.   But it is decidedly an error to trace him back to the pedagogue Lidus in the *Bacchides* of Plautus, as Riccoboni does,[3] as well as Klein.[4]   The Pedagogue is a perfectly serious character, who has nothing in common with the always ludicrous Pedant. The queer, absent-minded scholar, who gives himself airs with his Latin and learned subtleties, is much more likely than any of the other masks to be a study from nature of the Renaissance period.   The many Italian universities no doubt abounded in originals, whose counterfeits on the stage would be sure to excite laughter.

But another type, the Captain (*il Capitano*) can be

---

[1] Comp. the coloured illustrations in Maurice Sand, ii. pl. 27.

[2] Comp. the illustration, "Habit de docteur moderne," Riccoboni, ii. pl. 6.

[3] Riccoboni, ii. 312.

[4] *Geschichte des Dramas*, iv. 905, n. 6.

22

23

22—Pantalone (after Riccoboni).   23—The Doctor (after Riccoboni).

traced back to the *Miles gloriosus* of Plautus—though we can hardly suppose that the actors of the *Commedia dell' Arte* drew him directly from this source. The Capitano became quite a pet character on the Italian stage—in fact he was so at a very early period. As early as the fifteenth century there were excellent Capitanos, but at the time of Charles V. Spanish art and literature exercised their influence, and produced some change in the Italian original, which was hardly as much of a caricature as the Spanish type. "The novelty," says Riccoboni, "was unanimously applauded by the public ; our Italian captain had to yield, and the Spanish captain was master of the camp. It was his nature to be grandiloquent, but in the end he got soundly thrashed by Harlequin."[1]

Innumerable were the odd ideas, exaggerations, mad boastings, which the Italians put into the mouth of their hero. Once during the siege of Trebizond he penetrated into the camp of the Sultan, took hold of his beard, and dragged him across the camp, being forced all the time to ward off his assailants and keep in check the whole army of the enemy. When he came home, his cuirass was so pierced with arrows, that he might have been taken for a hedge-hog. Since that day he has carried a hedge-hog in his coat-of-arms.

Under these circumstances it is not inconceivable that he should dress all his servants in the material of the turbans which belonged to the Infidels, whose heads he has cut off. His sword also is a curiosity, for it was

[1] Riccoboni, ii. 315.

forged by Vulcan, the smith of all the gods. When he had made it, he gave it to the god of fate, who laid it in the hand of Xerxes ; he gave it to Cyrus, Cyrus to Darius, Darius to Alexander, Alexander to Romulus, Romulus to Tarquinius, Tarquinius to the Roman Senate, the Roman Senate to Cæsar, and finally it came down to the Captain.

His fatiguing life compels him to take substantial food, and, indeed, he eats three dishes of meat for lunch : Jew's flesh to begin with, then Turk's flesh, and at last Lutheran's flesh.

His mere name inspires terror. Il Capitano Spavento della Valle inferno[1] is the name he usually bears, but under Spanish influence he is also called el Capitano Sangre y Fuego, el Capitano Cuerno de Cornazan, el Capitano Escobombardon della Papirotonda, and so forth.

The ordinary Spanish name was el Capitano Matamoros, which also passed on to Italy and France.[2] In Germany the character was altogether rebaptized by Gryphius, and received the not very amusing name of Horribilicribilifax. The English type is called Ralph Roister Doister (in the play of this name by Nicholas Udall).

---

[1] Francesco Andreini, the Italian comedian *dell' arte*, whose theatrical career for the most part fell in the sixteenth century, published a collection of " Capitano-bravades " under the title : *Le bravure del Capitano Spavento, divisi in molti ragionamenti in forma di dialogo, di Francesco Andreini da Pistoia, Comico Getoso.* Venice, 1624. Some of the above examples are drawn from this source.

[2] In *l'Illusion comique*, by P. Corneille, the cowardly boaster, to whom particularly the success of the play was due, bore the name of Matamore, and in the Hôtel de Bourgogne he was called by the same name ; Fracasse was also a common name of this type.

Like our Jacob v. Thybo (Holberg) the Captain has the power of "inspiring both terror and love."

> "Quand je veux, j'épouvante, et quand je veux, je charme,
>
>   Et selon qu'il me plaît, je remplis, tour à tour,
>
>   Les hommes de terreur et les femmes d'amour,"

says the Matamore of Corneille, and this was the precise character of the Italian Capitano also.   Innumerable are the women whose hearts he has broken, and he is almost as ready to tell his adventures in love as his feats in war.

However, as soon as it comes to blows, or at the mere threat of it, he comes down a peg or two, and afterwards he has to find an explanation for the change in his behaviour.   Once Pantaloon threatens him with a pistol, and he disappears in a wink.   But afterwards, on being upbraided for his cowardice by Harlequin, he pretends that he "went to order a tomb for the old man."

As a dramatic character the Capitano reaped immense success in the sixteenth and seventeenth centuries, especially in the Romanic countries where braggadocia was probably a more typical characteristic than in the Germanic countries.   Such men as Scudéry, or especially Cyrano de Bergerac, were — except in cowardice — perfectly typical Capitanos.

There is another variety of the type.   In the earlier scenarios it is not unusual to find the Capitano represented almost as an ordinary lover, without any comic character at all.   In Riccoboni's first picture of the Capitano he is represented as a handsome, smart young man without any touch of caricature.[1]   In Callot's draw-

[1] Comp. Riccoboni, ii. pl. 9.

ings,[1] on the contrary, his comic character is more distinct, but there is a very marked difference between him and the other comic masks. The likeness reproduced in fig. 24, after an old engraving in the possession of our Royal Library in Copenhagen, no doubt represents the type in its Franco-Spanish form. From this engraving M. Sand has constructed his Capitan Spavento (*Masques et Bouffons*, pl. 12).

A deviation from the Capitano was the Neapolitan Scaramuccia, who did not rise to real honour and dignity till he came into the hands of his celebrated performer Tiberio Fiorilli. His costume was black from head to foot.

Finally, we come to the type of valet, the most varied and the most popular of all masks, the real pillar of the comedy.

The Italian valet of the *Commedia dell' Arte* went by the common name of Zanni, a name which has been explained as a derivation from Sannio, the fool of the Roman Mimes. He acted under many special names besides, and in his whole appearance and character as leader of the intrigue, he is closely akin to the Slave in the Græco-Latin comedy.

The *Commedia dell' Arte* nearly always requires more than one valet ; Pantalone has one, the Doctor one, and the young man, too, is frequently provided with a man-servant. In the earliest scenarios two types prevail : Pedrolino and Arlecchino, Pierrot and Harlequin ; but in those times these two types were very different from what they became afterwards, and especially from

[1] Jacques Callot, *I Balli di Sfessania.*

24—The Captain (after a print by A. Bosse).

the types we see in our own Danish pantomimes,[1] where Pierrot appears as a stupid, indolent fellow, and Harlequin as the nimble, smart, and cunning lover of Columbine.

In the scenarios of Flaminio Scala they seem to have exchanged parts : there it is Pedrolino who by a thousand devices spins the plot, disguises himself and others, takes in the old man and cheats him out of his money, who is the favoured lover of Colombina, the maid, and who boasts of all his knaveries.

In a play in which he is the servant of Pantalone, he is ordered to keep an eye upon the old man's wife, while the latter is asleep. Instead of doing this, he goes to drink with the Doctor and Captain Spavento ; they get tipsy, and commit the most ridiculous excesses, finally they lie on the floor as if dead. Pantalone, who hears the next day that his wife has been out while he was asleep, scolds Pedrolino for his negligence. But the servant, who is seedy and giddy after the revelry of the preceding night, has forgotten all about it, and does not understand his master's reproaches. Pantalone flies into a rage, uses his whip, and finally his teeth, with which he bites Pedrolino in the arm, after which he leaves him, crying with pain and vexation. He vows vengeance, and conspires with all the other persons in the play to mystify Pantalone by making him believe that his breath has a very bad smell, so that nobody can endure his presence. At last Pantalone believes it, and the malicious Pedrolino induces him to have some of his teeth pulled out. Arlecchino comes disguised as a dentist, and pulls out four excellent teeth. Afterwards the trick is

[1] By Casorti and Volkersen.

discovered, and Pedrolino pretends to be mad, in order to escape the lashes he has richly earned.[1]

Another time he makes both the Doctor and Pantalone believe that a lady is in love with them and asks for a meeting.   By his advice Pantalone disguises himself as a woman, for, he says, the lady is very anxious about her reputation, and wants to save appearances by this precaution.   The Doctor is told the same story, and the two old men meet, both disguised as women.   After an amusing love-scene, with the customary mistakes and *doubles ententes*, they recognise each other and come to blows.[2]

In a third case he is commissioned by his master to take a love-letter to the beautiful Isabella.   He loses it, cannot find it, and to avoid coming with empty hands and being punished for his negligence, he hits upon the expedient of stealing a letter from the postman.   He succeeds, and takes the stolen letter to Isabella, which causes the most complicated misunderstandings.

Though Pedrolino is occasionally stupid and easily taken in, he is most frequently represented in the oldest scenarios as the cunning, somewhat malicious plotter— indeed as the principal character of the play.   Arlecchino, on the contrary, is nearly always the foolish idiot, the tool and victim of Pedrolino.

A third type of a servant in Scala's repertoire is Mezzetino, who is even more idiotic than Arlecchino, and stupid enough to be taken in by him.

Finally, there is Burattino, who also appears as a

---

[1] Fl. Scala: Giornata 12, *Il Cavadenti.*
[2] Fl. Scala: Giornata 13, *Lo Speechio.*

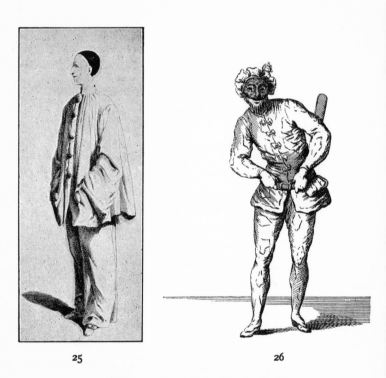

25

26

25—Deburau as Pierrot (after Maurice Sand).
26—The earliest type of Harlequin (after Riccoboni).

valet, but he is as frequently a cook, a landlord, a gardener, a shopkeeper, or a fool. Burattino is a mixture, so to speak, of Pedrolino and Arlecchino, of cunning and stupidity, now deceiving others, now being deceived himself. One of his comic effects is to appear with a *pot de chambre* in his hand. As landlord or cook he carries about his spit. No doubt, Maître Jacques in Molière's *L'Avare* is somewhat influenced by this mask.

With regard to the outward appearance of Pedrolino and Arlecchino, we regret to say that the original guise of the former is not known. It has been suggested that it was a French invention grafted upon the Italian masque. However, his mere presence as a principal figure in the repertoire of Flaminio Scala disproves this theory; for the French Pierrot neither could, nor is supposed to, have appeared till much later. It has not been ascertained whether the well-known white costume with the powdered face and soft felt hat is a French invention, but it is not impossible. The costume, as we know it from the Pantomime, comes closer to the type of Pagliaccio [1] (Bajazzo) with the immensely wide clothes and the enormous buttons, than to the Franco-Italian Pierrot (Pierò) of the seventeenth and eighteenth centuries, at which period the costume is smarter and more tight-fitting than our own. The costume of Deburau, however (fig. 25), the most celebrated Pantomime-Pierrot of our time, very much resembles our traditional guise, except that he wears a black velvet skull-cap or

[1] Compare the picture of Pagliaccio in M. Sand, i. pl. 18, the picture of Pedrolino of the seventeenth century, pl. 19, and Deburau as Pierrot, pl. 21.

serre-tête, as it is called, instead of our white cap, and that he does not paint his mouth and eyebrows in such a grotesque way. In one of Scala's scenarios the costume of Pedrolino is described as consisting of a long white shirt, a straw hat, and a long stick in his hand. This may possibly be the original costume, though it is by no means certain, as he appears in different guises in these plays (comp. fig. 27).

It has been mentioned that several of the French farce-players powdered their faces with flour.[1] Perhaps this was the Italian way of masking the type of Pierrot. So much is certain, that from the seventeenth century onwards he always appeared in snow-white, which had a striking effect among the variegated surroundings. He wore no mask—at least not in later times. An item of the Franco-Italian Pierrot costume is the broad outstanding linen collar. But this collar was abolished by Deburau, whom we mentioned before, because it was supposed to cast a shadow—from the footlights—on his face, thus preventing his facial play from being properly seen. Our Danish Pierrot does not wear such a collar either.

We are better informed as to the ancient costume of Arlecchino. In a private library Riccoboni found an old book published during the reign of Henry IV., which was written by a Harlequin-player, and contained an illustration of his costume. This drawing (comp. fig. 26) is reproduced in his book on the Italian theatre. It shows us a badly dressed person, with large irregular

[1] The white colour is no longer produced by flour or powder, but by grease paint of zinc white.

27—Gherardi as Harlequin (after a contemporary print).

patches both on his short coat, which is tied in front
with bows, and on his long tight - fitting "pantaloons."
He wears a belt with a small bag, and under his arm he
holds a wooden sword.   His feet are covered with low
light shoes, and his head with a soft cap, probably with
the afterwards traditional rabbit's or hare's tail.   The
upper part of his face is concealed by a black half-mask,
the lower part by bristling false whiskers.

Later this costume is arranged in a conventional
way.   The irregular patches become regular variegated
triangles, red, green, and yellow.   The long tights are
converted into close-fitting trousers, which come down to
the ankles and are buttoned on the inner side ; the bows
on the coat are replaced by metal buttons ; the cap by a
grey felt hat with the indispensable hare's - tail ; the
beard by a black chin-mask, which is joined to the upper
half-mask ; and his legs and feet are covered with white
stockings and shoes with buckles or bows.   The wooden
sword or stick is retained.

In nearly the same guise Harlequin has come down
to our own time, except that his coat has become a very
short close jacket, the whole costume is covered with
bright spangles, and the small grey felt hat and the
lower mask are abolished.   The other parts of the
costume are unaltered.

In the seventeenth century the character of Harlequin underwent a complete change through the influence
of a single distinguished actor.   From being the idiotic
fool, he became the witty jester, the spirited and
malicious censor of the other characters, quick and
nimble.   This actor was the idolised Domenico Bian-

colelli [1]—generally called Dominique in France, where he acted in the *Théâtre Italien*. Riccoboni says: "After the death of Trivelino, who acted as Harlequin in the king's company, M. Dominique adopted this costume. The character of Harlequin changed in appearance in the Italian Theatre in Paris. Hitherto Harlequin had always been a stupid fellow. Trivelino, the predecessor of M. Dominique, had not altered his character. After his death M. Dominique, who was a clever and well-instructed man, and who knew the mind of the nation which is fond of *esprit* everywhere, conceived the idea of supplying him with suitable jests and witty sayings. The authors of the *Théâtre Italien*, who began to write under Dominique, shared and encouraged his idea, and we know the stamp which they gave the character of Harlequin—a very different one from the ancient figure." [2]

And under this new form Harlequin made his tour throughout Europe, and not only—as Riccoboni says elsewhere—became "*les délices des plus grands Rois et des gens du meilleur goût*," but also the delight of plain people, who hailed his appearance with shouts of applause. Harlequin conquered all stages, and on some of them reigned so long and so supreme, that it became necessary at last to drive him away by force. We shall see afterwards how the German theatre groaned under his yoke.

Everything, of course, depended on the performer.

---

[1] Further information about him, and also other Italian actors, will be found in the following chapters.

[2] Riccoboni, ii. 320.

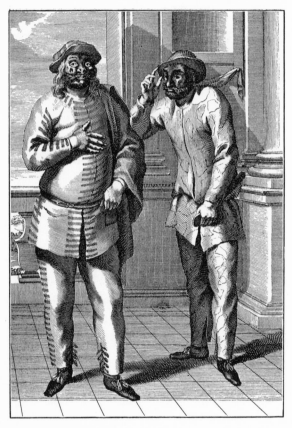

28—Scene between two Italian servants, Brighella and Trivellino (after an old print).

The character of Harlequin was more extemporaneous than any other, and required much inventiveness, tact and grace to become really amusing without being vulgar and exaggerated. " Improvisation is the stumbling-block of Harlequins ; if they are witty, a word or a situation easily tempts them to wander away from the subject ; if not, they are compelled to resort to *doubles ententes* which are badly invented and worse delivered. They lack the fund of talent and knowledge which might teach them to use the poison without being infected by it. It is a very difficult art, and I do not advise any actor to choose this career." [1]

After the change of type in Harlequin, Pedrolino naturally became his stupid and grotesque counterpart, and the comedy preserved its two indispensable types of *Zanni*. But besides these two, there were a number of other typical jesters which were closely related to the valets. Among others we may mention Brighella, a mixture of a pimp and a bandit, who serves everybody, but by preference helps young men in their love intrigues, and cheats old ones out of their money. His costume is like a kind of livery, white trimmed with green lace ; he wears a brown half-mask, and a big dagger in his belt (fig. 28).

Related—also in dress—to Brighella is Scapino, who has become famous chiefly through Molière. His costume is white, trimmed with blue, and a blue mantle, whereas the whole costume of the above-mentioned Mezzetino is red and white, striped. Both wear the characteristic wide soft cap or bonnet of the same colour

[1] Riccoboni, ii. 309.

as the costume (comp. fig. 36), and frills at the collar and wrists.

Another type—originally of the servant class—is the popular Pulcinella, the favourite of the Neapolitans, the rogue who has tempted so many learned men to write great works and long dissertations about his name, origin, and life.   And while they discuss his hunchback and his nose, he goes on cracking his jokes and pooh-poohing all the learned theories about what he ought to be and what he used to be.   "*Io son chi son*," he says, brandishing his stick contemptuously at all the learned nonsense.

However, he has not always had reason to plume himself on such great fame as he has enjoyed during the last century.   In neither of the two preceding centuries does he play a superior part among the Italian masks. He certainly exists : we see him among Callot's drawings, though somewhat different from the present type, and not differing much in costume from Fricasso, Fritellino, Franca Trippa, Trastullo, and others.

In Callot, who calls him Pulliciniello, he is seen dancing before Signora Lucretia (fig. 29).   He does not wear the black half-mask which afterwards became traditional, but he has a large nose and long moustaches (fig. 30).   His hat, like that of most of the others, is flat, pointed, cocked at the back, and divided in front, not high and pointed at the top as in later times.   He wears a shirt-like garment, gathered in at the waist, much the same as the one in use nowadays, and long trousers, a sword at his belt, and a short cape on his shoulders.

Pulliciniello.   *Sigª Lucretia.*

29

33

29—Pulliciniello and Signora Lucretia (after Callot).
33—Isabella Andreini (medal).

Nor does his character seem to have been the same then as it became afterwards. We rather suppose him to have been clever and graceful, whereas later he became coarse and clumsy.

Pulcinella is said to have been invented or introduced by the actor Silvio Fiorello at the close of the sixteenth or the beginning of the seventeenth century. He is not found at all in the scenarios of Flaminio Scala; in the edition published by Bartoli we meet him altogether in seven plays—four times as servant, three times as slave-dealer, landlord, and jailer; but his part is nowhere of particular importance. It is not till the latter half of the eighteenth century that he rises to the fame and important position which he still possesses. At that time he was introduced anew by the popular author Francesco Cerlone, a Neapolitan artisan and dramatist, whose comedies had a great success in the small theatres. In his play, *The Power of Beauty*, he introduced Pulcinella for the first time, and in the comic actor Domenico Antonio de Fiori he found an incomparable performer of his principal part. A contemporary—somewhat younger —colleague writes of him that he "was a clever and graceful Pulcinella, who met with an excellent reception and was much applauded in the Neapolitan theatres. His promptness of repartee, his natural and graceful mimicry, and a thorough comprehension of the impro-vised comedy together constituted merits which procured him fame and reputation."[1]

[1] Francesco Bartoli (actor from Bologna): *Notizie istoriche de' comici italiani che fiorirono intorno all' anno MDL fino ai giorni presenti.* Padova, c. 1781. The passage is quoted by Mich. Scherillo: *La Commedia dell' Arte in Italia,* p. 39 f.

Since that time Pulcinella has maintained himself as a permanent favourite type in Naples as well as in other Italian towns.   However, Pulcinella must not be confounded with the French Polichinelle, who is generally thought of whenever Pulcinella is mentioned.   Of course they have the same origin, but the French Polichinelle, who, like the English Punch, only exists as a puppet-show character, has developed very differently from the Neapolitan popular comic figure.   Polichinelle wears a richly bespangled red and green costume, a large three-cornered hat, exaggerated hunches on breast and back, white hair and moustache, and a glowing red, hooked nose.   But the genuine Neapolitan Pulcinella has no hunch at all, is clothed in white linen, with a large blouse gathered in by a belt or a string, with a bell fastened at one end of it, long trousers gathered at the ankles, and a high conical grey or white felt hat; his neck is bare, and the upper part of his face is covered by a black half-mask with an immense nose with a wart, and wrinkles on his cheeks (comp. fig. 31).

In this guise Pulcinella is a very ludicrous figure. Good performers represent him in a simple way.   He is a little indolent and drawling, his humour is dry and quiet.   He is rather chary of words and gestures, but what he says and does comes with a comic energy and precision which never fail to hit the mark.

Of course Pulcinella is a great scoundrel: he cheats and deceives wherever he can, but, like his townspeople, he does it in such an amiable, clever way that it is almost a pleasure to be taken in by him.   His devices are innumerable for appropriating everything that comes

30—Pulcinella and Pantalone (after an old print).

near him in the way of money or its equivalent.   One of the most fantastic is his stealing of the peasant's donkey.

This feat is performed when he belongs to a gang of gipsies, and has made up his mind to steal a donkey from a stupid peasant, who has his fortune told by one of the gipsy-women. While the peasant is thus occupied, Pulcinella slips the halter off the donkey's head, lets the animal run away, and puts his own head into the halter. After having listened to the prophecy, the peasant turns round, and is going to mount on his donkey, when, to his immense surprise, he sees Pulcinella calmly chewing at the halter; but his astonishment increases when the man begins to speak, and says: "I used to disobey my mother, and never had sense enough to do what I was told. So my mother cursed me and said: 'Go abroad and become a donkey, and may you remain so for five years, five months, five days, and five hours!'"

The peasant listens, dumfounded with wonder, while Pulcinella tells the history of his donkey-life. "But now," he says, "the curse is at an end, and I am again what I was before."

He shakes hands with the peasant, and thanks him for having treated him like a son while he was his donkey. The peasant is touched, and asks his pardon for the blows he has received, as he had no idea that he could be anything but a donkey, and invites him to come to his house. But Pulcinella only asks leave to keep the halter; he wants to hang it on his wall in memory of his time of trial. The peasant not only allows this, but gives him the few pence he has in his pocket. Suddenly Pulcinella begins to bray loudly: "Ooh, ah! ooh, ah!

ooh, ah!"—"What is the matter?" the other asks. "Nothing," the knave replies; "it is all right again. It was a reminiscence from my donkey-life."[1]

Besides the masks already mentioned, there are a multitude of characters, all of which, however, under different names, can be classified under the four principal types—Pantalone, the Doctor, the Captain, and Zanni, viz., the valet or jester.

But to these must be added the characters without masks, which occur in all plays and are quite as constant as the masks. These characters are: the male lover, the female lover, and the maid-servant.

The lover, *il comico acceso*, invariably appears as the elegant young man, about whom all we know is, that he is his father's son, and that he is in love. He is dandified after the latest fashion, *tiré à quatre épingles*, curled, pomatumed, perfumed, painted; he has a sword at his belt, a stick in hand, and waving feathers on his hat; he is equally enticing to the young ladies in the play and to the audience. His names are: Flavio (as in Flaminio Scala, who played this part himself), or Orazio, Valerio, Ottavio (Riccoboni's name as lover), Leandro, Fabricio, Cinthio; and he passes on to the French classical comedy without changing either character or name (Valère, Octave, Horace, etc.). As an example of his style let us take part of a dialogue from one of Gherardi's comedies.[2]

It is a conversation between Harlequin, who is dis-

---

[1] Related by Scherillo: *op. cit.* p. 43 f.
[2] *Colombine Avocat pour et contre*, comédie en trois actes, mise au théâtre par Monsieur D * * * (first performance on June 10, 1685). Gherardi, vol. i.

guised as a marquis, and is excessively smart, and Cinthio, the lover, who stares into his face, examines him from head to foot, takes hold of his sleeve, and asks : " Is that the fashion ? "

HARLEQUIN (*swaggering*).

Yes, sir, that is the fashion ! But it is no business of yours ! Indeed, I like that ! Yes, sir, that *is* the fashion !

CINTHIO (*coolly*).

Is not your name the Marquis of Sbrufadelli ?

HARLEQUIN.

It is, sir ; the Marquis of Sbrufadelli, that is my name. Have you any objection ?

CINTHIO (*coolly*).

And you are to marry Isabella, the Doctor's daughter ?

HARLEQUIN (*raising his voice*).

Indeed I am, and nobody shall prevent me. 'Sdeath, I am a man of quality, and a stout heart !

CINTHIO.

(*Laughs indifferently and strikes him on the nose with his sleeve.*) Ha, ha, ha ! a dainty creature !

HARLEQUIN.

(*Rams his hat down on his head and lays his hand on his sword.*) How dare you ? Death and pestilence, to a man like me ! . . . What the devil ! . . . I'll——

CINTHIO (*drily*).

What are you going to do with that sword?

HARLEQUIN (*growing meek at once*).

I am going to sell it, sir.   Will you buy it?

It deserves to be mentioned further, that in the pantomime composed after the *Commedia dell' Arte*, this type, under the name of Leandro, was changed into a comic character, the rich, dandified, but ridiculous wooer, who is deceived, while Harlequin is accepted as lover.

The first lover was generally played by the head of the company.

The female lover, *la comica accesa*, as a rule, had not much to do in the action of the play.   Nevertheless this part possessed a considerable attraction, because it was performed by women, and not, as was the custom in the Middle Ages, by men.   This reform also gained much ground for the Italian comedy abroad, where the handsome actresses contributed much to its success.   The female lover, like her male counterpart, dressed according to contemporary fashion.   Her name was most frequently Isabella (after Isabella Andreini, the celebrated actress in Scala's company), or Flaminia, Lucinda, Leonora, Ardelia, etc.

She was not always a shy, innocent, young maiden, but not unfrequently appears in very risky situations;[1] she responds to obscene and ambiguous allusions, and, as we have said above, is often seen in a costume that is

---

[1] Comp. *Le tre gravide*, by Francesco Ricciolini (Bartoli's collection), in which both the female lovers as well as the maid are *enceintes*, and where their condition is the subject of vulgar jokes.

anything but decent. It was a favourite contrivance to arrange the action so as to compel her to dress like a man.

This character was not necessarily represented as a young girl; it might be a married woman who deceives her old husband, or a young widow.

Finally, there is the maid-servant, who also differs considerably from the classical type (Dorine, etc.). The classical French maid, as a rule, is a steady, honest person, the favourite of the family, who represents common sense, and though her tongue may be a little sharp, she is very well-behaved, and does not even think of falling in love. But Colombina in the *Commedia dell' Arte* is a giddy Italian girl, in love, unfaithful, and jealous, flying at her rival at every opportunity. She is not always single either, but is sometimes the anything but faithful wife of Harlequin, Cola, or Pulcinella. If she appears as a servant-girl, it is not the glibness of her tongue or her lack of reserve that especially characterises her, as it is, for instance, in Molière, but her love intrigues and flirtations are her prominent features. Besides Colombina, which is her usual name, she appears also as Franceschina, Diamantina, Smeraldina, and later as Corallina (Anna Veronese), etc.

Originally her costume was the ordinary female dress, cut like that of her mistress, except for the traditional small apron, which was her constant attribute. In later times, about the year 1700, somebody conceived the idea of creating female counterparts of Harlequin and Pedrolino, and gradually there came to be a variety of Harlequinas and Pierrettas. The costume of Corallina

—according to a picture in Maurice Sand, which, we must admit, is not supported by documentary evidence—is a sort of imitation of the costume worn by Scapino and Mezzetino : a green and white striped cap, a tunic of the same material (comp. fig. 32) ; a skirt of white satin ; white shoes and pink stockings—cherry-coloured bows on tunic and shoes ; and a muslin frill at the neck.

In the pantomime, we know, Colombina is usually the daughter or ward of Cassander, and the subject of the plot is her love for Harlequin and their united efforts to overcome the obstacles which the old man lays in their way.

The counterpart and rival of Colombina is the somewhat older Pasquella. She is generally a widow, and possesses more experience, but not more virtue, than Colombina, with whom she quarrels and makes peace alternately. As a rule, she is plotting in order to bring about a good match for herself with one of the old men,[1] no matter which : age has taught her to despise love, and to look after the more material side of things. Nevertheless, she is not quite proof against the advances of younger men.

Both Colombina and Pasquella were played by women, not by men.

---

[1] Compare, *e.g.*, the scenario given in the Appendix.

31   32

31—The Neapolitan Pulcinella (after M. Sand).
32—Corallina ; Anna Veronese (after M. Sand).

III

Strolling Companies—The first Actresses—The Company named "The Jealous" and the Andreini Family—Writing Actresses—Beltrame—Favourite Comic Actors of Louis XIV.—Adventures of Mezzetino—The Riccoboni Family—Tommasino—The last Harlequin and the last Pantalone—Decadence.

IT is not known when the first companies of professional actors were formed in Italy. In the sixteenth century we find them flourishing, travelling from town to town, from state to state, from country to country. And they did not confine themselves to their native country. We may suppose that their reputation and the general interest in the new speciality of dramatic art was spread abroad by the multitude of foreigners who visited, and were influenced by, Italy during the Renaissance. Foreign courts sent for Italian actors, and we soon meet with little companies all over Europe: in Spain, France, Germany, and England. They came to France[1] as early as the first half of the sixteenth century, in the time of Francis I., but this is all that we know about them; we do not even know their names. In Spain a company under the leadership of a certain Ganassa visited the court of Philip II., and reaped immense success; afterwards, in 1588, there came another company under the brothers Tristano and Drusiano Martinelli. This same troupe, according to Collier,[2] had already, in 1577, been in England at the court of Queen Elizabeth.

It was the fashion of the time to form social or

---

[1] Comp. above, p. 141.
[2] Collier: *Hist. of English Dramatic Poetry*, iii. 201.

literary clubs, "Academies," which were called by the most absurd names, such as the Academy of "the Wet," "the Chilly," "the Obstinate," etc. The dramatic companies followed this example. They, too, called themselves Academies, and took such names as "the Familiar," "the Jealous," "the Faithful," "the Positive," "the Careless," etc.

Such a company, as a rule, consisted of from twelve to fifteen persons; sometimes, especially at a later period, there may have been more. It was ruled by a chief, *il Capocomico*. The majority of the members, of course, were men, but the more distinguished companies also included ladies—three or four, in later times even many more. In the sixteenth and the beginning of the seventeenth century, however, it was not quite unusual for young men to perform the female parts. We read this in a statement by one of the managers of the time, the very distinguished actor Nicolo Barbieri (Beltrame), who in his pamphlet *La Supplica*,[1] a kind of apologia for the dramatic profession, gives various information about the theatrical condition of his time. He writes: "I will never follow the custom of making boys play the parts of women or young girls, especially as I have seen the drawbacks of it in certain academies. In the first place, these young men do not know how to dress themselves in costumes which do not belong to their sex, so they are dressed at home by their women or flirting servant-girls, who frequently make fun with them; and those whose senses are not calmed by age or by

[1] *La Supplica, Disc. fam. intorno alle Commedie, di Nicolo Barbieri, detto Beltrame.* Bologna, 1636.

assiduous work may easily become vain and conceited, for thus disguised in female attire, these children go out and present themselves in the town, chatting and joking with everybody, and they arrive at the theatre in an untidy, disorderly state, so that their friends or teachers have to comb their hair again, paint them afresh, and arrange their collars and ornaments. If only they arrive in time, one must be contented; besides, they must be petted and flattered by way of encouragement; all of which offers plenty of opportunities of trying the patience of those who have to take care of them.

"It is more natural that women should perform their own parts; they are able to dress themselves, and as they are respectable, they set a good example instead of creating scandal. . . . But, somebody will object, 'I have courted an actress, and it did not take much time to gain my end with her.' But all women are not equally ready, and all men are not equally successful. There are men who pursue a woman for years, and sacrifice treasures for her sake, without obtaining anything but a dismissal.

"And besides, actresses are women like others, and nature has not favoured them with the privilege of resisting love more than others. They cannot err without its being known by all, and, religion apart, they are bound to be more careful and discreet in their behaviour than the women who can cover their fault with the cloak of hypocrisy."

So, if as late as the sixteenth century boys or young men still disputed the female parts with women, the victory *a priori* belonged to the latter, and this was a great step forward in the development of dramatic art—

an advance which was due to the old Italian comedians *dell' arte.* We have seen that even in the Middle Ages the appearance of women on the stage was not entirely excluded,[1] nevertheless it was the professional Italian actors who made a rule of their appearance on the boards, and established it as an artistic reform. The Italian actresses obtained such great success by their beauty and talent, and raised the level of the theatre so much by their generally decent and respectable private life, that other countries were soon compelled to introduce the new custom. Spain probably took the lead in the matter. The conquests of the Spaniards in Italy had acquainted them with Italian stage-matters, and as early as the first half of the sixteenth century we have evidence of the presence of women on the stage. Philip II., however, forbade their appearance on the boards, and ordained that young men should again undertake their parts, but as early as the close of the same century this command was no longer obeyed.

There is extant a novel by a contemporary author, Agustin de Rojas, who was a strolling actor himself. Its title is *The Amusing Journey*, and it gives us a first-hand, if somewhat comic, description of the elements and life of the Spanish companies in the sixteenth century— a description which, with trifling alterations, might apply to the dramatic companies of other Romance countries.

This is how Rojas describes the troupes : " There are eight classes of companies and actors, all differing from each other, viz., *bululu, ñaque, gangarilla, cambaleo, garnacha, boxiganga, farándula,* and *compañia.*

[1] Comp. above, p. 89 f.

"A *Bululu* is an actor who travels alone and on foot. As soon as he arrives in a village he goes to the priest and tells him that he knows a play and some *loas*.[1] Now, if the barber and the verger would come, and each of them give a little money to enable him to continue his journey, he would recite these pieces before them. The priest, the verger, and the barber assemble, the actor mounts on a box and performs his play, observing at each change of scene : 'Now comes such and such a person ; now comes the lady and says this or that.' Meanwhile the alms which the priest collects for him in his hat amount to about four or five coppers. Finally, our comedian receives a piece of bread and a bowl of soup, and continues his wanderings till fortune smiles on him again.

"*Ñaque* means two men who can perform an interlude, perhaps now and then an *auto*, a couple of 'octaves,' and two or three *loas*. They wear woollen beards, can beat the tambourine, and take an *ochavo* (two *maravedis*), or, here in Aragon, a *dinerillo* as entrance fee. They live a frugal life, sleep in their clothes, go barefoot, seldom have enough to eat, and catch each other's fleas in summer ; in winter the cold prevents them from being inconvenienced by vermin.

"A *Gangarilla* is a larger party, comprising three or four men, besides one who can play the fool, and a young man for the female parts. They perform the *auto* about the lost sheep, wear beards and wigs, usually borrow female dresses and hoods (which they sometimes forget

---

[1] *Loas* were a kind of introductory pieces or eulogistic monologues which frequently preceded the principal performance.

to return), act two comic *entremeses*, and charge a *quarto* (four *maravedis*) for a seat, but consent also to accept bread, eggs, sardines, and other victuals as payment. . . .

"A *Cambaleo* is composed of six — a woman who sings, and five men who howl. They carry with them a comedy, two *autos*, three or four *entremeses*, and a parcel of clothes—so light that a spider might carry it. The woman is sometimes carried on their backs, sometimes in a Sedan chair. In the farms they receive bread, grapes, and an *olla* for their play; in villages and towns they take six *maravedis*, a piece of sausage, a bunch of flax, and whatever people will give them, without despising anything. Remain between four and six days in one place, hire a bed for the woman, get—if they are on good terms with the landlady—a bundle of straw and a rug, and sleep in the kitchen. In winter the hayloft is their permanent abode. At noon they sit down round a table or on the bed, and eat an *olla* with beef, and six bowls of soup—one each. The woman distributes the food, and gives a portion of bread and wine (mixed with water) to each. But it gives them some trouble to wipe their mouths, for they have only one napkin between them.

"By a *Garnacha* is understood a party consisting of five or six men, a woman who acts the first lady, and a boy who plays the second. Their wardrobe, which they carry with them in a box, consists of two dresses, a wide mantle, three fur cloaks, beards and wigs, and a half-woollen woman's dress; their repertoire of four comedies, three *autos*, and as many interludes. The box is carried by a donkey, on which the woman rides, puffing and panting, while her companions drive it on. They remain for a week in one place, sleep four in one bed, eat *olla* of beef and lamb, and sometimes at night a good fricassee besides; they have wine by the pint, meat by the ounce, bread by the pound, and hunger by the hundredweight. They give private performances for a roast fowl, a boiled hare, four *reals* in money, and two quarts of wine, or for a lump sum of ten *reals*.

"In a *Boxiganga* there are two women, a boy, and six or seven men. The members of such a company have many vexations, as they seldom escape having among them a bravo, a ne'er-do-well, a man in love, or jealous, by which their safety, their contentment, and their purse are forfeited. They carry with them six comedies, three or four *autos*, five interludes, and two boxes (one with stage requisites and one for female dresses), and they hire four mules—one for the boxes, two for the women, and one for the remainder of the company, who ride by turns, each for a quarter of an hour. All seven generally have two cloaks between them, which are also used by turns, but frequently the donkey-driver runs away with them. They eat good meals, sleep together in four beds, and perform their plays at night, but on holidays during the daytime. On their journeys they generally sleep under the chimney for the sake of the sausages and bacon which are hung up there. They take what sausages they can get hold of, tie them round their waists, and carry them away with them. Such a *boxiganga* is dangerous, for it is more variable than the moon, and more unsafe than a border-country, if it is not conducted by a good manager.

" The *Farandula* comes nearest to the Compañia. Actors of this class have three women, eighteen comedies, and two boxes with luggage. They travel on mules or on cars, visit the tolerably wealthy districts, eat by themselves, are well dressed, at Corpus Christi give performances for two hundred ducats, and lead a merry life, with feathers in their hats or plumes in their helmets. Among their number we find gallants, who with their hats pressed down over their faces, with capes on their shoulders, and twisting their moustaches, cast killing glances all round, make signs with their hands, and put on amorous faces.

" The *Compañias* are composed in the most various manners, and they try a little of everything. Here are people of education and good manners, respectable men of good family, and also very respectable women (for where all classes are represented such women cannot be wanting). Such a *compañia* carries with it fifty comedies, three hundred *arrobes* [about 7500 lbs.] of luggage, sixteen persons who act, thirty who eat, one who has the cash-box, and Heaven knows how many who steal. Some of them travel on mules, others in carriages, others again on horseback, but none of them will put up with a cart, for they say their stomachs cannot bear it. On account of the many parts which they have to study, the constant rehearsals, and the changing taste of the spectators, their fatigues are excessive; but on this subject so much might be said that I had better say nothing at all about it." [1]

---

[1] Agustin de Rojas : *El Viage entretenido*, written in 1602, and published the following year. The above quotation is taken from the German

In spite of the playful tone of these lines, we see here how highly developed the dramatic companies, *i.e.*, the really good ones, were in the sixteenth century, and we notice in particular that only the inferior companies employed boys in their female parts.   Probably this was also the case in Italy ; we may assume, at least, that the superior companies which visited foreign countries, only employed women in the female parts, also for maids and elderly women.   The plays seldom contained more than three or four female parts.

In France the reform was speedily adopted with regard to female lovers.   It is proved that, as early as the middle of the sixteenth century, the strolling French companies carried actresses with them.   The proof consists in nothing less than the contract of an engagement,[1] concluded in the year 1545 between the woman Marie Fairet on the one side and the manager l'Espéronnière on the other.   Marie Fairet engages herself for a year to play "ancient pieces from Rome, or other stories, farces, or *soubresaults* (acrobatics), before the public wherever it may please l'Espéronnière," and she is even bold enough to promise that she will play these things "in such a manner that it will give pleasure to all who see it."   In compensation she is to have board and lodging, besides twelve francs a year, which even for those times cannot be called a liberal salary.   And if enthusiastic admirers

translation by F. von Schack (*Gesch. d. dram. Lit. und Kunst in Spanien*, i. 258 ff.).

[1] This interesting document was found and published ten years ago by Boyer, the keeper of the archives of the department (*Mémoires de la Société historique du Cher*, 4ᵉ série, 4ᵉ vol. 1888, p. 287, quoted by Bapst, *op. cit.* 177 f.).

give her presents after the performances, she is to share them with the wife of l'Espéronnière.

Certainly it did not occur to Marie Fairet that three hundred and fifty years after having concluded the twelve francs' engagement she would be remembered in history as the first French professional actress.

However, the custom of having old women and servant-girls represented by men survived as far down as the time of Molière. The author often put very bold replies into the mouth of the abigails, and the parts of the old women no actress wished to perform; so the men had to act them. In an earlier chapter we mentioned Alison, the actor of female parts at the Hôtel de Bourgogne; he played servant-girls in comedies and farces, and nurses in tragedies or tragi-comedies.

By degrees, as the parts of the soubrette became more decent, as in Molière's splendid Dorines and Toinettes, the actresses were quite willing to play them. But they persistently refused to undertake the ludicrous old women, and Molière's company still included a special actor for this branch. His name was Hubert; he had been trained by Molière in person, and had successfully played such parts as Mme. Jourdain, Mme. Pernelle, Bélise, in the *Femmes savantes*, Comtesse d'Escarbagnas and others. Hubert acted male parts besides, such as physicians and marquises, and confidants in the tragedies. He retired in the year 1685, and Beauval[1] succeeded him

[1] Jean Pitel, sieur de Beauval, came from the provinces, and was engaged by Molière in the year 1670, together with his wife (Jeanne Olivier Bourguignon), who acted the soubrettes; she was noted for her extremely querulous disposition, and for her sharp tongue. Beauval's parts were the foolish young men, and one of his particular successes was Thomas Diafoirus in the *Malade imaginaire*.

in his female parts, which he continued to perform down to the beginning of the eighteenth century; in 1704 he left the stage.   After Beauval the comical old women passed into the hands of actresses; and Mmes. Desbrosses and Champvallon distinguished themselves particularly in this line.

In England actresses made their way but slowly. Though in other respects the English theatre was highly developed, the conservative public hesitated to accept this reform.   It is true that in a book of travels of 1608 we read a statement which seems to indicate that by that time women had already appeared on the boards.   The author writes of his sojourn in Venice: "I went to one of their playhouses, where I saw a comedy acted.   The house is very poor and bare compared with our stately English theatres, nor can their drama be compared with our own as regards costumes, processions, and music.   Here I observed several things which I had never seen before: I saw women play comedy, a thing I had never seen before, though I have heard that it has occasionally been done in London, and they did it with as much grace, effect, good manners, and whatever else belongs to a play, as I have ever seen in a male performance."[1]

This statement might be, and has been, explained to the effect that women appeared as actresses in London previously to 1608.   This, however, has been nowhere confirmed.   And, indeed, it is much more natural to suppose that the author alludes to other Italian actresses, who in former times had occasionally appeared on the

----

[1] *Coryat's Crudities*, quoted by B. Baker, *London Stage*, i. 20.

boards at the court of Queen Elizabeth and in the English capital.

As late as 1629 the London public was so unaccustomed to the appearance of women on the stage, that actresses belonging to a French company were pelted with rotten eggs and apples when they appeared; and it was not till September 1656 that an English actress mounted the boards.   This was Mrs Coleman, the wife of Coleman, the actor, and she played a kind of operatic part: Ianthe in Davenant's *Siege of Rhodes*.[1]   By this time the constant intercourse with France and Italy had produced such a change in the public taste that, a little later, the royal licence obtained by Davenant—he was a manager—contained the following clause: "That whereas the women's parts in plays have hitherto been acted by men in the habits of women, at which some have taken offence, we do permit, and give leave, for the time to come, that all women's parts be acted by women."

At the same time probably women also appeared on the boards in Germany, but only in opera.   We first meet with professional French actresses in the company of Magister Velthen, when in the year 1685 it was officially nominated as the Company of the Electoral Court of Saxony.   Just as in England, it was an actor's —the manager Velthen's—wife who made the first start. A sister of hers appeared on the stage at the same time, and in the following year one actress more, Sara von Boxberg.

---

[1] This piece was a landmark in the history of the English stage in another respect also, for it was the first English opera, and, on the whole, the first piece in which real stage decorations were employed.

In Denmark, where professional dramatic art was not introduced till the first half of the eighteenth century, it was natural that the appearance of actresses should coincide with the foundation of a regular theatre. Nevertheless, we find many female parts performed by men.

The history of the Italian *Commedia dell' Arte* companies falls into three divisions : in the sixteenth century they gain their fame, during the seventeenth they maintain it, and in the eighteenth they lose it. It would be an overwhelming task, and one of less profit than labour, to pursue the changing fate and theatrical achievements of the various companies. Here we will only point out a few among the actors and actresses who distinguished themselves, and whose names are inseparably associated with certain characters.

One of the most celebrated companies of the sixteenth century was that of " The Jealous," and it gained its fame especially under the management of Flaminio Scala,[1] and through the distinguished and accomplished Andreini family. We have already spoken of Scala as author. He was the first who made a careful and accurate collection of the scenarios in use. He had them printed, and moreover—as his friend and companion Andreini tells us—added to each a list of all the properties needed in it, a custom which was preserved

---

[1] " The Jealous " (*i Gelosi*) was one of the first companies which visited France. Together with *i Confidenti* they formed for a time one company under the name of *i Comici Uniti* ("the united actors "), but *i Gelosi* soon separated from the other company, and after 1576 acted alternately in France and in Italy. The chronicler L'Etoile writes of them : " The Italian actors named *i Gelosi* . . . took four *sols* a head in payment from all French spectators, and there was such a crowd that the four best preachers, taken all together, had not so many hearers when they preached."

in later times. That he was a skilful manager seems evident, but as to his acting, all we know is that he acted lovers' parts under the name of Flavio.

Francesco Andreini, the most distinguished member of his company, also began his career by playing lovers. He was a well-educated and clever man, an author like his chief, versed in several languages, an able singer, and a performer on many instruments. He was born about 1548; when young, he became a soldier, was taken prisoner and sold as a slave by the Turks,[1] escaped again, and became an actor. It was not as a lover that he made his reputation, but essentially by his famous Capitan Spavento, his own invention, a character whose innumerable and fantastic pieces of bravado he afterwards published under the title of *Le Bravure del Capitano Spavento*. He also acted Dottores, and invented the Dottore Siciliano as well as the sorcerer Falcirone. Such versatility was unusual in those times, for, with this exception, each actor used to have his speciality, beyond which he did not go. After the death of his wife Isabella in the year 1604, Francesco left the stage, and never afterwards returned to it, though he did not die till 1624.

He loved his wife above everything, and her sudden death caused him such grief that he could no longer make up his mind to act. And indeed, according to all contemporary testimonies, she was well worthy of love.

---

[1] We know that the Turkish piratical states on the north coast of Africa drove a lively trade in kidnapped Christian prisoners just at this period. So the commonly used intrigue in the Italian plays of kidnapping sons and daughters was not so improbable in those times as it appears to us now.

Isabella Andreini was, beyond comparison, the most celebrated actress of her time, a really talented authoress, beautiful in appearance and noble in mind : *bella di nome, bella di corpore e bellissima d' animo*, as her husband wrote about her. No wonder that she was the idol of her time.

Isabella was born in Padua in 1562, and as a young girl of barely sixteen she was engaged as *accesa*, female lover, by Flaminio Scala. Francesco Andreini fell in love with her, and married her the same year, 1578. Wherever she appeared, she gained the greatest success by her beauty and intelligence ; the French and Italian poets vied with each other in paying her homage in their finest verses. Tasso wrote sonnets to her ; Henry IV. honoured her by offering her magnificent rooms for her residence while staying in Paris. She was a Laureata in the most distinguished *Accademia degli Intenti*, and at a festival in Rome, given by her admirer the Cardinal Aldobrandini, her portrait was hung, crowned with laurels, between those of Tasso and Petrarch.

Numerous eulogies were written on her and her art, but all these general and high-sounding phrases give us no impression of her style of acting. The comedies in themselves did not give the female lovers much opportunity of exhibiting their talent ; but it must be borne in mind, that improvised dramatic art extended its domain to serious historical and to tragic subjects, and perhaps we may suppose that these were the fields in which Isabella especially shone. Her noble, somewhat severe profile, as shown in the medal engraved after her death (fig. 33, p. 260), seems to indicate that serious characters were the most appropriate to her.

When, after a sojourn of three years in Paris, *i Gelosi*, of which, of course, she was the shining star and principal support, were to return to Italy, Isaac de Ryer wrote an enthusiastic poem to Isabella in order to persuade her to remain. The first and last verses run as follows :—

> Je ne crois point qu'Isabelle
> Soit une femme mortelle ;
> C'est plutôt quelqu'un des dieux
> Qui s'est déguisé en femme,
> Afin de nous ravir l'âme
> Par l'oreille et par les yeux.
>
> .   .   .   .   .
>
> Divin esprit dont la France
> Adorera l'excellence
> Mille ans après son trépas,
> (Paris vaut bien l'Italie)
> L'assistance te supplie
> Que tu ne t'en ailles pas.[1]

In spite of this pressing invitation, Isabella left Paris, but got no further than Lyons. She was *enceinte*, was prematurely confined, and died on July 10, 1604.

Before her death she published a pastoral play, *Favola pastorale*, called *Mirtilla*. Later her husband and Flaminio Scala published her letters and other writings.[2]

In the year 1579 Francesco and Isabella Andreini had a son, Giambattista Andreini, who became a clever actor, an energetic manager, and a very fertile author, and was altogether a strange, complex character. He acted under the name of Lelio in the same company as

---

[1] The whole poem is quoted in M. Sand, ii. 173 f.

[2] Adolfo Bartoli in his above-quoted work gives some specimens of her verse. They seem very pretty.

his parents, till the death of his mother. Then he
retired from the stage together with his father, and like
him he meant never to return to it. However, as early
as the following year, he formed a new company under
the name of *i Fideli*, and as its leader he acted for
several years in Italy, until in the year 1613 he was
summoned to Paris by Marie de Medici. In the same
year he had published a mystery, *rappresentazione sacra*,
called *Adamo*, which he dedicated to the same princess.
This made her wish to know him and his company, so
he went to Paris and acted there for some years, returned
to Italy in 1618, went to Paris again three years later
and played four years in the Hôtel de Bourgogne. His
father died, and thereupon he took a very solemn leave
of France and the theatre in general, in a little pamphlet
under the title of *Teatro celeste*. It is a collection of sonnets
of a very religious, almost ascetic character, in which he
sings the praise of several saints and of certain virtuous
actors and actresses, his mother among the number; on
the title-page he exhorts "poetically those who exercise
the theatrical profession to cultivate their art without
offending virtue, both in order to leave a distinguished
name on earth, and because they must not allow vice to
bar their way to Paradise." The book is dedicated to
Cardinal Richelieu, and the sonnet in which he takes
leave of the stage begins thus: "False stage, I leave
thee! Nevermore shall I stand in pride and splendour
on thy boards. Yea, I leave all this empty show, and
at the same time withdraw from the beautiful land of
France. . . ."

In spite of these solemn words he remained on the

false stage till his seventy-third year, when at last he retired for good, honoured with princely favours, with the title of chief huntsman to the Duke of Mantua, and a member of the *Accademia degli Spensierati.* During his long dramatic career he composed, besides several ecclesiastical dramas and ascetic poems, a number of comedies, which were very frivolous, besides a fantastic poem in twenty-five songs, *Olivastro, or the Unhappy Poet,* written in the over-elaborate and complicated style of the time, and full of the most remarkable absurdities.[1]

Among his dramas there are some regular Italian comedies in the ordinary style, but written with dialogue and all, not in the form of scenarios, like those of Scala; others are fantastic, fairy, and spectacular plays; others again, which are utterly absurd in form and subject, constitute a speciality apart.   Thus one of them, *la Centaura,* is a perfect monster: its first act is a comedy, the second a pastoral, and the third a tragedy.   In the pastoral the characters consist of a whole family of centaurs, father, mother, son and daughter.   The parents who fight in order to win the throne of Cyprus, commit suicide in despair, after a number of romantic adventures, and the young Centaura, daughter of the Centaur, ascends the throne, which, as Magnin,[2] who describes the play, justly observes, must have been easier for her than to sit on it.

Giambattista Andreini was married twice, each time

---

[1] A. Bartoli, *op. cit.* cxiv.

[2] "Teatro céleste, les commencements de la comédie italienne en France."—*Rev. de deux Mondes,* Déc. 15, 1847.

to a clever actress—first to Virginia Ramponi, named Florinda, and after her death to the actress Lidia, whose family name is unknown.

Besides this celebrated Andreini family, another actress of the sixteenth century, who deserves to be mentioned, is Vincenza Armani, who vied in fame with the beautiful Isabella. She was a poetess too, besides being an actress, and in addition to this was a sculptor, a singer, and a musician as well.

Of her acting it is said that "she played in three different styles—the comic, the pastoral, and the tragic—and that she observed so correctly what was appropriate to each of them, that the Academy *degli Intronati* in Siena repeatedly expressed the opinion that this young lady succeeded better in speaking *ex tempore* than the most perfect authors in writing with reflection.[1] And in another contemporary author we read that "by imitating the eloquence of Cicero, she has brought dramatic art into competition with rhetoric, and through her wonderful beauty and indescribable grace she has built herself a very magnificent monument in the world of spectators, and made herself known as the most excellent actress of our time."[2]

Her poems are commended for the warm and natural tone in which they are written. She does not seem to have been infected with the Petrarchism which rendered so many of the sixteenth century lyrics unreadable.[3]

---

[1] Bartoli : *Notizie istoriche de' Com. Italiani*, Padovo 1782 ; quoted by A. Bartoli, *op. cit.* cxviii.

[2] Garzoni : *Piazza Universale*, 738, quoted by A. Bartoli.

[3] A single specimen is found in Bartoli, p. cxix. It is a passionate love-poem, but very natural in tone, and yet melodious.

Giambattista Andreini's company, *i Fideli*, included a member who afterwards formed a company himself, which visited France among other countries, and reaped great success. This was the inventor of the Beltrame type, Nicolo Barbieri, a man of importance in the history of the Italian theatre, not least by reason of the often-quoted work which he published under the title of "The Petition [*la Supplica*], a confidential speech by Nicolo Barbieri, called Beltrame, addressed to those who by mouth or pen occupy themselves with actors, and have no regard to the merit of virtuous actions.—Reading for persons of distinction, who are neither completely critical nor perfectly foolish." This pamphlet is a kind of apology for the histrionic profession, but at the same time it gives much information about the actors of the time, which has been of great use to later investigators.

The dramatic character which he created, as an actor, was a kind of "heavy father," a more intelligent, more refined, more human Pantalone, whom he baptized Beltrame. Riccoboni, and after him Maurice Sand, have erroneously taken Beltrame for a servant, a kind of Scapin. In the plays left by Barbieri, who, like nearly all his distinguished colleagues, was a dramatic author, Beltrame is exclusively the sensible, cautious father. In outward appearance he is less striking, less of a caricature than Pantalone. His costume consists of a grey cloth garment, knickerbockers and "trousses," *i.e.*, short loose trousers, which were usually worn over the tight-fitting long "pantaloon," and a wide mantle, all of grey cloth. Round his waist he wore a leather belt with a small bag. His nose is hooked, though not excessively, and he has a dark, full beard.

Barbieri's best play was *l'Inavertito, overo Scapino disturbato e Mezzetino travagliato*, which he wrote and published with dialogue complete, though it was originally acted as an improvised play. It is the prototype of Molière's *l'Etourdi ou les Contre-temps*.

But the greatest name and the greatest fame were won by the highly distinguished comic actors, the Scaramucci, the Harlequins, the Mezzetinos, whatever their names might be. By their Italian subtlety of mind and body, their multifarious musical and mimetic accomplishments, which were based on an accepted artistic tradition, but appeared spontaneous because of the talent with which they were produced, they enchanted the public of the European courts, and lured many subventions, many gifts and favours from kings and princes, and these gifts constituted the essential, sometimes the only livelihood of the actors.

Thus, for instance, Tiberio Fiorilli gained immense fame by his highly admired Scaramuccia. Though he was not precisely the inventor of the type, which is previously found among the drawings of Callot, it was he who created its fame, and who supplied it with its new and final form. In France, especially, where Fiorilli ran the greater part of his career, Scaramouches became the fashion. In Italy he had always been a Capitano, but Fiorilli adapted him to every kind of play, and supplied him with an infinite variety of mimetic and musical hotch-potch, which, thanks to his spirited acting, appeared so witty and attractive, that, according to

Riccoboni, in France Scaramouch "was in every sauce."[1] Tiberio Fiorilli was born in Naples in the year 1608, and died in Paris in 1694. His long life is described in a little book which appeared the year after his death, the author of which is, or pretends to be, Angelo Constantini, a younger colleague of Fiorilli.[2] This book, however, is hardly anything but an accumulation of absurd and insipid anecdotes, which describe the actor in a number of extraordinary situations : on the galleys, in prison, in distress at sea, but always as a perfect rascal, who, like a magpie, steals all the objects of value which come under his eyes. As a biography this—at present rare—little book has no value, and is strongly repudiated by the author and actor Gherardi, who as the successor of Fiorilli must have known the real state of things. However, some parts of the book are not quite so absurd as others. Thus it gives a tolerably clear description of his appearance, which is corroborated by a portrait reproduced from an engraving by N. Bonnart (comp. fig. 34).[3] It shows Fiorilli as a tall, somewhat high-shouldered, but erect man, rather stout, for he was a great eater, but extremely active. His agility and his straight carriage distinguished Fiorilli

[1] "En Italie ce personnage n'a jamais fait d'autre caractère que celui du Capitan ; mais en France on l'a mis à toute sausse."—Ricc. ii. 315.

[2] *La Vie de Scaramouche, par le sieur Angelo Constantini, Comédien ordinaire du Roy dans sa Troupe Italienne, sous le nom de Mezzetin.* Paris, 1695.

[3] The biographers of Fiorilli (among others the usually correct Jal in his *Dictionnaire Critique*) say that the following quatrain is found at the bottom of this engraving in Bonnart :—

Cet illustre Comedien
Attegnit de son art l'agreable maniere.
Il fût le maître de Molière,
Et la nature fut le sien.

34—Tiberio Fiorilli as Scaramuccia (after a print by Bonnart).

even in his old age. It was he who at the age of
eighty-three could give boxes on the ear with his foot.
His performances were chiefly mimetic, and his mimicry
had attained a perfection which won his greatest success
as an artist.   In the Preface to his biography we read :
" We may even say that every part of his body spoke,
his feet, his hands, his head, and that the most insignificant of his postures was studied."   Molière was an
ardent admirer of his, and is said to have learned an
immense amount from him as actor.[1] We can find no
better authority to testify to his excellence.   However,
Gherardi gives us a description of one of his mimic
scenes, which conveys even a better idea than mere

But this is a mistake.   Under the engraving in question we read the
following lines :—

> Scaramouche est inimitable
> Pour faire des sauts périlleux
> Et quand il a le ventre à table
> Il s'en acquitte aussi des mieux.

The other lines, which are so often quoted, I have never found on any of
the likenesses of Scaramouch which I have seen ; that is, seven in all,
besides the little reproduction in Constantini's book.

[1] According to other statements it might be thought that Molière
simply took lessons in mimicry of the Italian " buffo."   Thus in the
lampoon which Le Boulanger de Chalussay wrote on Molière, under the
title of *Élomire* [anagram of Molière] *hypocondre*, we read :—

> . . . Par exemple, Élomire
> Veut se rendre parfait dans l'art de faire rire ;
> Que fait-il, le matois, dans ce hardi dessein ?
> Chez le grand Scaramouche il va soir et matin.
> Là, le miroir en main et ce grand homme en face,
> Il n'est contorsion, posture ni grimace
> Que ce grand écolier du plus grand des bouffons
> Ne fasse et ne refasse en cent et cent façons :
> Tantôt, pour exprimer les soucis d'un ménage,
> De mille et mille plis il fronce son visage,
> Puis, joignant la pâleur à ces rides qu'il fait,
> D'un mari malheureux il est le vrai portrait.
> Après, poussant plus loin cette triste figure,
> D'un cocu, d'un jaloux, il en fait la peinture ;

commendatory words. "Here," he says,[1] "we see Scaramouch, who, after having arranged everything in the room, takes his guitar, sits down in an easy-chair and plays, while he is waiting for his master. Pasquariel comes quite gently up to him from behind and beats time on his shoulders, which makes Scaramouch jump with fright. In short, here it is that the incomparable Scaramouch, who was the adornment of the theatre, and a model to the most celebrated actors of his time, whom he had taught the difficult art so necessary to people of their class, to stir the passions and express them correctly by the play of their face;—here, I say, it was that he made people nearly die with laughter for a quarter of an hour by a scene in which he expresses his fright without saying a single word. It must also be confessed that this excellent actor possessed this remarkable talent to such a degree of perfection, that he touched more hearts merely by simple natural means, than the ablest speakers by the beauties of the most persuasive rhetoric. This called forth the following remark from a great prince who once saw him act in Rome : 'Scaramuccia non parla e dice gran cose . . . ,' and as a mark of his high appreciation, he sent for him after the performance, and made him a present of the coach and six horses in which he had been fetched."

Besides his mimic play, his delivery of songs accom-

> Tantôt à pas comptés vous le voyez chercher
> Ce qu'on voit par ses yeux, qu'il craint de rencontrer ;
> Puis s'arrêtant tout court, écumant de colère,
> Vous diriez qu'il surprend une femme adultère,
> Et l'on croit, tant ses yeux peignent bien cet affront,
> Qu'il a la rage au cœur et les cornes au front.

[1] *Colombine Avocat pour et contre*, Act ii. Sc. 7.

panied by the guitar (Fiorilli's inseparable companion) imparted colour to the scenes of Scaramouch. Constantini's book describes vividly enough how Fiorilli wins the favour of Louis XIV. by a little very characteristic song. "As soon as he found himself in the presence of His Majesty, he threw his cloak on the floor, and there he stood with his guitar, his dog, and his parrot. He performed a very amusing concerto with these two animals, which he had trained to act each its part, one of them sitting on the neck of his guitar, the other on a little stool, while he sang the following words :—

> " Fa la ut a mi modo nel cantar
> Re mi si on non aver lingua a quel la
> Che sol fa profession di farme star
> Mi re resto in questo
> La berinto ch' ogni mal discerno
> Che la mi sol fa star in questo inferno.

> " La mi fa sospirare la notte è il dì
> Re mi rar la non vol el Mi-o dolor
> Là fa par ogni canto sol per mi
> Mi mi sol moro ristoro
> Non son mai per aver in sin ch' io spiro
> Che la sol fa la-mor, io Mi-ro-mi-ro.

" These three animlas did their duty so well that the King was pleased with the one in the middle, which was Scaramouch ; so that since that time he had the honour of diverting this great king for more than thirty years, each time appearing new in his gestures, though he did not change his guise." [1]

[1] *Vie de Scaramouche*, p. 89 f.   I dare not undertake to offer a translation of this remarkable specimen of a song.

Scaramouch's repertoire included other burlesque songs, such as the one about "the donkey in love," in which he copied the braying of the popular animal in the ascending gamut from do to la,[1] or another about "the gelded cat," in which he expresses the poor animal's impotent pangs of love in such a droll manner that, as his biographer tells us, the Duke of Florence, before whom he had sung it, "rushed up and fell upon his neck, swearing that nobody had ever amused him so well."

We see that it was not the most refined states of mind that Fiorilli's art represented, and his subjects for the most part remind us of the buffooneries of modern clowns. But even these may be performed with superior talent, though at present we do not often see it. And that Fiorilli's talent for burlesque was unique is beyond doubt, judging from all we read about it. That Louis XIV. valued him extremely, is a fact of which we possess palpable proofs in the large number of gratuities which, according to old account-books,[2] he received personally of the King, besides the annual subvention of 15,000 frs. granted to the Italian theatre in Paris.

His acquaintance with the great King, however, was of far more ancient date than is indicated by his bio-

---

[1] The first verse of this song runs thus :—

> L' Asinello innamorato
> Canto, è raggia à tutte l' hore
> Pare un Musico affamato
> Quando narra il suo dolore,
> È cantando d' amor va,
> Ut re mi fal sol la.   (*He brays.*)
> *Vie de Scaramouche*, p. 22.

[2] Extracted by Jal, *Dictionnaire Critique.*

grapher Constantini. As early as 1639 he came to Paris during the reign of Louis XIII., and on one occasion was summoned to the court together with his companion, Brigida Bianchi. But the young Dauphin, Louis XIV., a baby at the time, chose to be in a very bad temper, crying and screaming incessantly, and it was impossible to stop him. Then Tiberio Fiorilli promised the Queen that if he might take the child in his arms, he would be sure to calm him. The Queen consented, and the actor made such droll gestures and grimaces that the child's bad temper changed into frantic gaiety, with the result that, to the great amusement of the assembled court, Fiorilli's costume was entirely spoilt. Many years afterwards the King remembered this first meeting with Scaramouch, and always regarded him with favour.

Fiorilli was twice married and many times in love. His first wife was a very distinguished performer of soubrettes, Marinette or Signorina Del Campo (her family name). She died in Italy, while Fiorilli was about to settle in Paris. Here a young and very frivolous girl of inferior station, Marie Duval, ensnared his old heart, so that, in spite of her evident infidelity, he married her in his eightieth year, after which she decorated his head with an ornament much more prominent than any of those which he had ridiculed in his merry art. In the end, Fiorilli had to complain to the King of his unfaithful wife, and she was placed in a house of correction for women of bad repute.

According to his biographer, Fiorilli at his death left about 300,000 frs. to his son, who was a learned and respected priest, besides a considerable legacy to a convent.[1]

Fiorilli's successors as Scaramuccia were Gandini, Rauzini, Benozzi, and others, but none of them equalled him in fame ; in fact, the character died with him.

The only Italian actor whose fame reached the same height as that of Fiorilli, was his somewhat younger colleague, Giuseppe Domenico Biancolelli, born in Bologna in 1640, died in Paris in 1688. He belonged to a family of actors, and from early childhood had been educated for the profession, acting with his parents, who belonged to a company at Bologna. Even as a young man he had gained himself a good name, and was engaged by the company of Tabarini in Vienna. Thence he was called to Paris, in his twentieth year, and here he remained till his death.

In Paris he took an engagement as "second Zanni"— Harlequin, while Locatelli played Trivellino, the first Zanni. We have described above[2] how Domenico, or Dominique as he was usually called in Paris, altered the previous character of Harlequin and created a new type, more intelligent, more witty, and more active than the old. He played nothing but Harlequins, but he knew how to vary them infinitely, just as Fiorilli varied his Scaramuccia.

By his elegance and his adroit manners he became a great favourite at the court of Louis XIV., where he rivalled Fiorilli in the good graces of the illustrious king.

---

[1] *Vie de Scaramouche*, p. 133. Scaramouch, by the way, had many (legitimate and illegitimate) children.

[2] Comp. p. 258.

Within the oval frame: HARLEQUIN · JOSEPH DOMINIQUE · BOULOGNE · EN ITALIE

Decedé à Paris le 2.e Aoust 1688.

Ferdinand Pingeret.   N. Hubert Sculpebat.

Bologne est ma patrie et Paris mon Séjour,
J'y regne avec Eclat sur la Scene Comique
Harlequin sous le masque y cache Dominique
Qui reforme en riant et le peuple et la Cour.

35—Domenico Biancolelli, the Harlequin (after a print by Hubert).

Probably, however, the two comic actors differed very much in style. We have reason to think that the art of Domenico was a good deal more polished and graceful than that of the coarser Scaramuccia. We need only compare their portraits : Domenico in the excellent engraving of Hubert (fig. 35) wears the dress of a duke and smiles like a diplomat ; the whole appearance of Fiorilli—tall and crooked—is one broad grimace.

Domenico was short, and in his later years somewhat fat, which hampered him a little in his art. His face is rather handsome and intelligent, with a touch of irony about his small mouth, and a pair of large, sad eyes. His temperament was indeed melancholy,[1] as is frequently the case with people of much humour.

His death occurred very suddenly and under peculiar circumstances. The dancing-master of Louis XIV. had danced before the King in a ballet in one of the Italian pieces. Now Domenico, who was a very good dancer, took it into his head to mimic the French master, and he did it with such indescribably comic power that the King was exceedingly amused. Domenico, noticing this, went on longer than was good for him. Stout as he was, he became very hot, but had no time to change his clothes, as he had to act immediately after the dance ; so he caught a severe chill, took inflammation of the lungs, and died after a week's illness. The fashionable paper at the time, the *Mercure de France*, among other things had this verse about him :—

[1] Of course the imperishable anecdote told of most comic actors is repeated about Domenico—that the doctor, in reply to his request for a remedy against melancholia, says : " Go and see Domenico as Harlequin." Where this anecdote originated, it is difficult to say ; probably nowhere.

Cependant il est mort ; tout le monde en soupire :
Qui l'eût jamais pensé sans se désespérer,
Que l'aimable Arlequin qui nous a tant fait rire
Dût sitôt nous faire pleurer !

For about seventeen or eighteen years Domenico had been the main pillar of the Italian theatre in Paris. So his sudden death was a very severe blow to the actors. The theatre was closed for a month, and before it was reopened, the following characteristic bill was posted :— " We have long shown our despondency by our silence, and we should prolong it further, if the fear of displeasing you were not stronger than our just grief. We reopen our theatre on Wednesday next, the first day of September 1688 [Domenico died on the 2nd of August]. Impossible as it is to compensate for the loss we have sustained, we offer you the best which our care and diligence have been able to produce. Please receive us with some indulgence, and be convinced that we shall not omit anything by which we may add to your pleasure." [1]

After his death a little book about him was published in Paris, bearing the title: *Arlequiniana, ou les bons mots, les histoires plaisantes et agréables, recueillies des conversations d'Arlequin* (1694). The book was written by the actor Carlo Cotolendi, and it is as unreliable, insipid, and devoid of taste as Constantini's *Vie de Scaramouche.* Nevertheless its tedious anecdotes are repeated in all the handbooks.

Unlike Fiorilli, Domenico Biancolelli had many excellent successors. The very year after his death,

[1] Related by Maurice Sand, i. 78.

on the 1st of October 1689, Evariste Gherardi (comp. fig. 27) made his first appearance.   He distinguished himself not only in his profession, but also by publishing a large collection of plays under the title of *Théâtre italien de Gherardi,*[1] *ou le Recueil gén. de toutes les coméd. et scènes Françoises jouées par les Coméd. Ital.*

The son of Domenico, Pietro Francesco Biancolelli (b. 1680), was also a clever Harlequin.   He acted under his father's name, Domenico, in the French provinces and in Italy, in Paris from 1710 to 1717 at the Fair of St Germain, and elsewhere.[2]

In the year 1697 all the Italian actors were dismissed from the service of Louis XIV., and the Italian theatre in Paris was closed.   Hitherto Paris had been the favourite resort of all the Italians, the place where they gained their name and fame, where they basked in the sunshine of the grace of *le roi soleil,* and enjoyed his gold, and where most of them remained till their death.   The reason of their dismissal was, that in order to give additional attraction to a play, they had committed the blunder of giving it the title of a prohibited novel, *La fausse prude* (The False Prude), and this was considered as an offence against Mme. de Maintenon, the King's mistress, well known for her bigotry.   The theatre was closed without mercy.   In fact the play had nothing whatever to do with the supposed allusion.   Its original

---

[1] It is stated everywhere that Gherardi died on the very day when he had been in Versailles and presented his newly-published book to the Dauphin.   As far as I know, however, the *Théâtre italien* did not appear till 1717, and Gherardi died in 1700.

[2] He was not therefore, as stated by Ad. Bartoli, who is usually so trustworthy (*op. cit.* clxxvi.), the immediate successor of his father; besides, he was only eight years old when his father died.

title was *La finta matrigna* (The Pretended Step-
mother), but it was never performed, so the Italians
never had an opportunity of proving their innocence.

The chief pillar of the company, and perhaps also
the originator of the stupid blunder, was — besides
Evariste Gherardi—the frivolous and impudent Angelo
Constantini, or Mezzetino (his stage name), the biographer of Scaramouch. He had been acting in Paris
since 1682, had played with Domenico, and gained
success by his fresh and cheerful acting, which was supported by a very expressive and lively face (fig. 36).[1]
He had good ideas off as well as on the stage. Thus
the Brothers Parfait, historians of the French theatre
from the preceding century, relate a really amusing
story about him. He had dedicated a play of his own
composition to the Duke of Saint-Agnan, and was going
to lay the book in his hands, hoping to receive a handsome gratuity for his attention, for the Duke was noted
for his liberality. So one morning he went to the
Palace, but the Swiss guard would not admit him on
any consideration. In order to dispose him more favourably, Constantini promised him one-third of the fee he
expected to receive, and he was admitted. But on the
stairs he met the chief lackey, who was as unmanageable
as the guard. Constantini promised him the second
third, and now he advanced as far as the antechamber
of the Duke. But here he was met by the valet, who
was even more inflexible than the two others, and it was
with the greatest difficulty that he was admitted to the

[1] In the excellent engraving by Vermeulen it bears no slight resemblance to the well-known features of the elder Coquelin.

36—Angelo Constantini as Mezzetino (after a print by Vermeulen).

Duke's presence, after promising the valet the last third.

No sooner had the door opened, than he went straight up to the Duke, presented him with the book and said: "Your Highness, here is a book which I have taken the liberty of dedicating to you, and for which I desire you to give me a hundred lashes."

The Duke of course asked why he wished for such an uncommon reward. Constantini explained the difficulties he had had in obtaining admission, whereupon the Duke gave his servants a good scolding, and sent a hundred sovereigns to Constantini's wife, who had promised nothing.

When the Italian company was dissolved, Constantini accepted an engagement in Brunswick, where Augustus II., Elector of Saxony and King of Poland, sent for him to form an Italian company of actors and singers to give performances in Dresden.

He was glad to accept the offer, and acquitted himself of the task with so much skill, that Augustus ennobled him and made him a chamberlain.

But here again it was a king's mistress who became fatal to him. Constantini, who in Paris had been very successful with the fair sex, fell in love with the favourite mistress of Augustus—we know he had a large number of them—and made her a declaration of love. But this was not all; in her presence he ridiculed his patron, the King, and tried to lower him in her eyes. Augustus got wind of the matter, and concealed himself in her room at a time when the lovers were to have a meeting.

What happened on that occasion never transpired, except that the King rushed out from his concealment, sword in hand, and threatened to cut off the actor's head. However, he changed his mind, and contented himself with having the culprit arrested and put in prison in the castle of Königstein.

Here poor Mezzetino had to remain for twenty long years. Then another mistress of Augustus—we do not know why—took pity on him, and persuaded the King to visit the State prison. The actor—formerly so bold and elegant, now an old man with a beard which had been allowed to grow ever since he entered the prison— fell on his knees before him. Some months after he was released, and his property was returned to him, but he was banished from Dresden, and from the dukedom of Saxony.

Then Constantini went to his native town, Verona. But after some years his restless mind, and perhaps want of money, called him back to Paris. Meanwhile, in 1716, a new Italian company had been formed in this town after the death of Louis XIV. ; it was the so-called *Troupe du Régent*, under the leadership of Luigi Riccoboni. And old Mezzetino, who was now past sixty, applied to his old colleagues and proposed what we should call a series of star performances. His companions, to whom it was a joyful surprise to see Mezzetino again after so many years of fateful vicissitudes, and who perhaps expected a sensational success, at once engaged Constantini for five performances for the tolerably large sum of 3000 frs. And they were not deceived. The concourse was so enormous, that in spite of the doubled entrance-fee, the multitude of people who had to remain outside equalled the number which the playhouse could hold. Luigi Riccoboni had written a prologue for the occasion, in which Mezzetino presents himself before Momus[1] as a venerable old man, and thus by his order strips off his old man's clothes and stands forth in his former Mezzetino costume. Then he tells a dream he has had. He dreamt that he was again in Paris, in the Italian theatre. Out of the floor came a guitar, and he felt as if he would still be able to sing, though he was so old. While he was talking, of course a guitar came up through a trap-door, and Mezzetino took it and sang an insinuating song to the enthusiastic public.

After this last triumph, Angelo Constantini returned to Verona, where he died at the close of the same year, 1729.

The troupe he had joined was one of the most celebrated Italian companies, and had won its fame both by the excellence of its actors and by its good repertoire. Its leader, Luigi Riccoboni, has several times been mentioned and quoted as author of one of the principal sources of the history of the Italian comedy of masks. His private character was the reverse of Constantini's, and he was one of the actors who by his education and intelligence contributed most to the honour of the profession.

He belonged to an old and distinguished family of actors. His father, Antonio Riccoboni, was an excellent Pantalone at the court of the Duke of Modena, and won

[1] The deity of ridicule and raillery.

particular fame by his boldness in refusing the invitation of Louis XIV. when this king summoned him to Versailles in 1670. His son Luigi also began his career in Modena, which was his native town as well as his father's. He was born in 1675 or 1677. At that time the company in the service of the Duke was managed by a lady, a clever and energetic actress named Diana.[1] She christened Riccoboni with the stage name of Lelio, under which he acted ever afterwards, instead of Federigo, which he had chosen himself, but which she did not consider theatrical enough.[2] She also supplied him with a wife, a young actress of the company, whom she made him marry, but who died soon after; and Riccoboni was married again in 1707 to the clever actress Elena Balletti, well known under the stage name of Flaminia.

Both Lelio and Flaminia were deeply interested in literature. It was Lelio's ambition to revive the drama of the classical Renaissance, comedy as well as tragedy, which by this time had almost entirely disappeared from the boards of the Italian theatre. In these efforts he was strongly supported by the Marchese Maffei, who wrote his *Merope* for him, or rather for his wife; but not so much by the public, which preferred to see the improvised comedy to which it was accustomed. He was an author himself, and both wrote and translated after the best models; thus he produced Racine's *Britannicus* in Italian.

---

[1] E. Campardon, in his *Comédiens du roi de la troupe italienne*, thinks that her real name was Teresa Corona.

[2] Comp. A. Ademollo: *Una famiglia di Comici Italiani nel secolo decimottavo, Firenze*, 1885, p. 7.

Flaminia, who was called the Isabella Andreini of her time, was perfectly at home in the poetry of her country, and was herself a talented authoress. The best among her tolerably numerous writings is perhaps her sharp critique of Mirabaud's bad French translation of Tasso's *Gerusalemma liberata*, a critique which was written in the form of a letter to the well-known Abbé Conti ; with the result, by the bye, that the French translator in a subsequent edition corrected a number of the worst faults, and thanked his beautiful reviewer for her censure. It is also interesting to read her opinion of the so-called "new manner" of the French actor Baron.

In the year 1716 the two Riccobonis came to Paris on the invitation of the Regent, Philippe of Orléans, and reopened the Italian theatre with a first-rate company, which included, among others, the excellent Harlequin Tommaso Antonio Visentini, called Thomassin, the Pantalone Pietro Alborghetti, the distinguished and cultured Giuseppe Balletti, *secondo amoroso*, under the name of Mario, and his wife, the charming Rosa Benozzi (Silvia). Riccoboni himself played the first lovers and the tragic parts, his wife all the prima-donnas. In a certain sense we may say that the appearance of the Riccoboni company in Paris marked the culminating period of the Italian *Commedia dell' Arte*, but at that time it had already lost something of its peculiar and national character, and by degrees, as the actors gained a firmer footing in France—both Riccoboni and his wife were naturalised there—their repertoire and their style of acting were strongly influenced by their Parisian surroundings, so that even their language became a jargon, half Italian half French, which as a curiosity might for the moment produce a comic effect, but which in the long-run could not help foredooming Italian art to extinction. It is characteristic enough that the principal work of Riccoboni, the *History of the Italian Theatre*, is written in French, whereas his didactic poem, *On Representative Art*, which he wrote during a sojourn in London, is in Italian.

As an actor, Riccoboni's strongest point seems to have been the expression of violent passion, and he is commended for his lively and natural acting. However, the criticisms of those times are seldom descriptive ; and, as a rule, they are one-sided in their praise and blame. Therefore it is very difficult to form a clear opinion of the different artistic characters.

Riccoboni, like many of the Italian actors, was very religious. In the year 1729 he retired from the leadership of the Parisian company, and went with his wife and son to Italy, where he had been nominated "Superintendent of Court Entertainments" by the Duke of Parma ; but when the Duke died shortly afterwards, Riccoboni retired altogether from the theatre from religious motives. In a work which he composed and wrote in French during his leisure, and which he called *An Essay on a Reform of the Theatre*, he expresses his opinion that the best thing would be to abolish the theatre altogether. But considering the great difficulties which such a radical measure would meet with, he suggests that the governments should at least forbid dancing in the theatre, as well as the acting of plays which are exclusively built on love intrigues.

Though his wife also was, or at least became, bigoted, she nevertheless returned to the Italian theatre, and continued acting quite up to the year 1752. In her youth she was idolised by the Parisians, but we suppose that, like many other actors and actresses, she had the weakness not to discover that she had grown old; for in later times she was not always spoken of with enthusiasm.

The adventurous fortune-hunter, Jaques Casanova, in his *History of my Life* describes a visit which he paid the old Riccobonis in Paris in the year 1750. He writes as follows : " Under her stage name of Flaminia she was known in the literary world by some translations.[1] . . . As I had been introduced to Flaminia as an aspirant in the literary world, she thought I should feel honoured if she talked to me ; but she was mistaken, for I found her unpleasant in face, style, accent, and everything, even in the tone of her voice. She made me understand, though not in words, that famous as she was herself in literature, she knew she spoke to an insect. She seemed to dictate, thinking that at her age of sixty years or more, she had a right to do so, particularly with a novice of twenty-five, who had not enriched any library as yet. In order to please her, I mentioned the Abbé Conti, and occasionally quoted a verse of this deep author. In a kindly way the lady corrected my pronunciation of the word *scevra*, which means 'apart,' and said it ought to be pronounced *sceura*, asking me not to take amiss being taught this on the first day I spent

---

[1] Casanova does not do the old actress justice. She had published much more than some translations.

in Paris, and adding that it would make an epoch in my life.

"'Madam, I have come here in order to learn, not to lose what I have learned; and you will allow me to tell you that one ought to say *scevra* with a *v*, and not *sceura* with a *u*; for the word is a contraction of *scevera*.'

"'Well, we shall see which of us is wrong.'

"'It is you, Madam, according to Ariosto, who rhymes *scevra* with *persevra*, a word which would rhyme badly with *sceura*, which is not Italian.'

"She was persisting in her opinion, when her husband, an old man of eighty,[1] told her that she was wrong.   She said no more, but henceforth she told everybody that I was an impostor.[2]

"The husband of this woman, Louis Riccoboni, called Lelio, the same who in 1716 had taken the company to Paris in the service of the Duke-Regent, was a man of merit.

"He had been a very fine man, and justly enjoyed public esteem, on account of his talent as well as on account of the purity of his life."

Clearly enough, Casanova's description is rather

---

[1] In 1750 Luigi Riccoboni was seventy-three or seventy-five.   He says himself that in 1690 he was thirteen years old.   Comp. *Hist. du Th. ital.* i. 73.

[2] As a matter of fact, Casanova was something of an impostor, and as Elena Riccoboni no doubt through her correspondents in Italy knew all about his deserts, it was quite natural that her manner towards him should not be particularly gracious.   By this time she had withdrawn entirely from the world, if not from the theatre.   Casanova was himself the son of an Italian actress, and it is not likely that his antecedents were unknown to the leading members of the Italian theatre.—The above description is found in the *Mémoires de Jaques Casanova de Seingalt*, Paris, 1843, i. 547.

biassed, but other authors as well have spoken somewhat depreciatingly of her in her later years.   Nevertheless, she died deeply respected (in 1774), and—unlike the French actors—was buried with all ecclesiastical honours in the Church of St Sauveur.   Luigi Riccoboni died in 1753.

In 1707, the first year after their marriage, the Riccobonis had a son, Anton Francesco Valentino, who adopted the profession of his parents, and at the age of nineteen mounted the boards for the first time in Marivaux's *La Surprise d'Amour*.   Two years previously a dramatic work of the young actor had been performed, and his first appearance seemed to augur for the best. According to the custom of the time, his father introduced him to the public from the stage, soliciting the indulgence of the audience for the young beginner, and a poetic spectator expressed his good wishes and encouragement in the following lines :—

> Pour ton fils, Lelio, ne sois pas alarmé,
> Il n'a pas besoin d'indulgence ;
> D'un heureux coup d'essai le parterre charmé
> N'a pu lui refuser toute sa bienveillance :
> Pour ses succès futurs cesse donc de trembler ;
> Que nulle crainte ne t'agite,
> Si ce n'est d'avoir dans la suite
> Un généreux rival qui pourra t'égaler.

However, these glorious predictions were not to be entirely fulfilled.   Francesco Riccoboni was certainly a clever man, but owing to his restless disposition he never came quite to the front, either as an actor or as an author.   He left the stage several times — once on account of a quarrel with a *machinist*, afterwards in order to devote himself to the study of alchemy and to the culture of silk-worms, by which two pursuits he succeeded in ruining himself entirely. In his fifty-second year he had to return to the theatre. One of his specialities was parody, which he cultivated as actor and author with his colleagues and collaborators Romagnesi and Biancolelli. At that time parody was one of the chief attractions of the Italian theatre. When the French stage had a success in tragedy, the Italians soon after produced a parody on the same subject. Voltaire, in particular, was chosen as a victim. Thus by the joint efforts of the literary partnership, Romagnesi, Biancolelli, and Riccoboni, *Zaïre* was converted into *i Trovatelli*, or "The Sultan Civilised by Love."[1] He was a member of the well-known select company *Le Caveau*, which included, among others, Collé and Crébillon fils; and, like his colleagues, he wrote verses in honour of wine and love. We also possess a critical work from his pen on dramatic art: *L'art de théâtre*, printed in 1750. He died in 1772. The malicious Abbé Voisenon made the appropriate remark about him: "He is a man on whom God seems to have bestowed great gifts in order that he should perpetually make the wrong choice in his use of them."

In the year 1734 he had married a young Parisian girl of a somewhat doubtful family, Marie Jeanne Laboras di Mézières, who, like all her relations, chose

---

[1] Voltaire feigned great indifference to these parodies, but when in 1748 he learned that a parody on *Semiramis* was in preparation, he at once hurried to the Queen and obtained an interdict against it.—Ademollo, p. 33, note 1.

the theatrical career; but she was a bad actress. A contemporary chronicler writes of her : " Madame Riccoboni, a witty authoress, and a gay lady of fashion, but a very bad actress, has played lovers' parts for twenty-six years. Her age and appearance have compelled her to abandon this speciality and to undertake the maternal parts, which she has never acted in private life, though she has been perpetually working for this purpose."

Mme. Ricoboni was much more successful in literature than on the stage : she wrote several novels in the English style,[1] which won great favour, though she was rather advanced in age when she began writing. In the year 1792 she died, old and poor, in Paris, ruined by the Revolution, which deprived her of her pension.

We have mentioned already that the Ricoboni company included the Harlequin-player Thomassin (Antonio Tomaso Visentini). He had acted for a long time in Italy, before Paris set a seal on his fame. He was a great acrobat, but his break-neck performances all round the theatre, on the highest balconies of the auditorium, frightened the public more than they amused them, and were peremptorily forbidden. It was he, too, who in *Don Giovanni* performed the trick we have mentioned before, of turning a somersault with the full wine-glass in his hand.

However, in addition to this dexterity, he possessed real dramatic gifts, which, strange to say, were in the serious line. In the midst of his jokes he would bring

---

[1] Grimm speaks very favourably of her books in his correspondence, and they were still appreciated at the time of Sainte-Beuve. The most noted among them are: *Fanny Butler*, *Mylady Catesby*, *Lettres d'Elisabeth-Sophie de Vallière*, etc.

out pathetic points which brought tears to the eyes of
the spectators.   The brothers Parfait write of him : . . .
" Nature had made an excellent actor of him, taking
the term in its widest sense.   True, simple, original,
pathetic, amid roars of laughter called forth by his jokes,
he could make the tears flow by the touch of feeling
which he imparted to a thought or a word, thus surprising the author as well as the public ; and this effect was
so much the more astonishing, if we consider that he
appeared under a mask which was meant to cause fright
as well as laughter.   Frequently, when you had begun
by laughing at the way in which he expressed pain, you
ended by sharing the emotion which apparently filled
him."

He does not seem to have been equally fortunate in
comic improvisation ; this, at any rate, is the opinion of
Collé.[1]   He writes as follows about him and his successor
Carlino on the occasion of the appearance of a third
Harlequin : " Monday 21st inst. [June 1751] I went to
the Italian play and saw a new Harlequin, who has been
acting there for several days.   He is a pretty nimble
scamp, a vaulter, a kind of rope-dancer, a juggler, but
a feeble actor ; as he is only here on his passage through,
the Italians would not have committed the blunder of
allowing him to appear on the stage, if he had surpassed
or merely equalled Carlin, their present Harlequin.   The
latter, who has been acting this part for some years,
does not acquit himself badly, though he frequently

---

[1] Charles Collé, 1709-1783, author of comedies and songs, member of
the company *Le Caveau*, in his *Journal historique* gives a pretty sharp
criticism of the contemporary Italian company.

lacks ease in his action, and is always stupid at repartee [that is, improvised repartee], whatever the adherents of this bad kind of play may say. Thomassin, the predecessor of Carlin, was at least as stupid as he, even more so perhaps ; but in compensation for this defect, there was a constant fire in his action and an inimitable grace. Besides, this actor possessed a strong point— and a very surprising one in a Harlequin,—he was pathetic : he moved you to tears in certain plays, as in *The Double Inconsistency*, *Timon*, *The Island of Slaves*, etc., which, considering the Harlequin mask, has always seemed a miracle to me." [1]

Tommasino died at the age of fifty-seven, in 1739, and after two years was succeeded by Carlin, mentioned above by Collé. His real name was Carlo Bertinazzi. Collé, no doubt, is too severe in his judgment ; at least nearly all other contemporary critics are unanimous in exalting him both as a man and as an actor. Most important of all is the judgment of Garrick. This great English actor was his good friend, and appreciated him highly. But the story about the friendship between Carlin and Pope Clement XIV. is no doubt a fiction. It has been made the subject of a novel and a play,[2] in which we see the Holy Father rehearse the parts of Harlequin and borrow money of him. At least we do not suppose the connection between these two men to have been more

[1] C. Collé : *Journal et Mémoires*, ed. Bonhomme, i. 328.
[2] The novel was called *Clément XIV. et Carlo Bertinazzi Correspondance inédite*. It pretended to be a genuine correspondence between the two men, but it was composed by a man named De la Touche, and was full of absurdities. The play is by Rochefort and Lemoine. Ademollo in his above-mentioned book very ingeniously unravels the whole tissue about the friendship between the Pope and the comic actor.

than an early acquaintance which was afterwards discontinued.

But of the success of Carlo Bertinazzi in Paris there can be no doubt whatever; it found expression in many ways, among others in admiring verses. Perhaps we may also consider it as a proof of his fame that the small Russian pug-dogs, whose black faces recall the mask of Harlequin, were, and still are, called carlins. Like his namesakes, Bertinazzi became very stout in his old age; yet he continued to act till his death, which occurred in his seventy-third year. Goldoni writes of him in his Memoirs, that " Nature had bestowed matchless gifts upon him: his appearance, his gestures, his movements, predisposed people in his favour; his manners and his talent gained him admiration on the stage and favour in society. Carlino was the favourite of the public." It is said, by the bye, that Bertinazzi was the model of Goldoni's *Le bourru bienfaisant*.

Just as Carlo Bertinazzi was "the last Harlequin," that is, the last who gained real fame in this part, and with whom, so to speak, the character died out, so we may say that Antonio Mattia Collalto was "the last Pantalone." Originally he was an officer, but he abandoned the military career and gained great reputation in Italy as Pantalone. In the year 1759 he came to Paris, where he continued to act till his death in 1777, and gained unanimous praise for the naturalness and variety with which he performed the part of the not particularly interesting Pantalone. He reaped his most glorious success in a play of his own composition, *The Venetian Triplets*, in which he acted the three brothers

with the most wonderful characterisation of each, so that
in spite of the simplicity of his acting, and though he
had taken off the traditional mask, the spectators could
scarcely realise that it was indeed the same man who
represented the three different characters.   Francesco
Bartoli, the old writer on the stage, describes his acting
in the following way : "All he did was to change wigs ;
according to the character he performed, he wore a black
or a grey (round) wig, or a third one, after the French
fashion, with a pouch attached to it ; with this small, yet
important change, and by disguising his voice and varying his carriage, many of the spectators never could
understand that it was he alone who performed the
three characters."

Even critics who did not care for the Italian comedy
of that time were bound to acknowledge his talent, and
his unassuming and domesticated private life was
respected by all.   Grimm, who elsewhere deals many a
sharp blow at the comedian's *dell' arte*, says in his *Correspondence* (September 1777) on the death of Collalto :
"Among the irreparable losses which art and literature
have suffered this year, we must not forget Sieur Collalto,
who acted the part of Pantalone in the Italian Comedy.
Besides being an admirable actor, he possessed the
merit of having composed several excellent plays, *e.g.*,
The Triplets, a work with a masterly constructed plot, full
of original situations and genuine comic art.   Under the
most hideous and ludicrous mask, there was no feeling,
no passion, which he was not capable of representing with
much warm feeling and truth ; his talent overcame the
difficulties which lay in the incongruity of the costume

with the subjects represented.   In the above-mentioned comedy, where he acted without mask, he was seen to produce the most complete illusion, to act simultaneously, so to speak, three absolutely different parts, to appear by turns passionately in love, brusque and stern, awkward and idiotic, and all this with a truly magic spell, so that even eyes which knew him well could hardly recognise him.   His private character bore the stamp of a modesty and simplicity which are not common in his class.   He knew no other happiness than to live peacefully with his family and to do good to the poor and suffering who appealed to his liberality."

We have pursued the history of the Italian comedy of masques beyond the proper limit of time prescribed by the present volume ; for such as this peculiar speciality of dramatic art was born during the Renaissance, such it remained essentially unaltered till the earlier part of the eighteenth century.   At this period a turning-point occurs in its life.

In foreign countries people were tiring of it.   Even in France, where it had rooted itself so deeply, its ground began to shake, and in Germany, where the improvised comedy had passed into the hands of national actors, it had come to be considered as a dangerous weed, which ought to be rooted out.

Even in Italy its own adherents turned against it. Carlo Goldoni, who had been one of the most fertile and skilful authors of scenarios, afterwards wished to do away altogether with the character in the comedy of masques ; and Carlo Gozzi, their most zealous advocate and adherent, did not remain quite faithful to the end.

It must not be supposed, however, that the improvised comedy is dead, any more than its masks. It still
lives and thrives in Italy, though it has fallen somewhat
low in its old age ; it no longer receives subventions and
pensions from great European princes, but has to be
content with small popular booths, and with the *soldi*
which the poor but enthusiastic audience are willing to
pay.

But there is an end of its going abroad. In other
European countries it is only seen in effigy at puppet-
shows, where Polichinelle, Guignol, Punch and Judy,
Hans Wurst, Master Jakel are the last relics of the
masks of the once all-powerful Comedy of Art.[1]

But though out of Italy the *Commedia dell'Arte* is
no longer alive amongst us, it has left many important
traces everywhere. What Molière owes to it as author
and actor is incalculable. Many of his comedies are
simply imitations of the Italian scenarios, and not only
in subject and construction ; even the dialogues bear a
distinct stamp of their prototypes, in the short, quick
repartee *à coups de ricochet*, occasionally interrupted by
long, set speeches, which form a kind of rest or culminating point after the feverishly rapid verbal combat. As
an actor Molière studied directly after Italian models, and
in the provinces as well as during the first part of his
career in Paris he played his comic parts entirely in the
Italian style, improvising and wearing a mask.

In Spain, as in England, the Italian influence is also
unmistakable, though it has not left quite such deep

---

[1] In its Tivoli-Pantomime Copenhagen possesses a more distinct reminiscence of the Italian Comedy of Art.

marks as in France; in Germany improvised dramatic
art and harlequinades, direct imitations from the Italian,
reigned supreme on the boards for a long time.   How
much of the Italian influence passed into our own
(Danish) dramatic art through Holberg it is difficult to
ascertain; but that Holberg himself received very important impulses from this theatre seems unquestionable.

So comedy has been of incalculable importance
to dramatic art everywhere in Europe.   Just as
the insects who flutter about from flower to flower,
help to bring about the fecundation of the otherwise helpless plants, so the bright variegated masks
whirled from country to country in ignorance of the
civilising fecundation which they brought with them,
and equally ignorant of the fact that the magnificent
fruit which was developing itself before their eyes was
a production of their own.

Later they got a clearer understanding of their own
value, and went so far as to consider themselves the
only supporters of pure dramatic art.   They despised
those who could only recite what they had learned by
heart, and were of opinion that the genuine dramatic
gift lay in improvisation alone.

They forgot that the strength of dramatic art does
not consist in *what* is said, but in *how* it is said.

THE DEVELOPMENT OF THE STAGE
OF THE RENAISSANCE

The Stage a simple Platform—Construction of the English Stage in the time of Shakespeare—The Spanish Stage—" *Le décor simultané* " in France—The Olympian Theatre of Palladio—The Italian Principle of Decoration—Lighting of the Stage.

THE theatre of the Renaissance is distinguished from that of the Middle Ages by two principal features: dramatic art passes into the hands of professional actors, and the performances are removed from the open air into roofed buildings.

So long as plays were popular public festivals, to which everybody contributed his share in proportion to his capacity, it was possible to surround them with the magnificent display which we noticed in the great mysteries, and to spend so much time and money in the preparations that these performances became land-marks in the history of the town or country-district in question.

The conditions became very different when dramatic performances slipped into the hands of professional actors, who were just beginning to form a separate class. The first actors were poor people, whom the struggle for bread compelled to wander from place to place. Like all vagrants, they were looked upon with suspicion by the magistrates and by sedate domiciled citizens, and since the payment they took for their performances was considered as a kind of begging, the authorities always took good care that they should not ask too much. But even if they had gained more than they did, the great apparatus of the mysteries would have far surpassed their capacities, and matters took such a turn that plays sank from the greatest extravagance to the uttermost simplicity. Thereupon, as a matter of course, the mysteries were excluded from the stage, for they could not exist without pomp, splendour, and great expense, and repertoires came to consist of farces and moralities, and afterwards also of comedies, tragedies, tragi-comedies, and pastorals, all written for and adapted to the requirements of the new stage.

It was, moreover, of vital importance to the new class of actors to play much more frequently than had hitherto been customary. But this circumstance soon compelled them to seek refuge inside a building. They could not repeatedly expose themselves to the risk of having their performances spoiled by torrents of rain or other inclemencies of temperature.

In Italy, with its equable climate, the risk was not so great, and even to this day there are many open-air theatres in that country. But while these modern *arenas* —as they are called—have only their auditorium un-covered, the ancient Renaissance theatre in its simplest form was as free and open as possible.

It consisted of a square wooden platform about six feet high, covered by canvas all round the bottom. The front and sides of the stage were open ; the back con-sisted of a decorated curtain fastened to a partition of laths. Behind this background was the dressing-room used by actors and actresses together, into which they retired also during the intervals of their acting. For the mediæval custom that all performers remained visible to the audience during the whole play, no longer suited the conditions of the stage, for one thing, because in the small professional companies the same actor had frequently to play several parts, and because the new repertoires required various entrances and exits, in some cases with constant changes of costume.

The decorative back-cloth was either painted as a landscape in perspective, a street, etc., and in this case the actors went in and out by simply pulling the curtain a little one way or the other. This is shown in the small but very distinct and instructive etching by Callot, seen above (fig. 18). Or the background consisted simply of draperies, and in this case the actors went in and out in different places, and where they were supposed to listen unseen to some speech on the stage, they put their heads between its folds. The latter kind of background seems to have been most commonly used; at least in most illustrations we notice such a richly-folded back-cloth with heads peeping out; comp. fig. 19. Undoubtedly this was the older arrangement, and the painted curtain a later reform.

French engravings of the sixteenth century show exactly the same scenic construction, except that the theatre is found inside a building. The engravings both of Jean de Gourmont and of Liefrinck (figs. 14 and 15) have the same wooden platform—in the former it is a little more than a man's height—and the same richly-folded drapery as background. In a third French engraving (fig. 37)—a small page of an edition of Terence of the close of the sixteenth century—we find a somewhat more defined and detailed construction.   Here the drapery is divided into four parts, each with its super-scription, *i.e.*, there were four distinct indications of localities on the stage.

In all the pictures of those times which have come in my way, the stage proper was quite empty ; but the pictures alluded to, it must be observed, all represented scenes from comedies or farces.   There is no reason to suppose that in tragedies, tragi-comedies, and pastorals, they did not make use of certain properties, such as trees, rocks, caves, though they may have been of the simplest description.

A peculiar scenic construction is shown in fig. 38, also a French engraving of the sixteenth century.   In the middle of an oval hall there is a low raised platform, much lower than those hitherto mentioned, which were either in the open air or at one end of a hall.   The plat-form in this illustration is divided into two parts : the larger division, which is in front, is quite low and open, and it seems as if this were the part on which the action proper was represented ; the back division is raised some steps higher, and is evidently covered by a roof resting on pillars.   Here the actors are seated during the intervals between their appearances.   The spectators are placed all round, standing or sitting on the floor, and also in boxes higher up along the walls all round the hall.

We do not know what Parisian theatre this drawing is meant to represent, but we cannot doubt that it was used by some amateur company, being the hall of a convent or a university, in which the stage was arranged

37

38

37—Draped stage of the 16th century (title-page of an edition of Terence).
38—A Parisian theatre of the 16th century.

for this particular occasion. But the picture is of special importance, because it brings us into contact with, and throws light upon, the contemporary English theatre.

The English theatre was peculiar both in its outward and inward construction. While other nations, when the stage was transferred from the open air to the interior of a building, adapted themselves to circumstances and made use of the rooms at hand—tennis-courts, banqueting halls, yards, etc.—and raised their platform at one end of the space, the English adhered more persistently to ancient customs; though not to the stages formerly used for pageants, which were only suitable for festal processions, or occasionally for acrobatic performances on market-days and the like. But why not use the old remains of Roman amphitheatres, or imitations of them, in which had been acted mysteries and miracle-plays? Why not adhere to the form which was appropriate to all kinds of plays? With their habitual common sense, and with a clever calculation of public taste, the English arranged their first theatres with a double purpose.

There already existed arenas on which such popular entertainments as bear-baiting and bull-baiting, fencing, rope-dancing, and so on, were performed. On such an arena it was easy to construct a movable stage; and with the addition of a building to which the actors might retire, and in which costumes, properties, and other material might be kept, the national English theatre would be complete.

Except, however, for one thing. The standing difficulty was to make the public pay for admission. In the open arenas the managers had to depend almost entirely on the liberality of the people, and could not effectively ensure the payment of the proper fee by everyone. But this difficulty was overcome as soon as the first real theatre was constructed in London.

It was the actor and master-joiner, James Burbage, the father of Richard Burbage, the famous player of Shakespeare, and a leading member of the Earl of Leicester's company, who built the first stage and called it briefly "the Theatre"; and in order to secure the proper fee from each spectator, he surrounded the boxes of the arena by the high tower-like wall, which gives such a peculiar appearance to the oldest English theatres. There is no extant drawing of Burbage's "Theatre"— all we know is that it was circular—but we do not suppose that it differed very much from the other old stages: "The Curtain," "The Rose," "The Hope," "The Swan," and somewhat later, "The Globe." The sub-joined drawing (fig. 39) represents the outward appearance of the Globe Theatre, and the pictures we have seen of other theatres are much in the same style.[1]

The English theatres were built entirely of wood, and not always very solidly constructed. Thus in 1583 the boxes in the "Bear-Garden" amphitheatre collapsed, and many persons perished. As this sad accident happened on a Sunday, it was considered a punishment from Heaven because the day of rest had been misused for worldly plays. The outward appearance of the English theatre is distinctly shown in our illustration. There is a high polygonal tower-like building enclosing a yard.

[1] In T. Fairman Ordish's *Early London Theatres*, Lond. 1894, there are excellent illustrations of "The Hope" and "The Swan."

39—The Globe Theatre in London.

Above the outer wall we see the top of the actors' building, which also serves as a store-house, and here the flag of the theatre is seen waving when performances are going on.

About the inside of the English theatre we have tolerably clear information, partly from contemporary descriptions and builders' contracts, partly from a unique drawing (fig. 40) by the Dutch scholar Johannes de Witt, a drawing which, rough as it is, illustrates the scenic construction better than many descriptions could do.

The illustration was found (in the Utrecht library) and published ten years ago by Dr K. Th. Gaedertz,[1] accompanied by a Latin description, also by Johannes de Witt, which in translation runs as follows: "There are in London four theatres (*amphitheatra*) worth seeing on account of their beauty, which bear different names according to their signs. Various plays (*varia scaena*) are performed in them daily before the people. The two most magnificent of them are situated south of the Thames, and are called after their signs 'The Rose' and 'The Swan.' The others are situated outside the town to the north, on the road reached by passing through 'Biscopgate.' There is also a fifth, but of a different construction, devoted to fights between animals, in which bears, bulls, and wonderfully large dogs are reared in separate cages and pits; they are incited to fight with

[1] In his pamphlet *Zur Kenntniss der altenglischen Bühne,* etc., Bremen, 1888. The importance of the drawing, and the explanation given of it by Dr Gaedertz soon after its publication, were the subject of an article of rare erudition by Mr William Archer ("A Sixteenth Century Playhouse") in *The Universal Review,* 1888.

each other, which is a very delightful sight to the people. Of all the theatres the largest and most magnificent is the one which has a swan for its sign (generally called ' The Swan Theatre '), as it holds three thousand people, and is built of a substance chiefly consisting of flint stone (of which there is a great abundance in England) supported by wooden pillars, which are painted in such admirable imitation of marble as to deceive even the sharpest eye. And as its form seems to be an imitation of Roman work, I have given the above illustration of it."

Of the history of the Swan Theatre we do not know very much. It was opened in 1595, and therefore was quite new when Johannes de Witt wrote his description of it, if Gaedertz is right in his assertion that the drawing dates from 1596. It is not at all likely that any company connected with Shakespeare ever acted in this theatre ; at any rate the three figures on the stage cannot, as has been suggested, represent Malvolio, Olivia, and Maria in *Twelfth Night*, as that play is probably of four or five years' later date.

But though this theatre never saw the performance of a Shakespearian play, there can be no doubt that it presents a normal stage of the time of Shakespeare, and that it was really considered as a model structure. This appears for one thing from the fact that some years later it was stipulated by contract that the Hope Theatre should be built in exactly the same style as the Swan. This contract[1] is still extant, and it tells us that

[1] It is reproduced in part in the above-mentioned work by Ordish, p. 257 f.

Posticus

sedilia

orchestra

mimorum aedes

ingressus

proscenium

tectum

planities sive arena.

Ex observationibus Londinensibus Johannis de Witt

40

41

40—Interior of the Swan Theatre (after a drawing by De Witt).
41—Sketch of a scene by Mahelot, a master of the scenery.

this theatre is to be arranged both for the performance of plays and for the baiting of bears and bulls. For the former purpose a tire-house is to be built, the edifice which in de Witt's drawing is designated as *mimorum aedes* (the house of the actors). In order that the arena may be cleared for the fights of animals, the stage must be movable; it is a " frame to be caryed or taken away, and to stande upon tressels " sufficient to bear such a stage. It is this part which de Witt calls the *proscaenium.*

The stage, we see, is open on three sides and divided into two parts : the front part is quite open, the back is covered by a roof supported by pillars; the latter part might, if needed, be covered by curtains, and the different material and colours of these curtains formed almost the only decoration of the stage.

Their practical use, however, was the chief consideration. Like the draperies on the Italian and French stages, these curtains were used to conceal the persons who had to listen unseen to a conversation between other persons acting on the open part of the stage. In this way the King and Polonius were hidden while listening to the conversation between Hamlet and the Queen; later, Hamlet kills Polonius through the drapery, and then pulls it aside and reveals the dead body of the old courtier.[1] In *King Henry VI.*, Part II.,[2] where the King is invited to step into Gloucester's room: " Warwick

---

[1] *Hamlet* [*Draws*]. How now ! a rat ? Dead, for a ducat, dead ! [*Hamlet makes a pass through the arras.*] *Polonius* [*Behind*]. O, I am slain ! . . . *Hamlet.* . . . Is it the king ? [*Lifts up the arras, and draws forth Polonius*].—*Hamlet*, Act iii. Scene 4.

[2] In the quarto edition " The first part of the contention "; in the later editions the passage is altered.

pulls aside the curtain and points at Duke Humphrey in his bed"; and later in the same play: "Enter the King and Salisbury, the curtain is drawn, and the Cardinal is seen in his bed." And no doubt such curtains were used on many other occasions which cannot be enumerated here; thus, for instance, where a stage was represented on the stage, as in *Hamlet* and *A Midsummer Night's Dream.*

When the curtains were drawn aside, the background of the stage was formed by the actors' house, which in de Witt's drawing has two large doorways leading to the stage, through which the actors entered and retired. Higher up we see a row of boxes, into which possibly distinguished spectators may have been admitted, but which probably as a rule were occupied by actors during the pauses between their appearances before the public. Anyhow these boxes would have been very bad places for spectators when the curtains were drawn, and as de Witt has not drawn spectators elsewhere in the auditorium proper, there seems to be some reason for supposing that the figures which we see in the boxes alluded to, belonged to the performers. The custom of admitting spectators on the stage proper is of a later date. It is possible also that the musicians were stationed in these boxes.

But this superstructure was also used as part of the decoration, *i.e.*, as a kind of balcony. Here we must imagine Richard III. coming forward between two Bishops[1] when playing the hypocrite to the Lord Mayor;

---

[1] "Gloster in a gallery above, between two Bishops."—*King Richard III.*, Act iii. Scene 7.

and hence Juliet sent down her sighs of love to young Romeo.

At the very top above this gallery there was an attic or a kind of look-out tower ; we do not know what the inside of it was used for, but it was here that trumpets sent out their fanfares above the roofs of London to announce that the actors were ready to exhibit their art to the public.

The auditorium consisted in part of the flat open space which surrounded the stage on three sides, the place which in de Witt's drawing is called *planities sive arena*. The admission to this part was cheap—in the Globe Theatre, 6d. ; in inferior theatres only 2d. or even 1d.—but then very little was done here for the accommodation of the public. The spectators stood on the bare ground—there were no seats—and there was no protection whatever against rain or sun. This part of the auditorium was called the *pit* or the *yard*, and the public which stood there was not credited with much sense of art by actors or authors. Shakespeare jeers at these rough spectators in the famous speech of Hamlet to the players : "O, it offends me to the soul to hear a robustious periwig-pated fellow tear a passion to tatters, to very rags, to split the ears of the groundlings, who for the most part are capable of nothing but inexplicable dumb-shows and noise. . . ."[1]

"Groundlings" was a nickname for the spectators who stood on the ground, but they were hardly so quiet as their namesakes, the little fishes. Ben Jonson also nicknamed them "the understandings, gentlemen of the ground."

[1] *Hamlet*, Act iii. Scene 2.

The more distinguished spectators were placed in the upper galleries.   They had the advantages of being seated, of having a roof over their heads, and of having a better view of the stage than the "groundlings." And here the price was at least twice as high as in the pit, generally one shilling.   Some boxes were no doubt more expensive and were decorated with especial elegance. Thus in the contract with the builder of the Hope Theatre we read the following article : "Two boxes in the lower story, decent and convenient for gentlemen to sit in ; and the partitions between the boxes are to be made like those in the said playhouse called the Swan." Whether these are the boxes which in de Witt's drawing are designated as *orchestra*, we cannot decide ; Dr Gaedertz thinks they are, but in our opinion this would be rather absurd, as the view of the stage from these seats must have been particularly bad, and the spectators must have seen most of the action from behind.   This, however, may be the fault of the draughtsman.

But what in the opinion of all experts is a mistake, is de Witt's statement of the number of seats for the audience.   He asserts, as mentioned above, that the Swan Theatre held 3000 persons.   This is unquestionably a gross exaggeration ; Ordish even thinks that 300 would come nearer to the truth.   However, we are not likely to obtain an accurate answer to this question, especially as it is difficult to determine the exact number of places in the open space of the pit.   We are also struck by another point in his description, viz., that the Swan Theatre was built of flint.   Other accounts state that all the English theatres of those times were built of wood. Thus another German traveller, Paul Hentzner, writes in the year 1598 : " Outside the town there are some theatres, in which English actors nearly every day perform tragedies and comedies before very numerous audiences, and these plays end with excellent music, various dances, and immense applause of the spectators.

" Not far from one of these theatres, *all of which are built of wood*, lies the royal pleasure-boat. . . .

" There is also another place built in the shape of a theatre, which is used for the baiting of bulls and bears ; the animals are tied at the back, and then worried by large English bull-dogs, but not without great danger to the dogs from the horns of the former and the teeth of the latter ; they are sometimes killed on the spot, but those which are wounded or tired, are instantly replaced by fresh ones. This entertainment is frequently followed by the whipping of a blinded bear that is led out by five or six men, who place themselves round the animal and whip it mercilessly ; as the bear cannot escape on account of his chain, he defends himself with all his might and dexterity, flings to the ground all who come within his reach and who cannot retire quickly enough, tears the whips out of their hands and breaks them. At these spectacles and in all other places Englishmen always smoke tobacco. . . . In these theatres fruit, such as apples, pears, and nuts, all according to the season, are carried round and offered for sale, also beer and wine."

The shape of the auditorium was usually oval or

circular, a "wooden O," as Shakespeare calls it,[1] thus affording the best conditions for seeing and hearing. Of course the boxes nearest to the actors' house were the worst, since part of the stage must be difficult to see from there when the curtains were drawn, and since the main front turns the opposite way, even if we may suppose that the actors of those times did not always play in one direction (so as to face the pit), but turned alternately towards different parts of the auditorium.

We must say that, on the whole, the English theatre of the time was admirably adapted for its purpose, and was arranged with extraordinary practical sense.

But for decorative purposes, according to our ideas at the present time, it was certainly not suitable. The English stage did not yet know—consequently did not miss—illusion produced by painted decorations. It was reserved for the Italians to create this new scenic attraction, and thereby to alter the whole appearance and character of the theatre.

But whether this development of stage decoration has been a reform of dramatic art, and whether we may be certain that the modern theatre with all its perfection in the way of picturesque effects, ingenious mechanisms, and magnificent light, realises the ideal stage, is a great question. Who knows whether we shall not some day prefer to return to a stage which affords the best conditions for seeing and hearing the art of the actor and author naked and undisguised, rather than to go on

[1]   . . . may we cram
Within this wooden O the very casques
That did affright the air at Agincourt ? . . .
                        King Henry V., Prologue.

developing a decorative scenery which seems more calculated to throw a veil over the defects of both.

At all events it must be confessed that the Shakespearian stage in all its simplicity, with its two sections, one at the back, which could be concealed, and one projecting in front, open on three sides towards the audience, afforded great advantages. No word and no movement could be lost, as in our theatres, where the retired and covered situation of the stage renders speech indistinct, and the great distance from the majority of the spectators makes the facial play almost invisible.

A very long time passed before the English theatre was provided with the kind of decorations which are meant to create illusion, and at the time of the Renaissance proper it only possessed the draperies above-mentioned, which, though they might be painted or woven with much art, never pretended to represent anything but drapery. Nevertheless in colour and style they might well be adapted to the character of the piece. For instance, we sometimes find the background draped with black, when the play performed was a tragedy.[1]

In Italy, where nothing but drapery had been in use till the more perfect system of scenic decoration was introduced, the curtains were sometimes painted by the most celebrated artists. Thus Raphael painted draperies for the *Suppositi* by Ariosto, and the celebrated painted hangings by Mantegna, which are kept as a rare

---

[1] Look here, what I have not observed till now,
The stage is hung with black, and I suppose
A tragedy is acted here to-day.
(Prologue of an old tragedy of 1599.)

treasure at Hampton Court, were originally painted by the old master as scenic draperies for the Duke of Mantua.

We know that the draped stage in England, as elsewhere, made ample use of movable properties, such as rocks, bushes, benches, etc. In order to indicate what the stage was meant to represent in each scene, the old mediæval custom was sometimes followed of hanging up a board, on which the name of the locality was written.[1] Sometimes it was the prologue or the chorus who told the spectators where the successive scenes were laid.

We may add, finally, that the cavity beneath the stage was used. In de Witt's drawing we only see it as an open space, but in other theatres it was probably a closed cellar, in which spectres and ghosts might conceal themselves. In *Hamlet* it is distinctly said that the Ghost cries his "swear!" from *beneath*, and Hamlet says to his companions: "You hear this fellow in the cellarage."

Though the general public did not as yet feel the lack of illusive decorations, objections were raised now and then against the meagreness of the scenic equipment, and especially against the absurdity—for as such it was considered by the authors who were enthusiastic admirers of the antique, though the classic stage committed exactly the same mistakes—of making the same stage represent now one locality, now another.

As early as 1583 Sir Philip Sidney derided the

[1] Comp. p. 72. Sir Philip Sidney, in his *Apology for Poetry*, scoffs at this custom: "What child is there that, coming to a play, and seeing 'Thebes' written in great letters upon an old door, doth believe that it is Thebes?"

defects of the English stage in the following terms :—

"Where you shall have Asia of the one side and Afric of the other, and so many other under-kingdoms, that the player, when he cometh in, must ever begin with telling where he is (or else the tale will not be conceived). Now ye shall have three ladies walk to gather flowers, and then we must believe the stage to be a garden. By and by we hear news of shipwreck in the same place, and then we are to blame if we accept it not for a rock. Upon the back of that comes out a hideous monster, with fire and smoke, and then the miserable beholders are bound to take it for a cave. While in the meantime, two armies fly in, represented with four swords and bucklers, and then what hard heart will not receive it for a pitched field?"

However, neither professionals nor public minded this sort of raillery, and though the English stage underwent some changes during the subsequent period, it was not till the seventeenth century, or, more precisely, till the year 1656, that a public theatre showed its patrons a proper decorative equipment, viz., at the performance of Davenant's *The Siege of Rhodes*.[1]

The Spanish stage during the early period of the Renaissance was even simpler in its equipment. Later Spain followed suit with the remainder of civilised Europe, and received impulses chiefly from Italy, whose theatrical technique became in general decisive for all the other countries.

But during the first part of the Spanish Renaissance,

[1] Comp. above, p. 280.

while Lope de Rueda was writing his plays and having them acted, the outward conditions were as primitive as possible, if the words of Cervantes are to be credited. In the preface to his *Eight Comedies and Interludes* he describes the state of things in the following words : " I found myself recently in a circle of friends, where the stage and similar matters were discussed, and they were investigated and criticised in such a way that, in my opinion, the treatment of the subject could not be more to the point. It was also debated who had been the first in Spain to take comedy out of its swaddling-clothes, equip it properly, and dress it in a fine and smart attire. As the oldest[1] of the persons present, I said that I quite well remembered seeing the great Lope de Rueda on the stage, him that was so distinguished for his power of representation and his artistic sense. He was born in Seville, and was a gold-beater by trade, that is, one who makes gold into plates. He was admirable in the pastoral, and in this special branch has up to this day been surpassed by none, either in his own time or later. Though at that time, because I was merely a boy, I could not form an adequate judgment of the value of his verses, now at a more advanced age, when I recall those that have remained in my memory, I still find that I was right in what I said ; and if it were not for exceeding the limits of this preface, I should quote some of them in confirmation of this truth.

" In the time of this famous Spaniard the whole apparatus of an acting manager might be packed up in a

---

[1] Cervantes was born in 1547, and the principal part of Lope de Rueda's career comes between 1544 and 1566.

bag, and it consisted of four shepherd's costumes of white skin, trimmed with gilt leather, four beards and wigs, and about four pastoral staves. The comedies were conversations, almost like eclogues between two or three shepherds and a shepherdess. They were enlivened or amplified by some interludes performed either by a negress or a Rufian,[1] a fool or a Biscayan. All these four parts, and many others besides, were acted by the said Lope with the highest degree imaginable of excellence and truth to nature. In those times there was no machinery; there were no duels between Moors and Christians, either on foot or on horseback; it was still an unknown thing to see a person appear through a hole on the stage, coming or pretending to come from the centre of the earth, still more to see clouds coming down from Heaven bearing angels or the blissful souls of the dead. The theatre (stage) consisted of four benches placed in a square, and four to six planks laid across them, so that the stage was raised four spans above the ground. The scenic decoration consisted of an old drapery, which could be pulled either way by two strings, forming the so-called tiring-room, where the musicians also stood and sang, without guitars, some old romance." [2]

The first professional actors in Germany, too, knew no other stage than the draped platform.[3]

The attempt was made for a while to combine the

[1] A kind of Scapino or Scaramuccio, who frequently appeared in the ancient Spanish theatre.

[2] After the German translation by A. F. v. Schack, in *Gesch. d. dram. Lit. u. Kunst in Spanien,* i. 227 f.

[3] Comp. Devrient: *Gesch. d. d. Schauspiels,* i. 195.

II.

stage of the Middle Ages with that of the Renaissance, by moving the mediæval equipment with its many localities, which were all represented simultaneously, on to the narrow Renaissance stage, representing in a kind of *résumé* all the places to which the poet's fancy transported the action of the play.

If one act was to pass at the seaside, another in a palace, a third in a churchyard, a fourth in a dungeon, a fifth in a wood, all these places were indicated simultaneously on the stage, remaining there as a permanent decoration as long as the play lasted.

But the limited space to which the stage was confined at the time of the Renaissance compared with the vast open stage of the Middle Ages, compelled the machinists of the time to arrange, condense, and conventionalise the decorations much more than had been the case hitherto.

We do not hear that such simultaneous decorations— *décors simultanés*, as they were called in France—were used in the English Renaissance theatre, the repertoire of which might otherwise have been favourable to such an arrangement. But in France they were adopted for a time, not for the regular classic tragedy or comedy which were constructed after the antique, and aspired to unity of place, but for the free popular genuine comedy, especially as it was represented by Alexandre Hardy, " the French Shakespeare."

That it was France in particular which maintained or resumed the mediæval decorative system was not a mere chance. Nowhere else was the equipment of the mysteries carried to such extremes as in this country, and the public, which was accustomed to see so many marvellous exhibitions of conjuring, still—at any rate in the serious plays—wished to have their senses tickled by the sight of gloomy dungeons, fire-spitting dragons, brilliant fireworks, streaming blood, and the like theatrical baits. All these *machines* and *feintes* were indispensable means of keeping hold of the attention of the public, and much more so in France than, for instance, in England or Spain, where the art of scenic construction for the mysteries had never reached such a degree of perfection.

The lists of scenic decorations and accessories by Leon Mahelot,[1] machinist and scene painter, show that the old mediæval effects were not withheld from the public. We meet in them with items such as "blood, sponges, a little bladder for the trick (*feinte*) with the blow of the sacrificing priest," and "an artificial stuffing for drawing blood out of a body with a sword made for the purpose," "an artificial head," etc.; but above all, his drawings and descriptions give a tolerably distinct idea of the particular scenic arrangement which is designated *décor simultané* or *multiple*, and which forms such an interesting transition from the mediæval to the modern stage.

As an example, we may quote Mahelot's directions for the permanent decoration used in *Agarite*, a play by Durval :—

" In the middle of the theatre there shall be a room

---

[1] *Recueil des décorations et accessoires qui ont servi pour les représentations jusqu'en,* 1673, by Mahelot and his successor Laurent. During the first half of the seventeenth century Mahelot worked as machinist at the Hôtel de Bourgogne.

provided with a magnificent bed, which can be opened
and closed according to the requirements of the play.
On one side of the stage there shall be an old castle,
where a little boat can be introduced, and this castle
must have a cave of the height of a man, out of which
the boat shall come.   Round the said castle there shall
be a sea, two feet eight inches deep, and close to the
castle a churchyard provided with a bell and of broken
and decayed bricks.   Three tombs and a chair on the
same side as the churchyard.   A window through which
is seen the painter's shop, which shall be on the other
side of the stage, provided with pictures and other paint-
ings, and close to the shop a garden or wood, in which
there shall be apples, pears (*des grignons*), will-o'-the-
wisps,[1] and a mill."

Taken in connection with the mediæval theatre and
with what we know about that of the Renaissance, this
description, though not very clear in itself, helps us to
form a tolerably good idea of what such a *décor
simultané* was like.

Thus "down stage"—or, in the modern French
technical term, in the first *plan*, that is the space which is
bounded by the lowest wing, that nearest the audience—
we see on one side a castle, or rather a fragment of a
wall with a moat and a vault; opposite to it, on the same
plan, part of a house, from which we look into a painter's

---

[1] The text has *des ardens*, which means the same as *feux follets*, will-
o'-the-wisps, a very popular and very simple means of effect which is still
in use.   It consists of a small bunch of cotton wool or tow, which is
fastened to a long wire and dipped in spirit, and after being lit, is moved
up and down from behind the scenes.   As the wires become invisible at a
few steps' distance, the dancing flames fairly well create the illusion of will-
o'-the-wisps.

studio through a large window. Higher up stage—in the second *plan*—we see on one side a bit of a church-yard wall with tombs and a church bell, on the other side a garden. The background is formed by the room above-mentioned with the magnificent bed, and, when necessary, this part of the stage, like the background of the English theatre, could be concealed from the eyes of the spectators by pulling together the curtains in front of it.

However chaotic this stage may seem to have been, mixing up together churchyards, bedrooms, castles, studios, and gardens, it comes much closer to our theatre than the contemporary stage-platform, which in France and Italy was soon considered a thing of the past.

Besides, the confusion is only apparent. The different localities were not heaped together unsymmetrically as on the mediæval stage; on the contrary, they were arranged with too much regularity, with a scrupulous symmetry and regard of perspective, which for ages became fatal to scenic painting, not merely in France, but all over Europe. Indeed this exaggerated love of regularity has but quite recently been superseded by a sense for irregular, and therefore more natural scenery.

We need only cast a glance at a decorative sketch by the machinist Mahelot (reproduced here in fig. 41, p. 326) to see how little it is removed from the kind of scene painting which was still fashionable at the close of the last century. The only difference is that in our illustration each of the wings represents a different locality, though they may not be so heterogeneous as those in the above description. Mahelot, no doubt, is strongly influenced by the Italian principle of decoration.   I have nowhere been able to find an illustration of the genuine *décor simultané.*

In Italy modern scenic arrangement received its first development.   The Italian architects dreamt of resuscitating the ancient Italian theatre, and constructed one stage after another from the designs of Vitruvius.   In the fifteenth and sixteenth centuries no permanent theatre existed in Italy.   Professional companies contented themselves with easily built platforms, and it was only at festivals of court and church, where theatricals formed part of the entertainment, that architects were allowed to carry out their ideas; but only light materials were used, as the edifice was not intended to last for more than the particular festival.

One single theatre, however, was allowed to remain, on account of its particular magnificence and the ingenuity with which it was built, and therefore this stage was of special importance to scenic architecture in Italy. We mean the Olympian theatre in Vicenza, built in 1565 by the famous architect Palladio.

It has been thought that Palladio carried out the idea of the antique theatre, probably because his stage was both originally built and afterwards used for old Greek and Latin tragedies in the Italian translations of the Renaissance.   That this was not so, however, will be seen from the adjoined illustration (fig. 42).[1]

The stage of Palladio consists in the first place of a

[1] This illustration is taken from a drawing in Riccoboni's *Hist. du Théâtre ital.*, and, as far as we know, has not been reproduced before.   In his *Essai sur l'histoire du théâtre*, which is supposed to be the authoritative history of theatrical architecture, Bapst goes so far as to assert that there is not a single illustration of the stage of Vicenza.

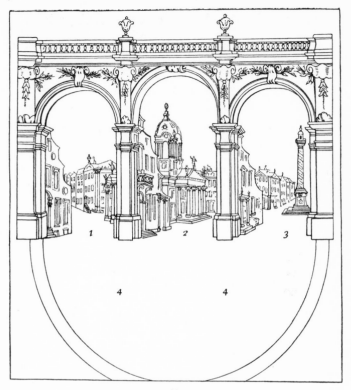

42

43

42—The Olympian Theatre at Vicenza (after Riccoboni);
43—Italian comedy scene of the 16th century.

semicircular open space, marked 4 in the illustration, then of an architectural façade elaborately decorated in the style of the time, and provided with three arcades (1, 2, 3) ; finally, through the three arcades we see three streets which run in different directions, and in which the houses are likewise built in the style of the Italian Renaissance with a touch of the antique.

These three streets, as Riccoboni[1] makes a special point of observing, were not reproduced in flat painting on canvas or boards, but built in relief, vanishing according to the rules of perspective, so that the house furthest removed did not exceed two feet in height.

Such a scenic arrangement must have been particularly appropriate to the Italian comedy of the time (even more than to the Greek tragedy, for which it was originally constructed) as well as to certain classical comedies which came under the influence of the Italian theatre.

This is also acknowledged by Riccoboni, who in somewhat involved sentences expresses his opinion about the matter : " For instance, when a servant, in looking for his master in order to give account of a commission he has had to carry out for him, appears on the stage through arcade 3, and his master who is looking eagerly for his servant and begins to talk in the middle of the street seen through arcade 1, stops to look down the small streets which turn sideways from the large street in which he is standing, he is at about 24 or 30 feet distance from the archway which he has to pass to arrive on stage 4. So the servant who stands on the part of the stage seen through arcade 3, cannot see his master who stays

[1] *Théâtre italien*, i. 115.

in the part behind arcade 1 ; and for the same reason the master is unable to see his servant till he has come forward through the arcade to stage 4, or till the servant has advanced as far as the front of arcade 1, where his master is. So they can perfectly well deliver several speeches without seeing each other."[1]

Excellent as this stage may have been, it did not suit the purposes of professional touring companies, partly because it was too expensive, partly because it took up too much room. Nor was it used by the actors of the *Commedia dell' Arte ;* yet most experts who have written on the subject, seem to have mixed up this unique festal building with the ordinary stages.[2]

But the principle of Palladio was to a certain extent introduced into the professional theatres. The object was to produce a scene, the total effect of which should be appropriate to every kind of play, but to avoid accumulating a multitude of absurd and heterogeneous objects simultaneously on the stage. As early as the sixteenth century it was generally acknowledged that each special branch required its particular scene, without going to the extremes of the present day and demanding a different scene—or sometimes many different scenes— each play.

The architect Serlio writes in his *Seven Books of Architecture*[3] : "Three decorations are sufficient for all kinds of plays. The first, which is intended for a comedy

---

[1] Riccoboni, i. 116.

[2] Compare Moland : *Molière et la comédie ital.,* 62, and Maurice Sand : *Masques et Bouffons,* i. 42.

[3] Serlio : *Les Sept Livres de l'Architecture,* edition of 1545, translated by Martin, quoted by Bapst, 255.

or farce, represents a tolerably narrow and deep street, with numerous shops with signs, and houses, all of which allows of multiplying the episodes during the action of the play. The second, intended for tragedy, is a public place in a severe style, like the Piazza della Signoria in Florence. . . . Finally, for the plays which in those times [*i.e.*, classical antiquity] were designed as satirical— idylls and *boscaresqui* or mythological plays, a sylvan decoration was used, which recalled the sacred groves in our modern ballets. The two first-mentioned were built of light material, timberwork covered with painted canvas ; the latter was simply painted."

At least a century before the other European countries Italy possessed scenery which was perfectly developed for the purpose of creating illusion. At a time when France, England, Germany, and Spain knew nothing but the troublesome and absurd mystery stage, or the plain unadorned platform, Italy possessed scenery which did not differ essentially from that of our modern stage.

If we cast a glance at the two scenes in figs. 43 and 44, we see two cleverly drawn and practically constructed stages, the former evidently for comedies, with its deep, narrow street crossed by side streets, by which the performers could come on or off, hide themselves, watch their fellow-actors, etc. ; the second is probably a stage for tragedies, according to Serlio's prescription, a public place in severe style, with a large monumental building in the background, side entrances right and left in the foreground, fountains, statues, movable balconies, etc.

Both scenes are built, not painted on flat wings, which

of course produces a stronger illusion and also requires more skill and labour.

Simultaneously with this complicated scenery, the stage took the shape which it has nowadays. It was no longer a projecting platform surrounded by the audience on three sides. It was a separate space, an enormous square box, the front wall of which had been removed, and in the inside of which the plays were presented to the spectators like pictures against a background.

Then first it became possible and natural to have a front curtain which concealed the setting of the scenes, and marked the close of the acts, or at least of the piece. On the mediæval stage there had been no use for such a curtain, nor could it be used on the platform stage of the Renaissance, where it was replaced by a back cloth separating the two sections of the stage.

The shape of the auditorium, which originally—where the plays were performed inside a building—had been square like an ordinary hall, now, according to antique models, assumed in several theatres the shape of a semi-circle or oval with rows of seats in several storeys along the walls, and a level or slightly sloping pit a few feet lower than the stage. Thus the inside of the theatre received the form which it has preserved in the main to this day, but which is sure to be altered in the future, as scenic experts no doubt will soon discover that the present construction by no means produces the greatest effect on the ear or the eye.

However, as it was, the Italian system of decoration and scenic construction were looked upon as an

44

45

44—Italian tragedy scene of the 16th century.

45—Scene for Corneille's "Andromeda."

important reform, and justly so, if compared with the awkward and absurd stage arrangements of the time.

France soon adopted the Italian system, which supplanted both the French platform-stage and *le décor simultané;* even plays which seemed written and calculated for the latter form of stage, were now performed with the simple, regular, and invariably recurring scenes : "a street," "a public place," or "a classical colonnade," and "a forest"; and in addition to these "a room" with five doors symmetrically placed—one in the background, two "upper entrances" and two "lower entrances," a scene which is still used in several of Molière's comedies, such as *Tartuffe, le Misanthrope, l'Avare,* etc. These plays, indeed, are so completely adapted to this scene that they cannot be performed with any others. But even dramas such as Corneille's *Cid,* which is evidently composed with a view to the *décor simultané,* since the action is constantly moving from place to place, was performed on its first production with one and the same scene, a room, throughout all its acts. Now it is represented with a series of shifting tableaux.

The professional actors naturally had to take the question of economy into account, and to them the Italian system was economical in so far as its few decorations sufficed for many pieces.

On the other hand, the ever-increasing demand for mechanical contrivances, which was gratified in particular by the numerous and splendid private performances given by kings, princes, and other potentates or Mecænases of art, in Italy as well as in France, for one thing entailed considerable expense on the theatrical managers ; and moreover, which was even worse, the insatiable public craving to see human beings flying, the sun rising and setting, houses collapsing, and so on, compelled authors to write and actors to perform absurd magic plays, which had no other object than to show to what pitch mechanical dexterity could be carried at the time. The modern theatre, by the way, suffers from the very same disease, and will continue to do so as long as the present form of theatre exists.

While, as early as the middle of the seventeenth century, the art of constructing machinery had reached a high standard, and in its effects certainly was not very inferior to present attainments,[1] in another respect—the matter of lighting—those times were very backward indeed.

Hitherto the performances had taken place by day-light, so there was no need to trouble about artificial light. But now when, to begin with, the stage was removed to the inside of a building, when it became a closed room, and when, finally, the taste of the public required later and later hours for the performances, artificial light became indispensable.

The question of light was eagerly discussed by the architects of the time. The usual way of lighting the stage was to hang up chandeliers or bracket lamps, which

---

[1] Thus Fig. 45 shows a magnificent scene for Corneille's *Andromède*, in which the goddess appears in the clouds, just as we see her nowadays. It is done in this way : clouds are painted in perspective on canvas curtains, which are cut in different forms and applied one behind the other, covered by thickly draped curtains of gauze. The goddess stands on a high scaffold ; at the moment when she is to appear, the gauze draperies are drawn up ; the goddess advances on the scaffolding with a strong light shining upon her, and seems to walk on the clouds.

were placed above and at the sides of the stage. Footlights do not seem to have been in use.[1] In the chandeliers were burned candles or oil. The oil lamps, which were generally double and boat-shaped, gave a red, smoky light. The wax candles, which were suspended in triangular frames, had a white, clear light, but they were expensive, and as a rule were only used at court festivals. Ordinary theatres used tallow candles. As a precaution against fire, which was always much dreaded, large sponges fastened to long sticks were employed, as well as ordinary hand-engines, for which water was always kept in store.

To us, whose eyes are spoiled by the many hundreds of brilliant electric lamps which nowadays shed their light on our stage, the light of those days would no doubt have appeared gloomy darkness. But what people did not know they could not miss, and it is much more probable that this otherwise fully developed theatre seemed to their eyes as a radiant revelation from the world of fancy.

In any case, with all its defects, fighting its way through the changes of time and of taste, through the absurd, the ludicrous, the awkward, and the tasteless, the stage had worked its way, and in the end acquired a fixed form.

The house stood ready to receive the approaching guests of honour, the great poets and the great actors.

---

[1] Ludovic Celler, in his *Les décors, les costumes et la mise en scène au XVII. siècle*, is of opinion that the system of footlights owes its origin to the small plain theatres, which could not afford to have chandeliers, and therefore placed tallow candles on the floor in front of the stage.

APPENDIX

THE INTRIGUES OF LOVE

OR

THE ENCHANTED WINDOW

[Italian scenario of the eighteenth century, published for the first time by A. Bartoli in his collection : *Scenari inediti della Commedia dell' Arte, contributo alla storia del teatro popolare italiano*. In Firenze 1880. In order to assist the memory of the actors, such scenarios were posted on the stage behind the wings.]

The Persons of the Play.

PANDOLFO, father of Lucinda and Ottavio.[1]

LUCINDA, his daughter, and sister of Ottavio.

OTTAVIO, son of Pandolfo (unknown).

COLOMBINA, maid to Lucinda.

COLA, servant to Ottavio.

UBALDO, father of Valerio.

VALERIO, his son.

STOPPINO, his servant [frequently called *Zanni*].

PASQUELLA, his housekeeper [she is called *serva*, but is a widow and occupies a somewhat different position from a servant-girl].

ACT I.

SCENE I.

PANDOLFO *alone ; then* COLOMBINA.

Pandolfo relates how he had sent his son away from home to be nursed, and how he was kidnapped by the Turks while out walking with his nurse and with his servant named Colafronio, and goes on to say that he has never received any information about them, that afterwards Heaven gave him this daughter, Lucinda, whom he loves above

---

[1] Mark the circumstantial observations about the mutual relationship of the characters, which were natural in the improvised comedy, where it was important to the actors to understand these things quickly. Molière, among others, follows this example.

everything, and whom he wishes to see well married; after this is done, he, being a widower, will also take a wife. Calls the maid-servant, commends his daughter to her, saying that she must not allow her to fall in love; tells her what to do, and that, when her young mistress is married, he will also find a husband for her too. The old woman promises. She goes into the house; he out.

Scene II.

PASQUELLA, *alone.*

Says that it is a bad thing to be a widow, and that she who is always arranging matches for others, can do nothing for herself, but that, when she has succeeded in making Valerio marry Lucinda, she will begin to act for herself.

Scene III.

VALERIO *and* STOPPINO.

Valerio expresses his love for Lucinda, applies to the servant, who says that it would be a good thing to speak to Colombina and to make her help him, because Pasquella, who does not live in the house, cannot so easily find an opportunity of speaking to Lucinda, and that it is necessary to give something to the person who helps in such a love affair; that as to himself, he will do what he can. Valerio is uneasy about his father's intention to marry; still he is in good spirits, and they go.

Scene IV.

UBALDO *and* PANDOLFO.

Ubaldo declares that he is in love with Pandolfo's daughter, catches sight of him, expresses his friendship for him, asks consent to marry his daughter. Pandolfo consents, after which Ubaldo gives him Pasquella, his housekeeper;[1] Ubaldo says that the only thing he has to do now is to get his son married, that he has already written to one of his friends in Venice to ask for a daughter of his, and presently

---

[1] Several other scenarios are even more complicated and sometimes quite incomprehensible.

SCENE V.

UBALDO, VALERIO, and STOPPINO.

Ubaldo tells Valerio that he has chosen a wife, but that as a good father he will see his son married before celebrating his own wedding; all are pleased; Ubaldo goes out, saying that he is going to the post-office to see if there are any letters; Valerio says that he does not know anything about it, expresses his pleasure to the servant; they say that they will find Pandolfo and rejoice with him; presently

SCENE VI.

The same, PANDOLFO, COLOMBINA.

Valerio expresses his joy to Pandolfo at the connection between the families; they perform a *Scena equivoca,*[1] so that the old man thinks he is pleased on his father's account; the mistake is not cleared up; Pandolfo gives Colombina to his servant in marriage.

SCENE VII.

OTTAVIO and COLA.

Ottavio says that after many years' slavery he has succeeded by his good qualities in obtaining liberty, not only for himself, but also for his servant, and that for this reason the latter ought to be a good servant to him; they say that they have been staying for many months in this town on their way to Leghorn, their native town, but because he has fallen in love with this Lucinda, he has not been able to tear himself away. The servant acts a scene about his slavery, advises his master to give up his love and to return to his home; he says that he cannot do it, and exit.

SCENE VIII.

VALERIO, STOPPINO, and PANDOLFO.

They repeat their mutual compliments with double meaning (*in equivoca*), at last they understand each other, and go away, all in anger.

---

[1] Comp. above, p. 228.

Scene IX.

Pasquella.

Says that she is longing to give Valerio to Lucinda, and that she has observed that Pandolfo is violently in love with her, that when he has given his daughter to Valerio, her wedding with Pandolfo will follow; presently

Scene X.

The same, Pandolfo.

They act a love scene, whereupon she requests the hand of Lucinda for Valerio, her master; he: that he has promised her to the father; she: that she loves him, but that she means to speak to Valerio and persuade him to allow his father to marry Lucinda; Pandolfo exit; presently

Scene XI.

Valerio, Pasquella, Colombina, Lucinda, *and* Stoppino.

Pasquella tells Valerio that his father wants Lucinda, therefore he has ordered her to dissuade Valerio from his love; that if the matter is not arranged, she will not become the wife of Pandolfo; presently Lucinda sees Valerio; they act a love scene; he says she must not doubt that he knows what to do; Pasquella and Colombina remain.

Scene XII.

Pasquella *and* Colombina.

Colombina says how violently she is in love with Stoppino; that if the marriage with Valerio comes to pass, she will not get Stoppino; Pasquella says that if the marriage with somebody else takes place, she will not get Pandolfo; they get angry and fight. *End of Act I.*

ACT II.

Scene I.

Ottavio *and* Cola.

Ottavio says that before going to Leghorn he will try his luck and ask Pandolfo for Lucinda; tells Cola to call Colombina, that she may tell him what her mistress is doing; Cola calls; presently

Scene II.

The same, Colombina, Lucinda.

Cola acts a love scene with Colombina; she calls her mistress and desires her to fall in love with Ottavio; he comes forward, makes love, she turns him off; Colombina renews her entreaties, she refuses. Cola says that she must try to dissuade her from her obstinacy, so that there can be two couples; Ottavio says that he is going to find Pandolfo and ask for the hand of his daughter, and they go.

Scene III.

Stoppino *as sorcerer.*   Ubaldo *and* Pandolfo.

Ubaldo says: when is this wedding to take place? Pandolfo says that his son has requested that Lucinda shall be his, and that if she is given to somebody else, he will kill him, whoever he may be. Ubaldo in a fury goes away to find Valerio; Stoppino makes some incantations aside towards the house of Ubaldo, says he hopes his trick will be successful; surprised at this, Pandolfo becomes suspicious, and he returns into the house.

Scene IV.

Valerio, Ubaldo, *and* Zanni (Stoppino), *then* Pandolfo.

Ubaldo comes shouting up to Valerio and says that he has chosen him a wife in Venice, so he has no more to say. Valerio replies in the same tone, yields in the end, and goes. Ubaldo calls Pandolfo, insists on the wedding ; Pandolfo leaves the house, pretends to be afraid ; says he has a feeling as if the sorcerer had worked some spell on him ; Zanni : that it is quite probable, since the sorcerer has done so to others, that he has done so to him ; Ubaldo says, why is he talking about a sorcerer ? Pandolfo says he cannot give him any other answer about the wedding, and goes into the house, frightened. Ubaldo goes away surprised. Zanni laughs at his trick and goes.

SCENE V.

PASQUELLA, LUCINDA, *and* COLOMBINA.

Pasquella expresses her wish that Ubaldo may marry Lucinda, for then her marriage with Pandolfo will also take place ; presently (enter) Lucinda, who says she will marry no one but Valerio. Pasquella comes forward, beseeches her to take the old man ; she refuses, Colombina scolds her, she flees, the others come in.

SCENE VI.

PANDOLFO *and* LUCINDA.

Pandolfo requests his daughter to marry Ubaldo, she refuses ; he says that if she does not take him, she will get nobody else, and goes away angry, saying that he is going to fetch Ubaldo ; Lucinda complains, and exit.

SCENE VII.

PASQUELLA, VALERIO, *and* ZANNI.

Valerio recommends himself to Pasquella, who says that he must doubt of the sincerity of her wish that this marriage may take place, as her own marriage with Pandolfo will follow after,—and exit. Stoppino tells Valerio to go and leave all to him ; and presently

SCENE VIII.

STOPPINO *and* PANDOLFO.

Zanni says to Pandolfo that he cannot understand why he thinks that if Ubaldo gets Lucinda he will have Pasquella, as she is in love with Cola, the valet of Ottavio, and if she has promised to become his wife, it is in order to make him give his daughter to Ubaldo; it is Ubaldo who has ordered her to do so; he believes it and goes, saying that since Pasquella is in love, he will certainly not give his daughter in marriage into the Lanterni [1] family. He thanks Zanni for informing him of the whole affair, acts a scene of contempt towards Pasquella, and goes; Zanni laughs and goes.

SCENE IX.

OTTAVIO, COLA, *and* PANDOLFO.

Ottavio says that he has not been able to find Pandolfo in order to ask for his daughter; Cola says he also is vexed on account of his interest for Colombina; presently he sees Pandolfo, greets him, and asks if he will give him his daughter; after some conversation he consents, and says that he has dismissed all the others, and moreover has given peremptory orders that they are not to have any intercourse with that house; makes compliments, Cola pleased, they go; Pandolfo enters the house to inform his daughter of the matter.

SCENE X.

VALERIO, UBALDO, *and* ZANNI.

The old man angry with Valerio because he has spoiled his prospects; they excuse themselves. Zanni says he has no doubt that he will succeed in satisfying Pandolfo; the old man goes, contented; Valerio and Zanni remain, they call Lucinda; presently

SCENE XI.

The same, PANDOLFO, LUCINDA.

Lucinda comes, Valerio makes love to her; Pandolfo scolds her from the window and comes down; while he is coming down, she goes into the house; Zanni engages his master in conversation; Pandolfo does not see his daughter, goes into the house again, saying that he

---

[1] Lanterni is identical with Ubaldo; in several other scenarios the name of one of the old men is Ubaldo Lanterni.

must have been mistaken; this lazzo is repeated three or four times; at last he tells Valerio to go away and not to speak to his daughter; Valerio tells Pandolfo that he is mad, that he has not spoken to his daughter at all, but to his valet, who says that this must be an effect of the sorcerer's trick; he believes it, makes excuses, and they go in; Lucinda comes out, they speak to each other again; the old man takes hold of her arm, beats her; Valerio defends her, so does Colombina, and Zanni too. *End of Act II.*

ACT III.

Scene I.

Ottavio *and* Cola.

Ottavio says that all is ready for the wedding. Cola says the same; both have made a list, they read it, find that some necessary things are wanting; they go to fetch them.

Scene II.

Pandolfo *and* Pasquella.

Pasquella sees Pandolfo, makes love; he listens to her, at last he reproaches her, saying that he has seen her false tricks in order to make him give his daughter to her master, not in order to marry him, and that he knows she is in love with Cola, but that she will be put to shame and not have him, as he means to give his daughter to Ottavio and Colombina to Cola; Pasquella wants to explain her reasons, he does not listen to her, and exit; she complains, and exit.

Scene III.

Ubaldo *and* Stoppino.

Ubaldo asks if Stoppino has kept his promise; Stoppino makes excuses, at last he tells how the whole affair has come to nothing; Ubaldo gets angry, says that he will send away both his son and his servant, that he is going to marry Pasquella, because he does not intend to be without a wife, and exit.

Scene IV.

Colombina *and* Pasquella.

Make peace; Pasquella says to Colombina that if she makes Pandolfo marry her, she will take care that Cola shall be hers; Colombina promises, Pasquella goes, and presently

Scene V.

Valerio, Stoppino, Lucinda, *and* Colombina.

Valerio grieves to see that all has gone wrong, and says that he will go away in despair; so will Stoppino; presently enter Lucinda; they take leave, she goes in crying, so do Colombina and Zanni, and they go.

Scene VI.

Ubaldo *and* Pasquella.

Ubaldo proposes to Pasquella; she turns him off, saying that it is not good for a servant to become mistress, or stepmother to Valerio, who would not approve of such a thing; Ubaldo says that he is master in his own house, and that he has already turned him out; Pasquella does not refuse, but first she wants to try if she cannot succeed in becoming the wife of Pandolfo; Ubaldo goes, saying that she must soon give him an answer; Pasquella remains; and presently

Scene VII.

The same, Pandolfo.

Pandolfo grieves over his son, who has been kidnapped by the Turks, also over his servant, complains that he can find no means of getting his daughter married, that he has not got Pasquella for his wife; sees her; she makes him understand that she has no other lover; they exchange vows and go into the house of Pandolfo.

SCENE VIII.

UBALDO, *alone.*

Ubaldo comes home, does not find Pasquella there, grieves at being left alone, repents of having sent away his son, goes into his house again, complaining.

SCENE IX.

LUCINDA *and* COLOMBINA.

Lucinda complains that she is going to have a servant as step-mother, grieves over her father; Colombina is desolate to find that her love is hopeless; they go in weeping.

SCENE X.

PANDOLFO, OTTAVIO, *and* COLA.

Ottavio says that he is longing immensely to hear from Pandolfo; sees him, they exchange compliments, they discuss the contract of marriage, and when he is to tell his name, he says that it is not Ottavio, but Flamminio, that the name of Ottavio was given him by some Christians in Turkey; Cola says likewise that his name is not Cola at all, but Paschariello Patana;[1] they tell about their slavery; Pandolfo recognises him as his son, calls his daughter, they show their joy, and exeunt.

SCENE XI.

VALERIO *and* STOPPINO.

Valerio says that he is going away because Lucinda is to be married to Ottavio, and that he does not wish ever to see this part of the Heavens again; Zanni complains; and presently

---

[1] In the first scene Pandolfo says that the kidnapped servant was called Colafronio.

Last Scene.

Omnes.

Ubaldo comes, sees his son, asks his pardon and beseeches him not to go away; Ubaldo persists; then comes Pandolfo, rejoices to find his son again; in his joy Ubaldo asks Pandolfo to give Lucinda to Valerio; he consents, the wedding takes place; Cola and Stoppino hold a tournament to see which of them is to have Colombina, Pasquella enters holding the hand of Pandolfo, Ubaldo scolds her, forgives her at last, and the comedy is at an end.

Properties.

Two cardboard horses for the tournament.
Lances of reed.
A cabbage for Cola to smell.[1]
A piece of Parmesan cheese for Zanni to smell.[1]
A stick.
Sorcerer's costume and beard.

[1] These two remarkable properties were given, I suppose, to the two fighting fools after the tournament.

BIBLIOGRAPHY

Adam: Drame anglo-normand du XII siècle. V. Luzarche. Tours 1854.

Ademollo, A.: Una famiglia di comici italiani nel secolo decimottavo. Florence 1885.

Ancien Théâtre Français. Collection des ouvrages dramatiques les ʳplus remarquables depuis les Mystères jusqu'à Corneille, publ. p. Viollet le Duc. I-X. Paris 1854-57.

d'Ancona, Alessandro: Origini del Teatro in Italia. I-II. Turin 1891.

Archer, William: A Sixteenth Century Playhouse (*The Universal Review*). London 1888.

Aubertin, Charles: Histoire de la langue et de la littérature française au moyen âge. I-II. Paris 1876-79.

Bächtold: Schweizerische Schauspiele des 16 Jahrhunderts. I-III. Zürich 1890-93.

Baker, H. Barton: The London Stage. Its History and Traditions from 1576 to 1888. I-II. London 1889.

Bapst, Germain: Essai sur l'histoire du théâtre. Paris 1893.

Bartoli, Adolfo: Scenari inediti della commedia dell' Arte. Florence 1880.

Birket Smith: Studier paa det gamle danske Skuespils Omraade. Copenhagen 1883.

Brandes, Georg: William Shakespeare. Copenhagen 1895.

Campardon, Emile: Les Comédiens du Roi de la troupe française. Paris 1879.

Casanova, Jacques: Mémoires écrits par lui même. I-IV. Paris 1843.

Celler, Ludovic: Les décors, les costumes et la mise en scène au XVII siècle. Paris 1869.

Clédat Léon: Le théâtre au moyen âge. Paris 1896.

Collé, Charles: Journal et Mémoires, éd Hon. Bonhomme. I-III. Paris 1868.

Collier, James Payne: The History of English Dramatic Poetry. I-III. London 1879.

Constantini, Angelo: La vie die Scaramouche. Paris 1695.

Creizenach, W.: Geschichte des neueren Dramas. I. (Mittelalter und Frührenaissance). Halle 1893.

Devrient, Eduard: Geschichte der deutschen Schauspielkunst. I-IV. Leipzig 1848.

    „   „   Das Passionsschauspiel in Oberammergau und seine Bedeutung für die neue Zeit. Leipzig 1851.

361

Ebert, A.: Die englischen Mysterien (Jahrbücher für roman. und engl. Literatur, Bd. 1). 1859.

Fournel, Victor: Curiositiés théâtrales. Paris 1859.

Gaedertz: Zur Kenntniss der altenglischen Bühne, etc. Bremen 1888.

Genée, Rudolf: Lehr- und Wanderjahre des deutschen Shauspiels. Vom Beginn. der Reformation bis zur Mitte des 18 Jahrhunderts. Berlin 1882.

„ „ Shakespeare's Life and Work. Translated by S. Birket Smith. 1877.

Gherardi, E.: Le théâtre italien de Gherardi, etc. I-VI. 5. édition. Paris 1721.

Grimm et Diderot: Correspondance littéraire. I-IV. 2. éd. Paris 1812.

Hase, Karl: Das geistliche Schauspiel. Leipzig 1858.

Jal, A.: Dictionnaire critique de biographie et d'histoire. Paris 1872.

Journal d'un bourgeois de Paris, etc., publ. p. Lalanne. Paris 1854.

Julleville, Petit de: Les mystères. I-II. Paris 1880.

„ Les comédiens en France au moyen âge. Paris 1874.

„ La comédie et les moeurs en France au moyen âge. Paris 1886.

„ Répertoire du théâtre comique en France au moyen âge. Paris 1886.

Jusserand J. J.: Le théâtre en Angleterre, etc. Paris 1881.

Keller, Adalbert von: Fastnachtspiele aus dem 15 Jahrhundert. I-III. Stuttgart 1853-58.

Klein, J. L.: Geschichte des italienischen Dramas. I-IV. Leipzig 1866-69.

„ Geschichte des englischen Dramas. I-II. Leipzig 1876.

Lacroix, Paul (Bibliophile Jacob): Sciences et lettres au moyen âge et à l'époque de la Renaissance. Paris 1877.

„ „ Recueil de Farces, Soties et Moralités du XV siècle. Paris 1859.

Lemazurier, P. D.: Galerie historique des acteurs du théâtre français, depuis 1600 jusqu'à nos jours. I-II. Paris 1810.

Lenient, C.: La satire en France au moyen âge. Paris 1888.

Levertin, Oscar: Studier öfver Fars ock Farøsrer i Frankrike mellem Renaissancen og Molière. Upsala 1888.

Magnin, Charles: Teatro celeste, les commencements de la comédie italienne en France. (Rev. d. deux mondes, 15 déc. 1847).

Maistre Pierre Pathelin, suivi du Nouveau Pathelin, etc., publ. p. P. L. Jacob. Paris 1859.

Mercey, F.: Le théâtre en Italie. (Rev. d. deux mondes 1840.)

Michels, Victor: Studien über die ältesten deutschen Fastnachtspiele (Quellen u. Forschungen, etc., 76-78). Strassb. 1896.

Moland, L.: Molière et la Comédie italienne. Paris 1867.

Mone: Schauspiele des Mittelalters. I-II. Karlsruhe 1846.

Monmerqué et Michel: Théâtre français au moyen âge. Paris 1842.

Moynet, A.: L'Envers du théâtre, machines et décorations. Paris 1873.

Nyrop, Kristoffer: En Theaterforestilling i Middelalderen. Copenhagen 1892.

Ordish, T. F.: Early London Theatres. London 1894.

Parfaict frères, François et Claude: Histoire du Théâtre François depuis son origine jusqu'à présent. I-XV. Paris 1754-55.

    ,,   ,, Histoire de l'ancien Théâtre Italien, etc. Paris 1767.

Picot, E.: La Sotie en France (Romania t. VII).

Pollard, Alfred W.: English Miracle Plays, Moralities and Interludes. Oxford 1890.

Pougin, Arthur: Acteurs et actrices d'autrefois. Paris s. d. [1897].

Prölss, R.: Geschichte des neueren Dramas. I-III. Leipzig 1881-83.

Prutz, R. E.: Geschichte des deutschen Theaters. Berlin 1847.

Riccoboni, L.: Histoire du théâtre italien, etc. I-II. Paris 1730.

    ,, Dell' Arte Rappresentativa, Capitoli sei. Lond. 1728.

Rigal, E.: Alexandre Hardy et le théâtre français. Paris 1890.

Ring, Herm.: Teaterns Historia. Stockholm 1898.

Sachs, Hans: Altdeutsche Schaubühne, herausgeg. v. J. G. Büsching. I-III. Nürnberg 1824.

    ,, Sämtliche Fastnachtspiele, herausgeg. v. E. Goetsche. Halle 1880-84.

Sand, Maurice: Les masques et bouffons de la comédie italienne. I-II. Paris 1859.

Sauval, Henri: Histoire et Recherches des Antiquités de la ville de Paris. I-III. Paris 1724.

Shack, A. F. von: Geschichte der dramatischen Literatur und Kunst in Spanien. I-III. Berlin 1845-46.

Scherillo, Michele: La commedia dell' Arte in Italia. Studi e Profili. Turin 1884.

Schiött, J.: Beiträge zur Geschichte der Entwickelung der mittelalterlichen Bühne. Herrigs Archiw LXVIII.

Smith, Lucy Toulmi: York Plays. Oxford 1885.

The Towneley Mysteries. Publications of the Surtees Society. London 1836.

W. [Will]: Geschichte der Nürnbergischen Schaubühne (Historisch-diplomatisches Magazin für das Vaterland, etc.). Nürnb. 1781.

Ward, A. W.: A History of English dramatic literature to the death of Queen Anne. I-II. London 1875.

Wright: Early Mysteries. London 1838.

INDEX